ICONLOGIC™

v112122
Page Count:218
Kindle KDP: 9781944607913
Vital Source PDF: 97819446079131
Kindle eBook: 9781944607920

Adobe RoboHelp 2022: The Essentials

Kevin Siegel

ICONLOGIC
"Skills and Drills" Learning

Rank Your Skills

Before starting this book, complete the skills assessment on the next page.

Skills Assessment

How This Assessment Works

Below you will find 10 course objectives for learning Adobe RoboHelp 2022. **Before starting this book**, review each objective and rank your skills using the scale next to each objective. A rank of ① means **No Confidence** in the skill. A rank of ⑤ means **Total Confidence**. After you've completed this assessment, work through the entire book. **After finishing the book**, review each objective and rank your skills now that you've completed the book. Most people see dramatic improvements in the second assessment after completing the lessons in this book.

Before Starting

1.	I can create topics.	①	②	③	④	⑤
2.	I can create a table of contents.	①	②	③	④	⑤
3.	I can create hyperlinks to topics.	①	②	③	④	⑤
4.	I can create a cascading style sheet (css).	①	②	③	④	⑤
5.	I can create a variable.	①	②	③	④	⑤
6.	I can create conditional build expressions.	①	②	③	④	⑤
7.	I can create a snippet.	①	②	③	④	⑤
8.	I can customize an output template.	①	②	③	④	⑤
9.	I can create a map file.	①	②	③	④	⑤
10.	I can publish a project.	①	②	③	④	⑤

Now That I Am Finished

1.	I can create topics.	①	②	③	④	⑤
2.	I can create a table of contents.	①	②	③	④	⑤
3.	I can create hyperlinks to topics.	①	②	③	④	⑤
4.	I can create a cascading style sheet (css).	①	②	③	④	⑤
5.	I can create a variable.	①	②	③	④	⑤
6.	I can create conditional build expressions.	①	②	③	④	⑤
7.	I can create a snippet.	①	②	③	④	⑤
8.	I can customize an output template.	①	②	③	④	⑤
9.	I can create a map file.	①	②	③	④	⑤
10.	I can publish a project.	①	②	③	④	⑤

IconLogic, Inc.
www.iconlogic.com

iCONLOGiC

"Skills and Drills" Learning

Contents

NOTES

NOTES

NOTES

NOTES

NOTES

ICONLOGIC

"Skills and Drills" Learning

About This Book

This Section Contains Information About:

NOTES

The Author

Kevin Siegel is a Certified Technical Trainer (CTT), Certified Master Trainer (CMT), and Certified Online Training Professional (COTP). Kevin served in the U.S. Coast Guard, where he was twice decorated with the Coast Guard's Achievement Medal. He also received the coveted Alex Haley Award for writing and photojournalism.

Kevin has spent decades as a technical communicator, face-to-face and virtual trainer, eLearning developer, publisher, and keynote speaker. Kevin has written hundreds of books for adult learners. Some of his best-selling titles include "Adobe Captivate: The Essentials," "Adobe RoboHelp: The Essentials," "Articulate Storyline: The Essentials," "Articulate Rise: The Essentials," and "TechSmith Camtasia: The Essentials."

IconLogic

Founded by Kevin in 1992, IconLogic is a training, development, and publishing company offering services to clients across the globe.

As a **training** company, IconLogic has directly trained tens of thousands of professionals both on-site and online on dozens of applications. Our training clients include some of the largest companies in the world including Adobe Systems, Inc., Urogen Pharma, Agilent Technologies, Sanofi Pasteur, Kelsey-Seybold Clinic, FAA, Office Pro, Adventist Health Systems, AGA, AAA, Wells Fargo, VA.gov, American Express, Lockheed Martin, General Mills, Grange Insurance, General Dynamics Electric Boat, Michigan.gov, Freddie Mac, Fannie Mae, ADP, ADT, Federal Reserve Bank of Richmond, Walmart, Kroger, Duke Energy, USCG, USMC, Canadian Blood, PSA, Department of Homeland Security, and the Department of Defense.

As a **development** company, IconLogic has produced eLearning and technical documentation for Duke Energy, World Bank, Heineken, EVERFI, Bank of America, Fresenius Kabi, Wells Fargo, Federal Express, Fannie Mae, American Express, Microsoft, Department of For-Hire Vehicles, DC Child and Family Services Agency, DCORM, Canadian Blood Services, Cancer.org, MLB, Archrock, NEEF, CHUBB Limited, Canadian Natural Resources, and Hagerty Insurance.

As a **publishing** company, IconLogic has published hundreds of critically acclaimed books and created technical documents for both print and digital publication. Some of our most popular titles over the years include books on HTML, Virtual Reality, Dreamweaver, QuarkXPress, PageMaker, InDesign, Word, Excel, Access, Publisher, RoboHelp, RoboDemo, iSpring Suite, Presenter, Storyline, Captivate, Camtasia, and PowerPoint.

You can learn more about IconLogic's varied services at www.iconlogic.com.

Book Conventions

In our experience, humans learn best by doing, not just by watching or listening. With this concept in mind, instructors and authors with years of experience training adult learners have created IconLogic books.

IconLogic books typically contain a minimal amount of text and are loaded with hands-on activities, screen captures, and challenge exercises to reinforce newly acquired skills. This book is divided into modules. Because each module builds on lessons learned in a previous module, we recommend that you complete each module in succession.

Lesson Key

Instructions for you to follow look like this:

❒ choose **File > Open**

If you are expected to type anything or if something is important, it is set in bold type like this:

❒ type **9** into the text field

If you are expected to press a key on your keyboard, the instruction looks like this:

❒ press [**shift**]

Confidence Checks

As you work through this book, you will come across the image at the right (which indicates a Confidence Check). Throughout each module, you are guided through hands-on, step-by-step activities. To help ensure that you are understanding the book's content, Confidence Checks encourage you to complete a process or steps on your own without step-by-step guidance. Because some of the book's activities build on completed Confidence Checks, you should complete each of the activities and Confidence Checks in order.

NOTES

RoboHelp Updates and How They Affect This Book

With each major update of RoboHelp, my intention is to provide a book to support that version and make it available within 30-60 days of the software being released by Adobe.

From time to time, Adobe releases updates for RoboHelp to fix bugs or add functionality. Usually, the updates are minor and have little or no impact on the lessons in this book. However, Adobe does sometimes make significant changes to the way RoboHelp looks or behaves, even with a seemingly minor update.

If something on your screen does not match what is shown in this book, please visit the RoboHelp 2022 book page on the IconLogic website for possible book updates or errata information (http://www.iconlogic.com/adobe-robohelp-2022-essentials-workbook.html) or email me at ksiegel@iconlogic.com.

Software Requirements for This Book

Before you start the lessons in this book, install the Adobe RoboHelp 2022 software on your computer. The RoboHelp software does not come with this book, nor can it be downloaded from the IconLogic website. Purchase the program or download a free 30-day trial version from Adobe at **www.adobe.com/products/robohelp.html**.

Downloadable Book Assets (RoboHelp2022Data)

You're probably eager to dive into RoboHelp and begin creating awesome Help Systems. As you'll learn as you work through this book, all you need to create help systems on your own is Adobe RoboHelp and some content.

Wait, content? What content? You'll need text files, images, multimedia... the list of supporting assets you'll need to create even a basic help system could go on and on.

If you have never used Adobe RoboHelp before, and this book assumes that you have not, I do not expect you to learn RoboHelp now, on-the-fly, *and* come up with content. Learning on-the-fly can be fine, but that takes, and wastes, time.

I've got a deal for you. You provide the computer, the Adobe RoboHelp 2022 software (the free trial version works great), and a willingness to learn. I'll provide all of the project files and supporting assets (topic content, images, and videos) to get you started.

Here are the steps you need to download the free book assets from my website:

1. Start your web browser and go to the following web address: **http://www.iconlogic.com/pc.htm**
2. Click the Data Files link.
3. Choose your operating system (PC or Mac).
4. Select **RoboHelp 2022: The Essentials**.
5. **Save** the zip file to your computer. (It's a good idea to note where the zip downloads so you can find it during the next step.)

6. After the **RoboHelp2022Data.zip** file has fully downloaded, you can close the browser.

7. Find the **RoboHelp2022Data.zip** file you just downloaded and **unzip** it. (On the Mac, the zip is typically extracted automatically.)

   Although you can unzip the assets anywhere on your computer, the desktop usually works well. If you have an unzipped folder on your computer called **RoboHelp2022Data** and the Adobe RoboHelp 2020 software, you're good to go.

   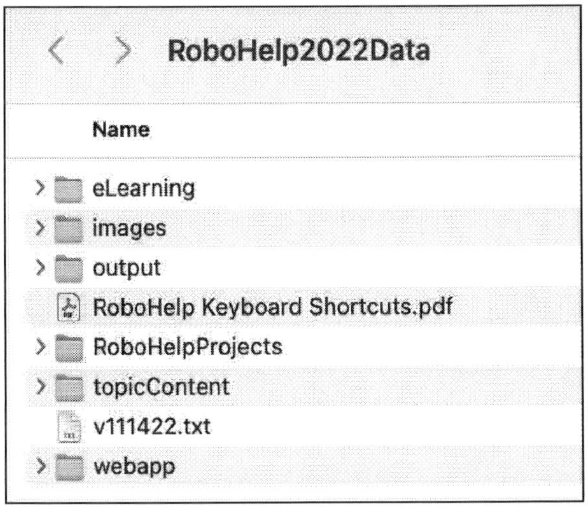

NOTES

NOTES

Project Scenarios

As you work through the activities in this book, I'm going to ask you to use your imagination and pretend that you are a technical communicator for an awesome, but fictional, company called **Super Simplistic Solutions**. As a technical communicator, it is your job to create all of the documentation for the company's products, services, and internal policies and procedures.

During the lessons presented in this book, you will use Adobe RoboHelp 2022 to create a Policies and Procedures guide that can be used by employees via a desktop computer, a laptop, smartphone, or tablet.

Although the information you create in the upcoming policies guide is fictional, the content will likely seem similar to information in many corporate policy guides. Nevertheless, none of the information in the guide is based on real people, events, or companies. Any similarities are purely coincidental.

Contacting IconLogic

Web: www.iconlogic.com
Email: ksiegel@iconlogic.com
Phone: 410.956.4949, ext 711

iCONLOGiC

"Skills and Drills" Learning

Module 1: Introduction to RoboHelp

In This Module You Will Learn About:

And You Will Learn To:

NOTES

RoboHelp's History

According to Adobe, "RoboHelp is an easy-to-use authoring and publishing solution." Adobe also says that RoboHelp allows you to "deliver content to tablets, smartphones, and desktops using output formats such as Responsive HTML5."

Everything Adobe says about RoboHelp is true, and you'll see that for yourself as you work with RoboHelp via the lessons in this book.

I started using RoboHelp when it was owned by a company called Blue Sky Software. That company re-branded itself as eHelp Corporation. Later, eHelp was absorbed by Macromedia (of Dreamweaver and Director fame), which was, in turn, gobbled up by Adobe.

There have been several versions of RoboHelp over the years (see the table below). RoboHelp versions have included names like RoboHelp 5, 6, 7, 2002, X3, X4, and X5. RoboHelp 6 was Adobe's first RoboHelp version. However, eHelp Corporation also had a RoboHelp version 6. Yes, that's right. There was once eHelp RoboHelp 6, and there was an Adobe RoboHelp 6, creating a bit of customer confusion.

Starting with RoboHelp 2015, Adobe changed RoboHelp's naming convention again, this time using the year that the software version was released.

While this book focuses exclusively on RoboHelp 2022 and is titled, "Adobe RoboHelp 2022: The Essentials," RoboHelp 2022 is really RoboHelp version **24**.

Here is a list of RoboHelp versions and their release dates.

Version	Release date	Company/Note
1.0	January 1992	Blue Sky Software First generally-available version of RoboHelp
2.0–12.0	1993–2003	Blue Sky Software/eHelp Corporation
13.0	January 2004	Macromedia
14.0	January 2007	Adobe Systems, Inc.
15.0	September 2007	Adobe Systems, Inc.
16.0	January 2009	Adobe Systems, Inc.
17.0	January 2011	Adobe Systems, Inc.
18.0	July 2012	Adobe Systems, Inc.
19.0	January 2014	Adobe Systems, Inc.
20.0	June 2015	Adobe Systems, Inc.
21.0	January 2017	Adobe Systems, Inc.
22.0	August 2018	Adobe Systems, Inc.
23.0	July 2020	Adobe Systems, Inc.
24.0	September 2022	Adobe Systems, Inc.

Exploring RoboHelp

During the lessons in this module, you will open a completed RoboHelp project, explore it a bit, and then generate outputs. As you work through subsequent modules in this book, you will learn how to build the completed project you're about to see from scratch.

Note: To complete the first activity below, you will need the **RoboHelp2022Data** folder on your computer (also known as data files or assets). If you have not already downloaded the data files to your hard drive, see **page x** in the About This Book section of this book for instructions.
The RoboHelp software is not included with this book. If you do not have RoboHelp installed on your computer, you can purchase the software, or download a 30-day trial, from Adobe at www.adobe.com/products/robohelp.html.

Guided Activity 1: Open an Existing Project

1. Start Adobe RoboHelp 2022.

   After starting RoboHelp, the first thing you will see is the Starter Screen. From here, you can open recent projects, create new projects, and find additional resources. If the Starter is not on your screen, you can choose **View > Starter Screen** to view it.

2. Open an existing project from the RoboHelp2022Data folder.

   ❒ on the **Starter Screen**, click **Open Project**

   ❒ navigate to and open the **RoboHelp2022Data** folder

   The RoboHelp2022Data folder contains several assets that support the lessons in this book, including images, HTML files, Word documents, and existing RoboHelp projects. You'll be instructed when and how to use these assets as you work through the lessons in this book.

   ❒ open the **RoboHelpProjects** folder and then open the **completed_project** folder

   There are several subfolders within the **completed_project** folder. Cumulatively, all of the assets within those folders support the main RoboHelp project file (the project file's name is **completed_project.rhpj**).

   ❒ open **completed_project.rhpj**

   When opening a project, you may see a message similar to what is shown at the right. The message appears if your version of RoboHelp is even slightly different than the one used to create the projects for this book. If you see the message shown at the right, click the **Upgrade** button.

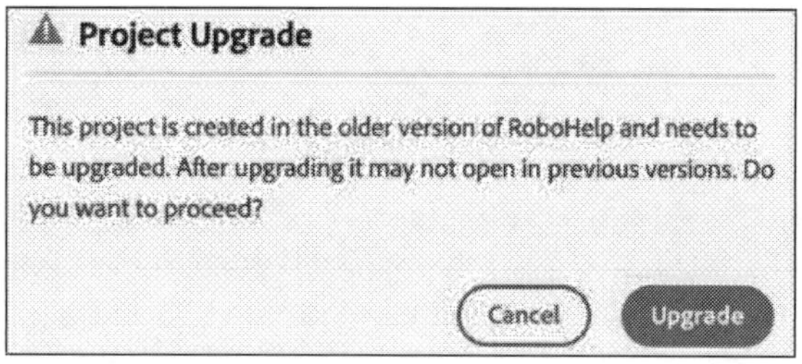

NOTES

The image below shows the PC version of RoboHelp 2022. RoboHelp is nearly identical on the Mac and PC. Because the interfaces are so similar, I'll randomly show one platform or the other throughout this book. Should there be significant differences between the Mac and PC version of RoboHelp, I'll note those differences as appropriate.

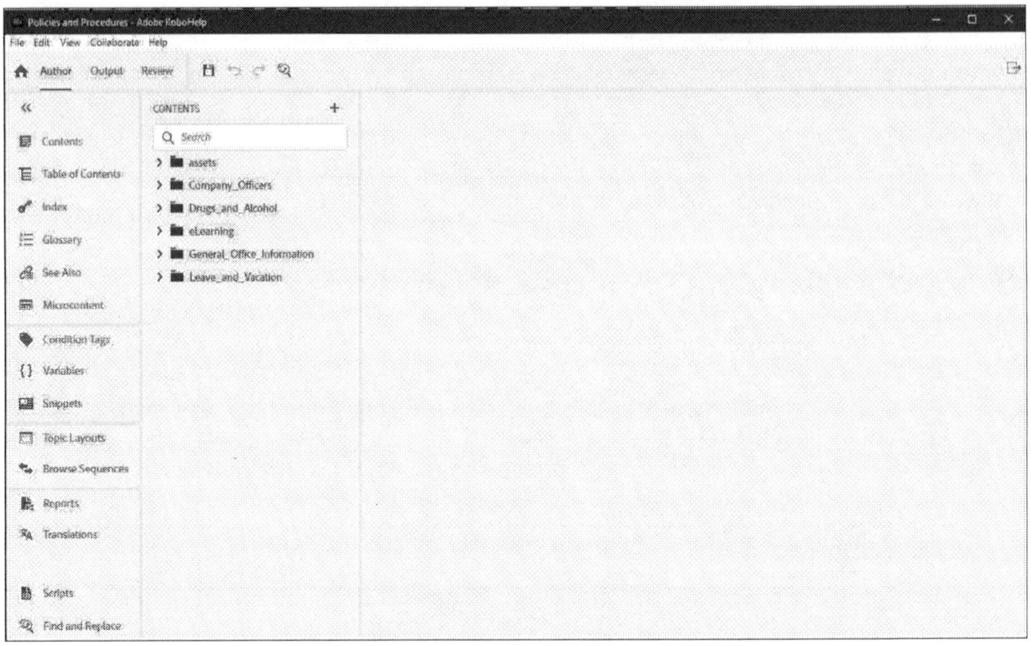

The completed project is a corporate policies and procedures guide for a company called **Super Simplistic Solutions**. During the activities presented throughout this book, you will learn how to create a similar project from scratch.

Before moving forward, I'd like to explain the role of the **rhpj** project file that you opened a moment ago. The image below shows the contents of the **completed_project** folder. Notice that the **rhpj** file is only **3 KB**. Although it's small and does not contain any project content, the rhpj file has a critical job. The project file keeps track of content, links, images, multimedia, table of contents, indexes, and other critical behind-the-scenes functions.

Name	Date modified	Type	Size
condition	9/28/22 3:45 PM	File folder	
contents	9/28/22 3:45 PM	File folder	
glossary	9/28/22 3:45 PM	File folder	
index	9/28/22 3:45 PM	File folder	
publish	9/28/22 3:45 PM	File folder	
seealso	9/28/22 3:45 PM	File folder	
settings	9/28/22 3:45 PM	File folder	
toc	9/28/22 3:45 PM	File folder	
variable	9/28/22 3:45 PM	File folder	
completed_project.rhpj	9/12/22 3:31 PM	RHPJ File	2 KB

While it's certainly important, the rhpj file is by no means the RoboHelp project. Everything you see in the image above is an important project component. When it's time to back up your work (and I encourage you to back up the project folder at least once per day), back up **the entire project folder** instead of just some of the files within the project folder.

Guided Activity 2: Set the RoboHelp Application Theme

1. Ensure that the **completed_project** is still open. (If you're not sure how to open the RoboHelp project, see page 3.)

2. Change the Theme.

   ❐ PC users, choose **Edit > Preferences**;
   Mac users, choose **Adobe RoboHelp 2022 > Preferences**

   The **Application Preferences** dialog box opens. Changes you make here will affect all RoboHelp projects created or opened on your computer.

   ❐ at the **left** of the dialog box, select **General**

   ❐ from the **Theme** drop-down menu, choose **Dark**

   The RoboHelp interface instantly switches from a light interface to dark. There are four RoboHelp Themes ranging from light to very dark. Personally, I like the contrast offered with the Dark Theme. The color scheme you use in RoboHelp is, of course, up to you.

   ❐ select **any Theme** that you like

   ❐ ensure that the remaining **General** settings match what is shown in the image below

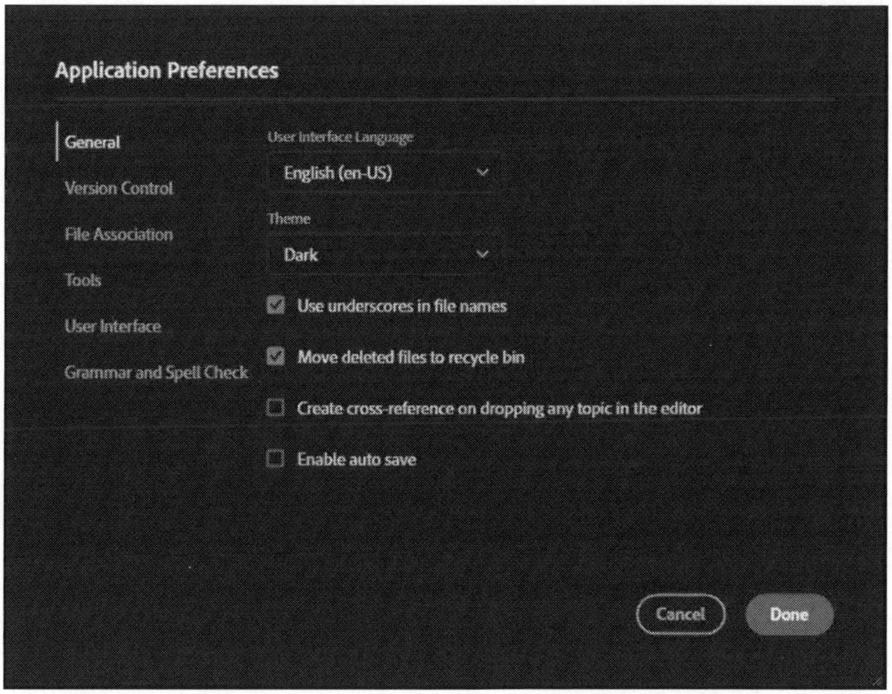

   ❐ click the **Done** button

Guided Activity 3: Explore Project Content

1. Ensure that the **completed_project** is still open. (If you're not sure how to open a RoboHelp project, see page 3.)

2. Explore the Author area.

❐ from the upper left of the RoboHelp interface, notice that there are three tabs: **Author, Output,** and **Review**

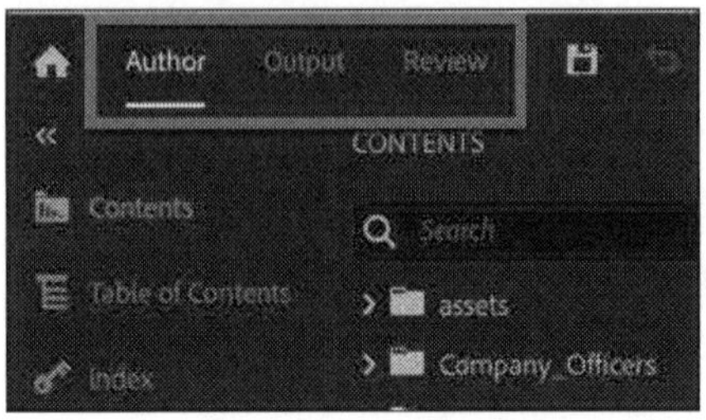

❐ from the upper left of the RoboHelp interface, click **Author**

When you work in RoboHelp, you create or import content while working in the **Author** area. When you're done authoring, you'll use the **Output** area to generate your content into a format appropriate for users who will not have Adobe RoboHelp on their computers or devices. The **Review** area is where you will set up your project content for internal review and feedback from your team members and stakeholders.

❐ from the **Author** area, click **Contents**

The project contents open. If the Contents area does not open, try clicking **Contents** one more time.

❐ from the **Contents** panel, double-click the **General Office Information** folder to expand the folder and view its content

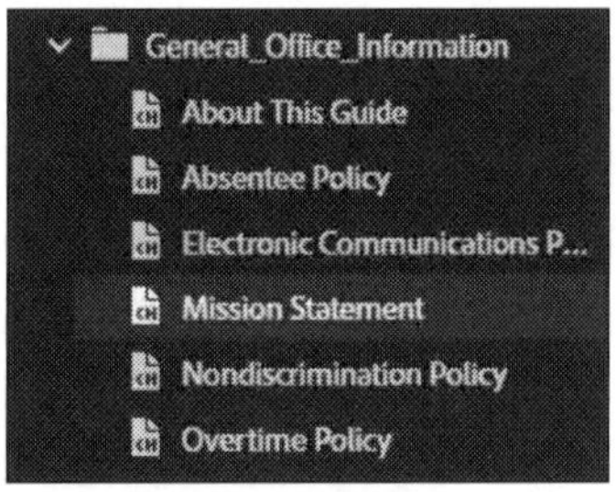

Note: If you see file names in the Contents panel, such as Electronic.htm instead of Electronic Communications Policy, choose **View > Show > Topics by Title**.

3. Open a topic.

❐ from the list of items in the **General Office Information** folder, double-click **Mission Statement**

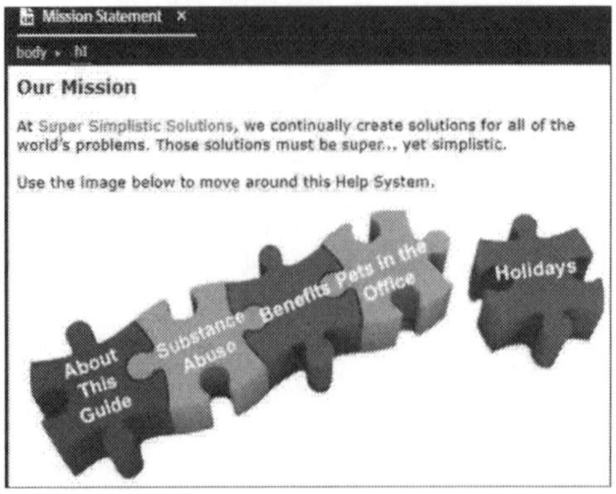

4. Open a second topic.

   ❒ from the **Contents** panel, open the **Drugs and Alcohol** folder

   ❒ double-click **Alcohol Policy**

   Two topics are now open in the **Authoring** area.

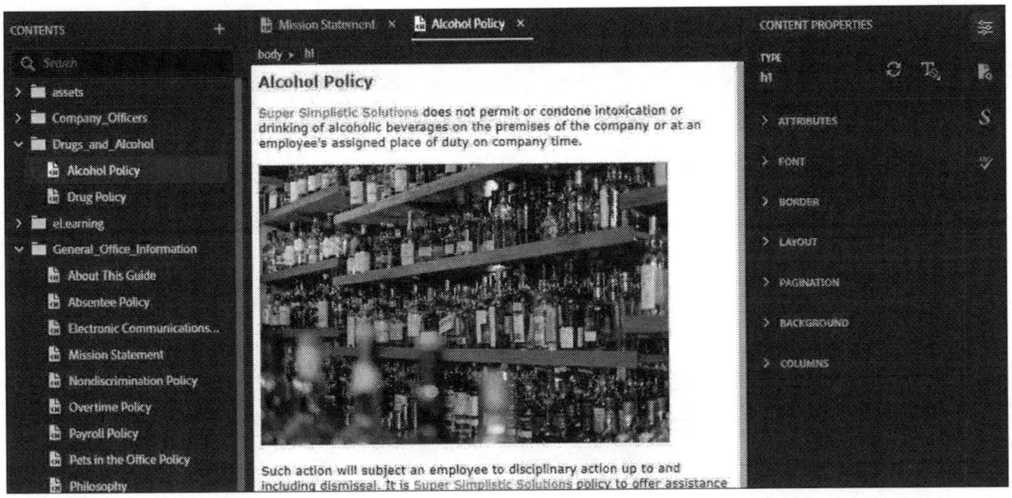

5. Switch between open topics.

   ❒ from just above either open topic, click the topic's **title tab** to switch between the two topics

   Note: While you can have multiple topics open at one time and quickly switch between them, you can only edit the content in the active topic. The active topic is denoted by the horizontal line beneath the topic's title. In the image below, two topics are open: Mission Statement and Alcohol Policy. The Alcohol Policy topic is the active topic.

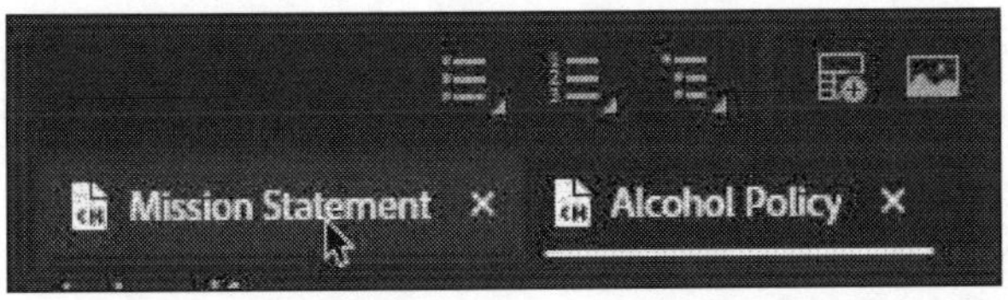

6. Close multiple topics.

   ❒ choose **File > Close All**

7. Close all expanded folders.

   ❒ on the **Contents** panel, right-click any folder and choose **Collapse All**

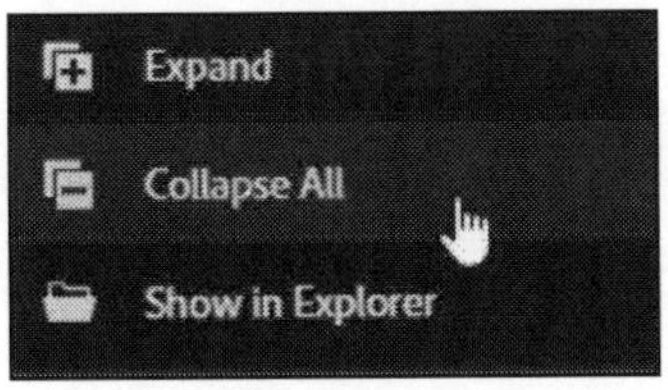

Topics

You've likely heard the saying that content is king. It's true. The heart of any Help System is its content and the information it provides. Most of the content in a RoboHelp project is contained within topics. Topics typically consist of text formatted with styles (page 43), images (page 80), hyperlinks (page 69), videos (page 89), tables (page 120), and more. In the next few activities, you will create, modify, and delete a topic.

Guided Activity 4: Create, Edit, and Delete a Topic

1. Ensure that the **completed_project** is still open. (If you're not sure how to open the RoboHelp project, refer to page 3.)

2. Create a new topic.

   ❐ on the **Contents** panel, right-click beneath the last folder

   ❐ choose **New > Topic**

   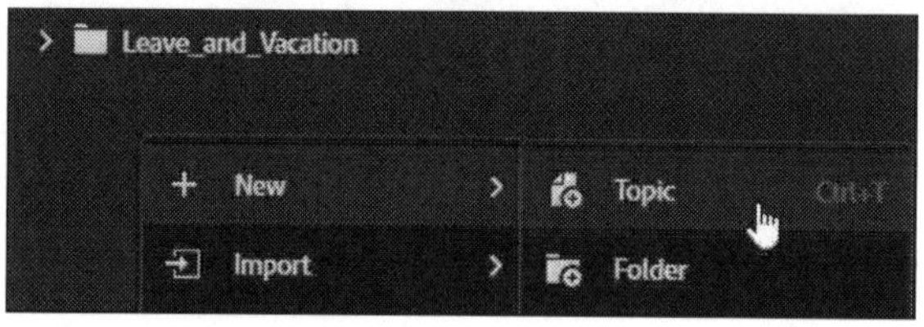

   The New Topic dialog box opens.

   ❐ change the **Title** to **My First New Topic**

   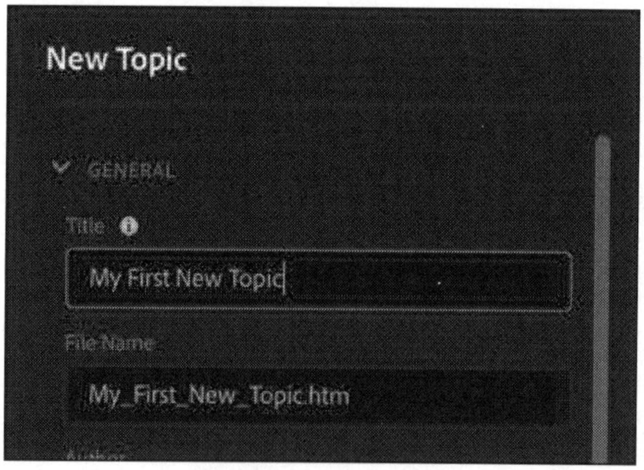

   ❐ from the bottom of the dialog box, click the **Create** button

   The new topic appears on the Content panel and opens for editing.

3. Edit the new topic.

❒ click in the white space below the heading "My First New Topic"

❒ type: **The best Help topic will contain only enough text to get my point across and no more. One paragraph or two is ideal, supported by an image or two.**

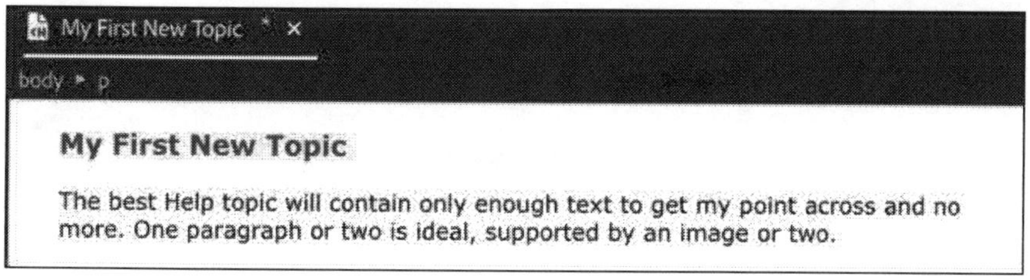

Above your new topic, observe the asterisk to the right of the topic's title.

The asterisk indicates an unsaved topic.

4. Save and close the topic.

❒ choose **File > Save**

The asterisk is removed, indicating that changes made to the topic have been saved.

❒ choose **File > Close**

5. Delete a topic.

❒ on the **Contents** panel, right-click the **My First New Topic** topic and choose **Delete**

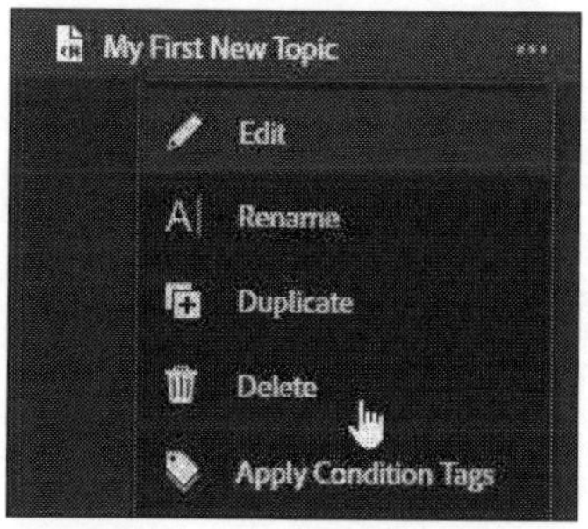

You will be asked to confirm the action.

❒ click the **Yes** button

NOTES

Adding and Deleting Topics Confidence Check

1. Create a new topic titled **My Second Topic**.
2. Change the title of the new topic to **Delete Me**.
3. Delete the **Delete Me** topic.

Table of Contents and Indexes

A Table of Contents (TOC) provides users with a high-level overview of the content in your RoboHelp project. The order of the content in a TOC is typically based on a logical organization of information that you set up when you build the project. Of course, that logical structure won't necessarily make sense to your users. So while a TOC is important, it will not be the first thing used when someone seeks help on a specific topic. Instead, users will likely turn to the Index or Search.

Unlike a TOC, which is most often a logical organization of content, an Index is an alphabetical listing of keywords, each targeted toward a specific topic. Users can quickly scan the list of keywords, find what they're looking for, and click the keyword to display the appropriate content.

Guided Activity 5: Explore a TOC and an Index

1. Ensure that the **completed_project** is still open.

2. Open an existing TOC.

   ❒ from the panel at the far left, click **Table of Contents**

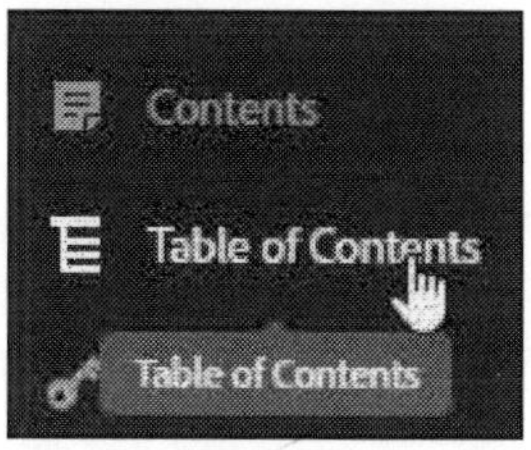

This project contains one TOC named **policies**.

❒ double-click **policies** to open the TOC

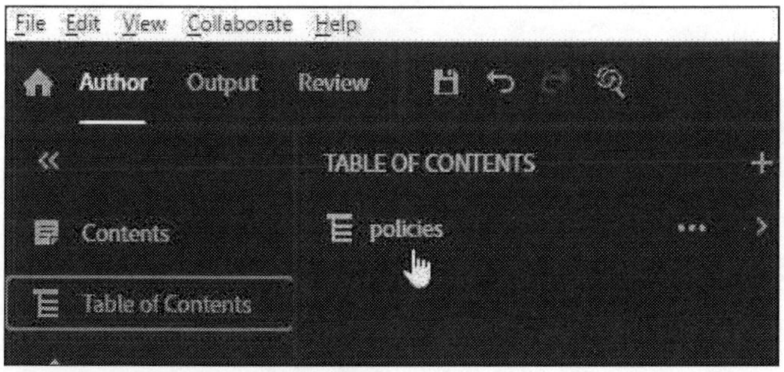

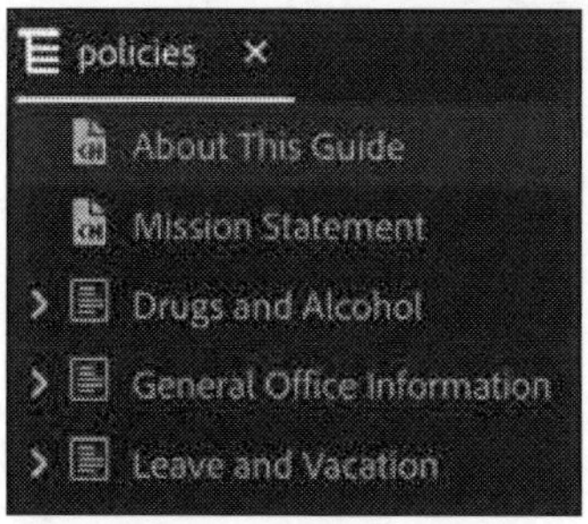

You will learn how to create a Table of Contents like this one beginning on page 39.

NOTES

3. Open an existing Index.

❒ from the panel at the far left, click **Index**

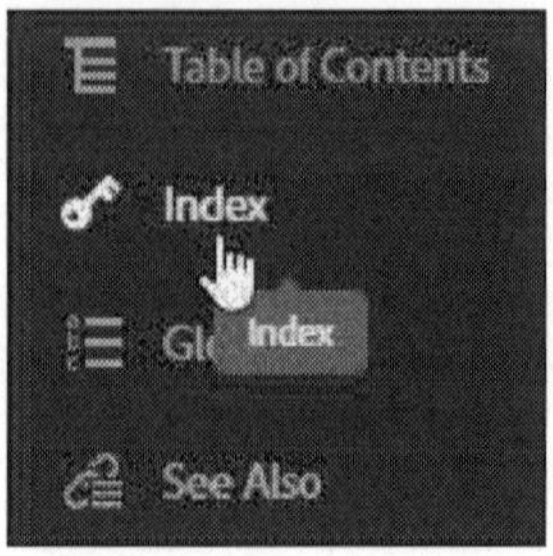

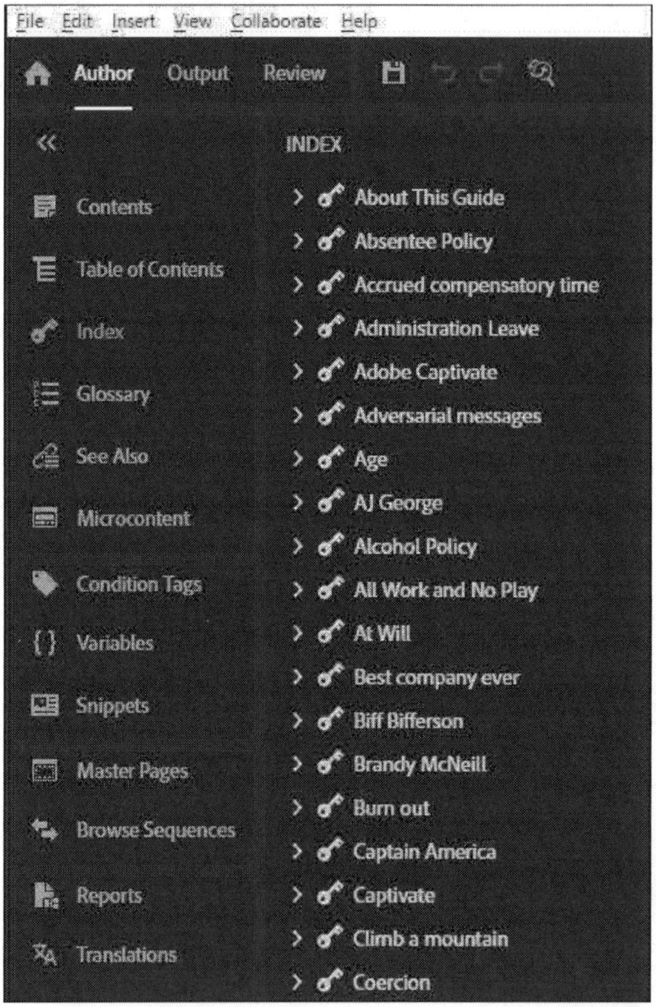

You will learn how to create an Index similar to this one beginning on page 127.

Frameless Output

If you'd like to get a sense of what your users will experience when accessing your finished RoboHelp project, you need to create **output files** from the project's content. Your users do not need RoboHelp to open the output you create with RoboHelp. However, depending upon the type of output you generate, the users' hardware and software needed to open the output will vary.

Frameless output can be viewed on the web or using a desktop application. This output works with any web browser, on Macs, PCs, and is highly customizable. When you generate Frameless output, you're creating a self-contained website with several codependent files that must always be kept together to ensure that the Help System works as designed.

Guided Activity 6: Browse the Outputs

1. Ensure that the **completed_project** is still open.

2. View the current outputs.

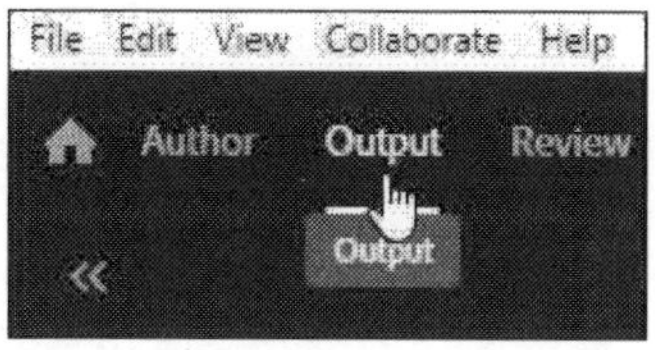

   ❒ from the upper left of the RoboHelp window, click **Output**

   ❒ from the list at the left, click **Output Presets**

   This project has a few outputs. There are several more outputs than those shown and you will explore some of them soon enough. Note that there is an output shown in the image below called **Microsoft HTML Help**. This output is unique to PC users. Because Mac's cannot open this type of output, it is not available in RoboHelp for Mac.

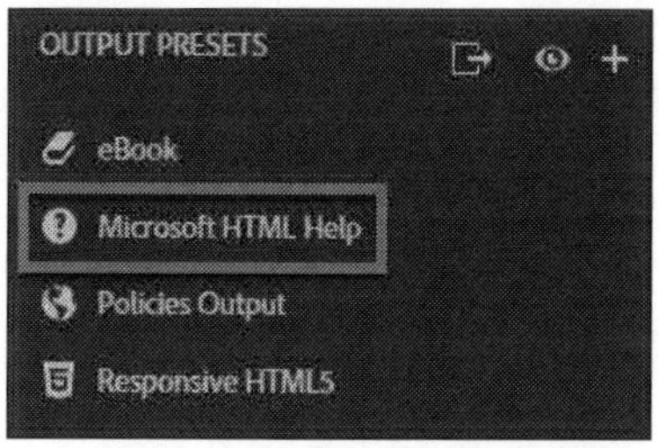

3. View all of RoboHelp's output formats.

   ❒ to the right of **Output Presets**, click the **plus sign**

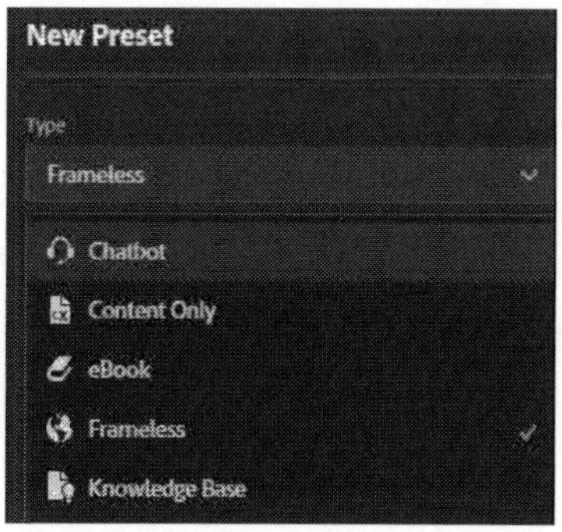

   The New Preset dialog box opens.

   ❒ click the **Type** drop-down menu

   Notice that RoboHelp can output Chatbots, Content Only, eBooks, Frameless, Knowledge Base, MicroHelp, Mobile App, and more.

   ❒ click on any of the **Preset names** to collapse the **Type** drop-down menu

   ❒ click the **Cancel** button

NOTES

NOTES

Guided Activity 7: Generate Frameless Output

1. Ensure that the **completed_project** is still open.

2. Generate and view Frameless output.

   ❒ from among the **Output Presets**, double-click the **Policies Output** to open the output for editing

   When an output is added to a project, it can be given any name. The developer who added the Frameless output elected to not use the name Frameless and instead went with the name Policies.

   ❒ select the **General** category

   ❒ from the **Output Path** area, click the **Browse** icon

   ❒ browse to and **Select** (PC) or **Open** (Mac): **RoboHelp2022Data > output > Frameless**

3. Close the Preset. (Save it when prompted.)

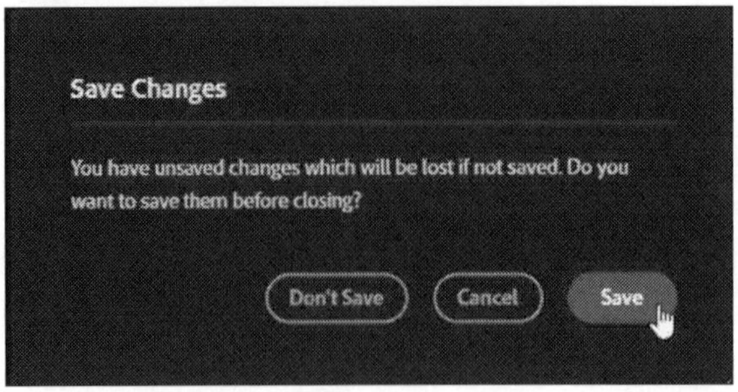

4. Generate Frameless output.

   ❒ right-click **Policies Output** and choose **Generate**

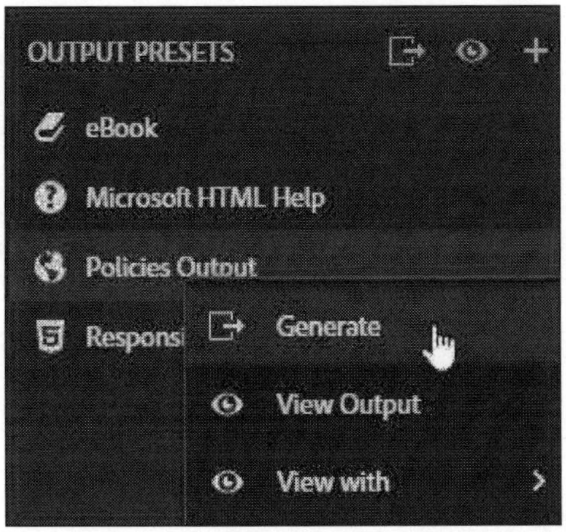

You'll see your Output Generation progress in the lower right of the RoboHelp window.

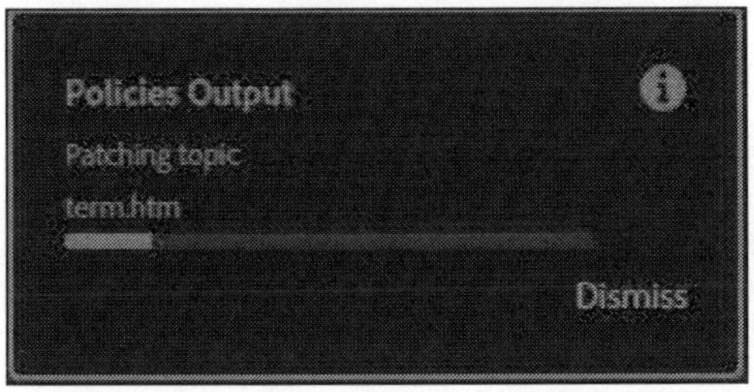

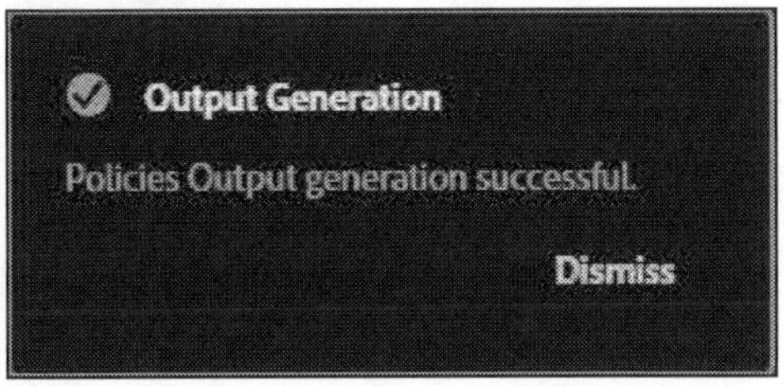

5. View the generated Frameless output.

   ❒ from the **Output presets** area, right-click **Policies Output** and choose **View Output**

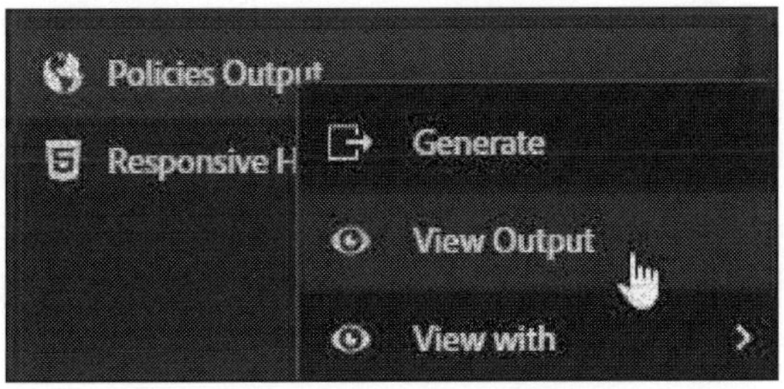

NOTES

The Help System opens within your computer's default web browser.

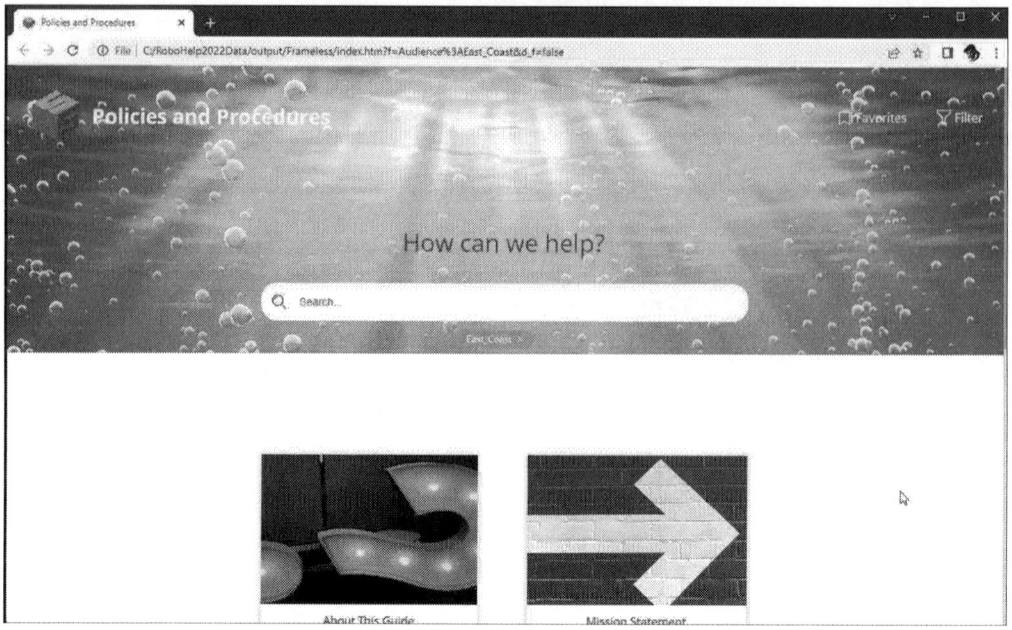

6. Spend a few minutes exploring the output by clicking the thumbnail images.

   I personally love the look of the Frameless output, and it's completely customizable. I also love how the page content reflows nicely as the browser window is resized.

7. When finished exploring the output, close the browser window and return to RoboHelp.

Responsive HTML5 Output

The sale of smartphones exceeds the sale of traditional phones; the sale of tablets exceeds those of desktop computers. These trends have led to a need for help authors to create content that can be accessed from both mobile devices and traditional computers.

When you output Responsive HTML5 with RoboHelp, just about everything in the Help window reflows, resizes, and adjusts to provide optimal viewing across a wide range of devices and screen sizes.

Guided Activity 8: Generate Responsive HTML5 Output

1. Ensure that the **completed_project** is still open.

2. Generate and view Responsive HTML5 output.

   ❒ from among the **Output Presets**, double-click **Responsive HTML5** to open the layout

   ❒ select the **General** category

   ❒ from the **Output Path** area, click the **Browse** icon 

   ❒ browse to and **Select** (PC) or **Open** (Mac):
   RoboHelp2022Data > output > Responsive HTML5

   ❒ close and save the **Responsive HTML5** preset

   ❒ right-click the **Responsive HTML5** preset and choose **Generate**

3. View the Output.

4. Resize the browser window.

   Similar to the Frameless output, observe how the appearance of the page changes (responds) as you resize the browser window.

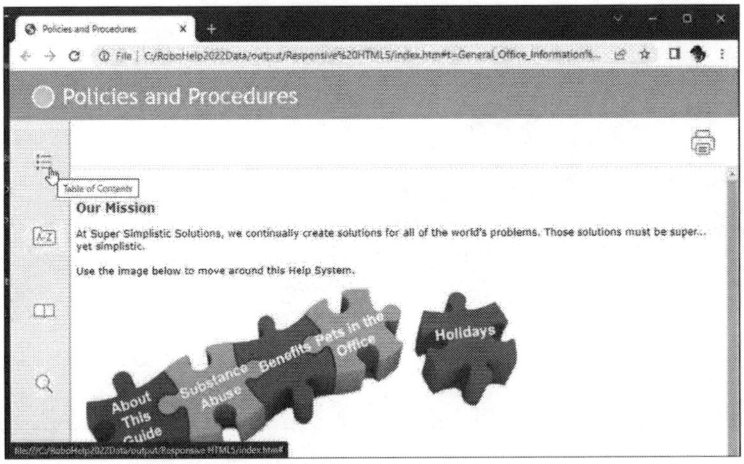

5. Close the browser window and return to the RoboHelp project.

NOTES

eBooks

You have learned that RoboHelp easily outputs web content by generating Frameless and Responsive HTML5. You can also use RoboHelp to generate an eBook (also known as an ePub or Kindle). When opened with an eBook reader, the text wraps to fit the size of the user's device or display. The user can control the font, font size, and font color. Although the eBook format is flexible, it does not currently support all of the bells and whistles that you can add to a RoboHelp project. For instance, eBook readers do not support expanding hotspots, glossaries, or interactive eLearning videos. (You will learn how to add these features later in this book.)

> **Note:** In the steps that follow, you will use RoboHelp to generate an eBook. After the eBook file has been created, you will need an eBook reader to open the eBook file. There are many eBook readers (some free, some not). Here is a list of free eBook readers: **https://www.techradar.com/best/best-free-ebook-reader**.
> For more information on the eBook format, visit **https://www.w3.org/publishing/**.

Guided Activity 9: Generate an eBook

1. Ensure that the **completed_project** is still open.

2. Output an eBook.

   ❒ from among the **Output Presets**, double-click **eBook** to open it

   ❒ select the **General** category

   ❒ from the **Output Path** area, click the **Browse** icon

   ❒ browse to and open/select: **RoboHelp2022Data > output > eBook**

   ❒ close and save the eBook preset

   ❒ right-click the **eBook** Preset and choose **Generate**

3. View the eBook output.

   The eBook opens in your computer's default ePub reader. In the image at the right, you can see a page from the EPUB as it appears using the Calibre reader for the Mac.

4. Close the eBook file.

5. Return to the RoboHelp project.

   The last activity in this module involves outputting Microsoft HTML Help and is for PC users only. Mac users, you can close the project and then move on to the next module.

Microsoft HTML Help

Microsoft HTML Help (HTML Help for short) is the oldest of the outputs and can be created and used only by PC users. When you generate HTML Help, RoboHelp outputs a single, compressed CHM file (pronounced "chum").

A CHM file works great if your users are accessing the Help System with a Windows-based PC and if the CHM file is installed on the user's hard drive. CHM files do not work if your users access the Help System with a computer or laptop running any other operating system, or if the user is on a mobile device, such as a tablet or smart phone. CHM files do not work well if opened by users over a server. And there are limits on how much you can customize the look and feel of the HTML Help window.

Given the limitations of a CHM file, you might think that HTML Help is an output that is best avoided. Not necessarily. There is much to like about CHM files. For instance, HTML Help files are self-contained Help Systems, and your users won't need other programs to use them outside of what is already installed on most PCs. And CHM files are typically smaller than any of the other outputs. The savings in size alone is one reason that many organizations still rely on CHM files, even given the inherent limitations of CHMs.

Guided Activity 10: Generate Microsoft HTML Help

1. Ensure that the **completed_project** is still open.

2. Generate HTML Help.

   ❒ from among the **Output Presets**, double-click **Microsoft HTML Help**

   The preset opens for editing.

   ❒ select the **General** category

   ❒ in the **Title** area, change the title to **Policies and Procedures**

   ❒ from the **Output Path** area, click the **Browse** icon

   ❒ browse to **RoboHelp2022Data > output > HTML_Help**

   ❒ click the **Select Folder** button

   ❒ in the **CHM File** area, change the name to **policies.chm**

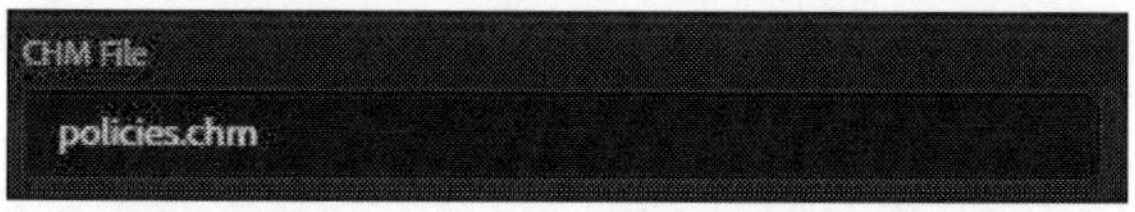

   ❒ close and save the Microsoft HTML Help preset.

   ❒ right-click the **Microsoft HTML Help** preset

   ❒ choose **Generate**

3. View the Output.

   - ❒ from among the **Output Presets**, right-click **Microsoft HTML Help**
   - ❒ choose **View Output**

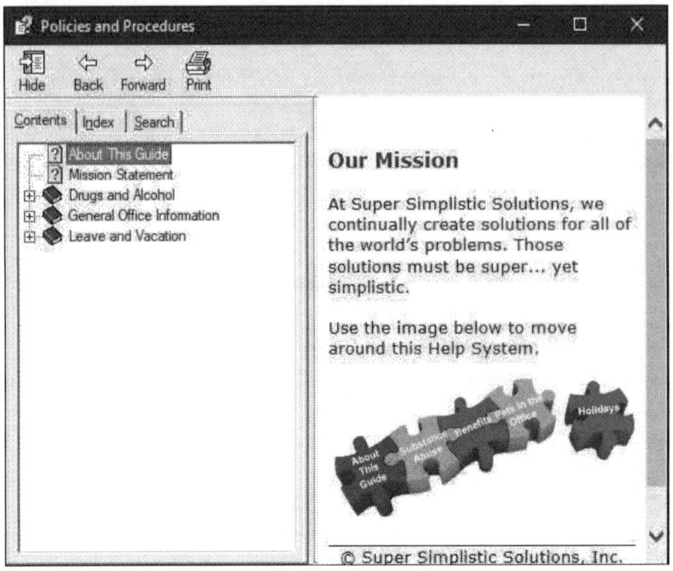

4. Open the **General Office Information** book.

5. Spend the next few moments viewing the topics contained within the book.

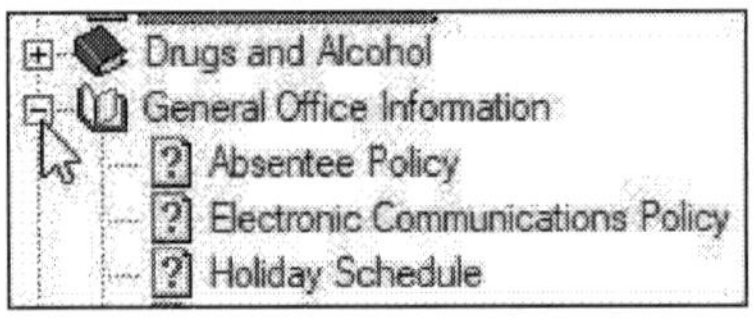

6. Close the Help window.

7. Right-click the Microsoft HTML Help preset and choose **Show in Explorer**.

   Within the HTML_Help output folder, you'll find the generated help file: **policies.chm**.

   Everything the Help System needs to work on a PC user's computer is contained within this one compressed CHM file.

8. Double-click the CHM file to reopen the generated output.

9. Close the Help Window and return to the RoboHelp project.

10. Close the project.

ICONLOGIC

"Skills and Drills" Learning

Module 2: Create a Project

In This Module You Will Learn About:

And You Will Learn To:

NOTES

New Projects

During the last module, you opened and explored an existing project. That module was designed to get you comfortable with the RoboHelp interface. Now that you know your way around RoboHelp a bit more, let's create a blank project that will become the Policies & Procedures guide for your mythical employer, Super Simplistic Solutions. The new project you create will have humble beginnings. It will not have much structure or content. However, as you work through the modules in this book, your project will evolve. In the end, your project will contain plenty of content, graphics, multiple forms of navigation, and many of the same type of high-end features you saw when you explored the project in the last module.

Guided Activity 11: Create a New Project

1. Create a Blank Project.

   ❒ choose **File > New Project** (or click the **New Project** button on the **Starter Screen**)

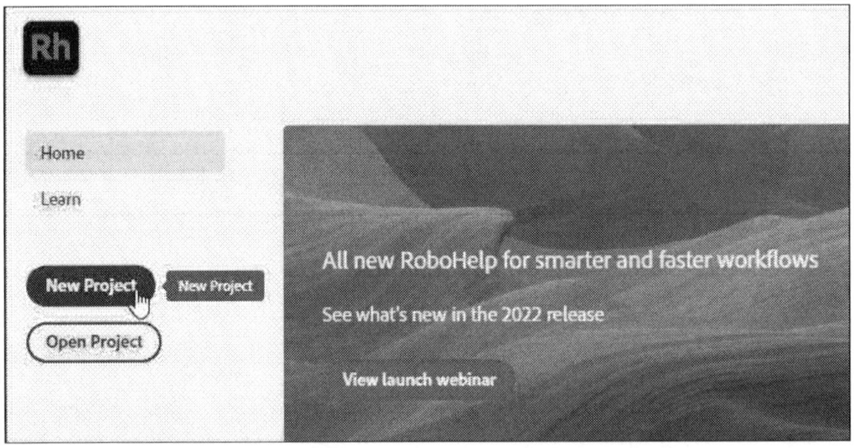

   Note: If the Starter Screen is not currently open, choose **View > Starter Screen** to open it.

   The New Project dialog box opens.

   ❒ in the **Title** field, type **Policies & Procedures**

   ❒ ensure that the **Language** is **English (US)**

   ❒ from the **Save location** area, click the **Select Folder** icon 

   ❒ navigate to and open the **RoboHelp2022Data** folder

   Note: You should have already downloaded and unzipped the **RoboHelp2022Data** folder to your hard drive as instructed in the "About This Book" section of this book (see page x).

   ❒ click once on the **RoboHelpProjects** folder and then click the **Select Folder** (PC) or the **Open** button (Mac)

   ❒ click the **Create** button

Your new RoboHelp project opens. By default, the project contains a single topic titled **First Topic.** If necessary, select **Author** from the left of the RoboHelp window and then select **Contents** to see the lone topic. Next, you'll change the default topic's Title, File Name, and then add some content to it.

2. Change a topic's Title and File Name.

❒ from the **Contents** area, right-click **First Topic** and choose **Properties**

The Topic Properties dialog box opens.

❒ change the topic's **Title** to **Mission Statement**

❒ change the topic's **File Name** to **mission**

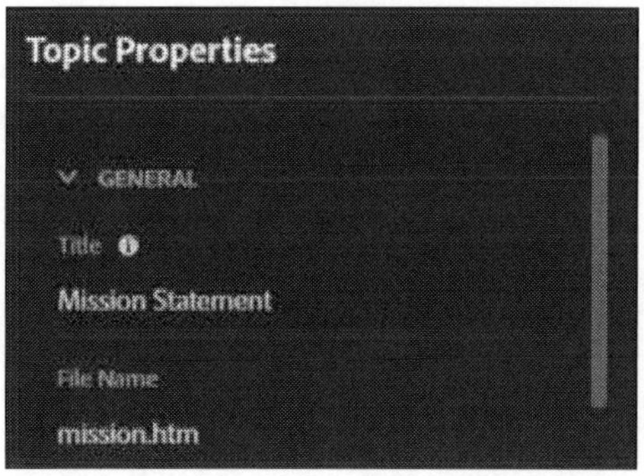

Every topic in your project has two names: Title and File Name. The title is seen by your users. It can and should contain spaces and can be descriptive. By contrast, a topic's File Name is not seen by the user. The name should not contain spaces or special characters. Also note that the .htm extension is added to the file name automatically by RoboHelp.

❒ click the **Apply** button

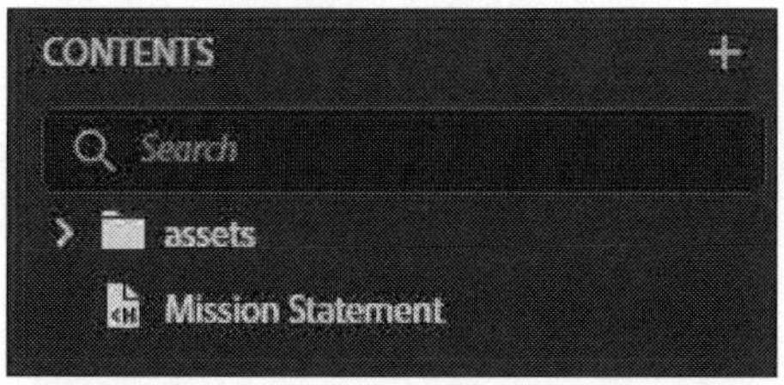

Note: You can elect to use upper or lowercase letters in file names. Some organizations require the use of one or the other (lowercase is the most common).

NOTES

3. Add topic content.

   ❒ from the **Contents** area, open the **Mission Statement** topic

   ❒ replace the heading text with **Our Mission**

   ❒ highlight the remaining text in the topic and replace it with the following content: **To continually create solutions for all of the world's problems. Those solutions must be super... yet simplistic.**

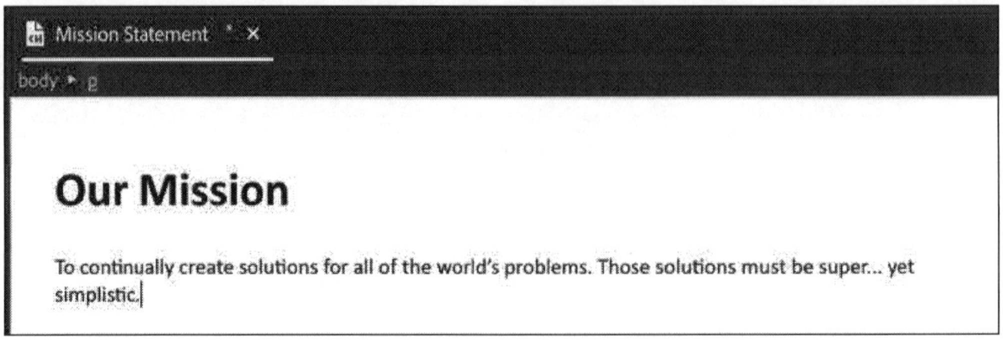

4. Save the project.

   ❒ from the toolbar at the top of the RoboHelp window, click the **Save All** tool

When you work within RoboHelp, multiple assets might be open at one time. For instance, it's possible to have several topics open, all in an unsaved state. As you make changes to project assets, the project file (the **rhpj** file) also remains in an unsaved state. It's a good idea to Save All frequently.

5. Close the Mission Statement topic.

   ❒ at the right of the topic's title, click the **X**

You are about to learn how to create topics on-the-fly. Because RoboHelp allows you to have multiple topics open and quickly switch between them, it's not necessary to close topics prior to creating new topics or editing existing topics. From this point forward, you can close topics—or not—as you see fit.

Topics

Your new project contains just a single Mission Statement topic. In the next few activities, you will learn how to create, rename, and delete topics. Each new RoboHelp topic you create is actually an HTML file. As I promised in the first module of this book, you do not need to know HTML to create HTML topics.

Guided Activity 12: Create a New Topic

1. Create a new topic.

   ❒ still working in your new **Policies & Procedures** project, from the **Contents** area click the **New File/Folder** icon

   ❒ choose **Topic**

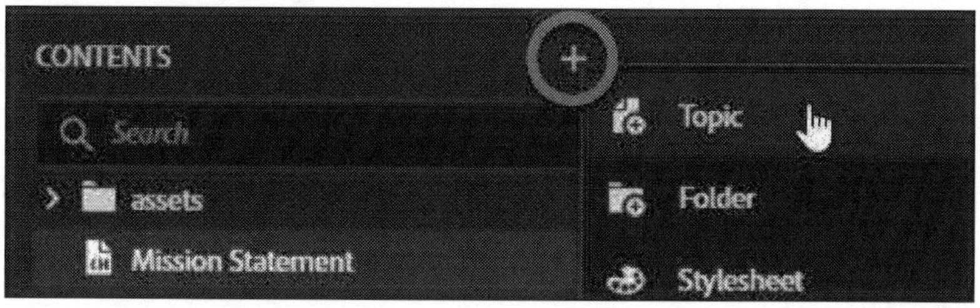

The New Topic dialog box opens.

❒ from the **General** area, change the **Title** to **Philosophy**

When deciding upon a topic Title, consider being fairly descriptive. A title can be a single word or multiple words, can contain spaces, and can include punctuation. A topic's title is displayed to users in the TOC, Index, and other areas of the output. Titles are also shown in search results. A misleading title could make it more difficult for users to find the help they need while using your Help system.

Notice that the File Name (Philosophy.htm) has automatically been added to the File Name field. Unlike topic Titles, a topic's File Name cannot contain spaces or special characters. Should you change your mind about a topic's Title or File Name, both can be edited at any time (you'll learn how on page 27).

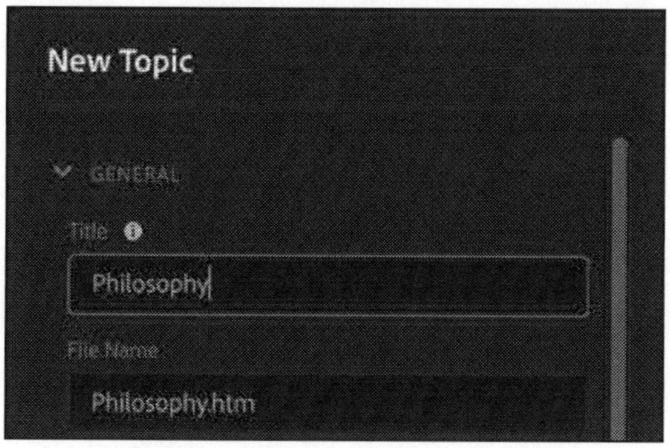

❒ click the **Create** button

The new topic automatically opens for editing.

NOTES

2. Add content to the new Philosophy topic.

   ❒ with the new Philosophy topic open for editing, replace the existing heading text with **Super Simple Tactics**

   ❒ press [**enter**]

   ❒ type **Tactics that focus on motivation, engagement, relevance and usability are standard operating procedures for all of our projects. Working with subject matter experts, we distill and render technical content in logical and easily digestible units. We link concept and application to the real world, with a user-centered perspective.**

   RoboHelp assumes that the text you just typed is supposed to be formatted as a standard paragraph (as opposed to heading text like the first paragraph). In this instance, RoboHelp made a good assumption. Soon enough you'll learn that it's easy to change the appearance of any topic text via Styles.

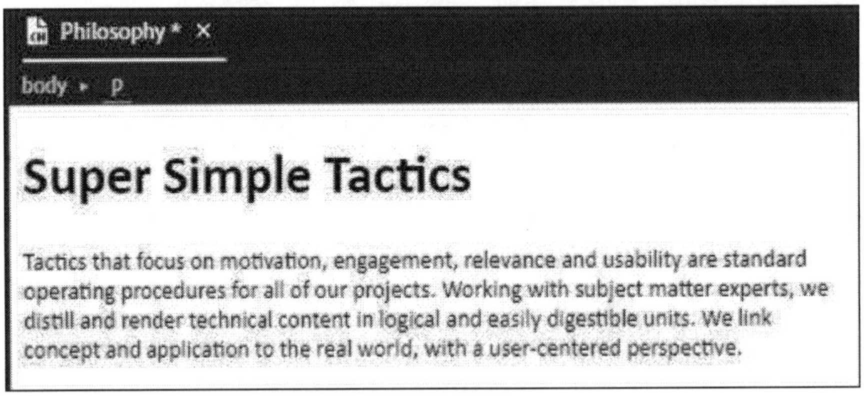

3. Save the project and project assets.

   ❒ choose **File > Save All**

Guided Activity 13: Rename and Delete Topics

1. Ensure that the **Policies & Procedures** project is still open.

2. Create a new topic.

   ❒ from the **Contents** area, click **New File/Folder** and choose **Topic**

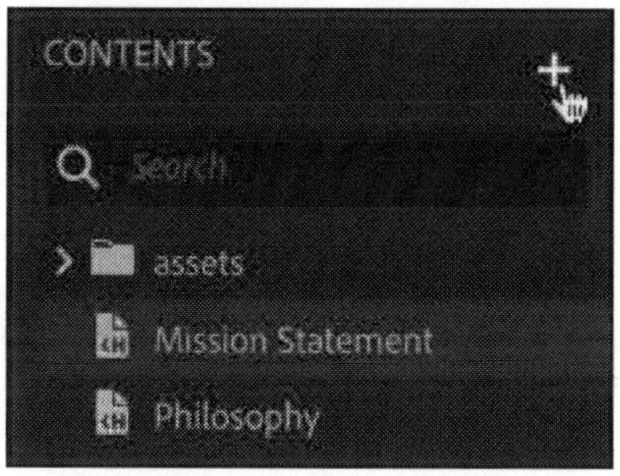

   The New Topic dialog box opens.

   ❒ from the **General** area, change the Title to **Ooops**

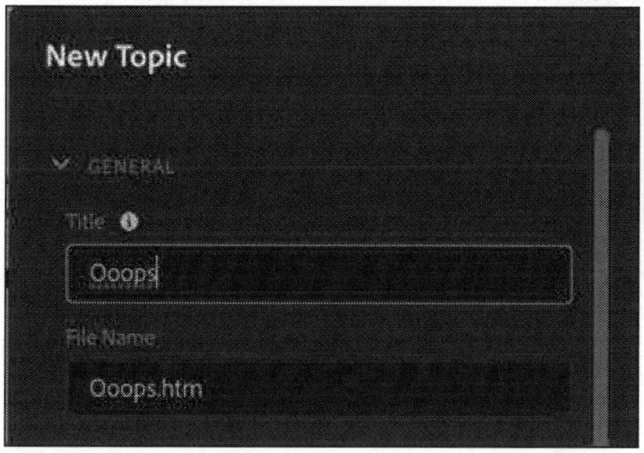

   ❒ click the **Create** button

3. Rename a topic's Title and File Name.

   ❒ from the **Contents** area, right-click the **Ooops** topic and choose **Properties**

   The Topic Properties dialog box opens.

   ❒ change the Topic Title to **Delete Me**

   Notice that the topic's File Name does not automatically change.

   ❒ change the File Name to **Delete_Me**

   ❒ click the **Apply** button

   Because you are viewing the topics by Title, the update to the Title appears in the Contents area after you Apply the changes. You can switch to File Name view by choosing **View > Show > Topics by Title** to toggle the option **off**. If you do so now, just

NOTES

remember to toggle Topic by Title back on so your screen matches the images shown in this book.

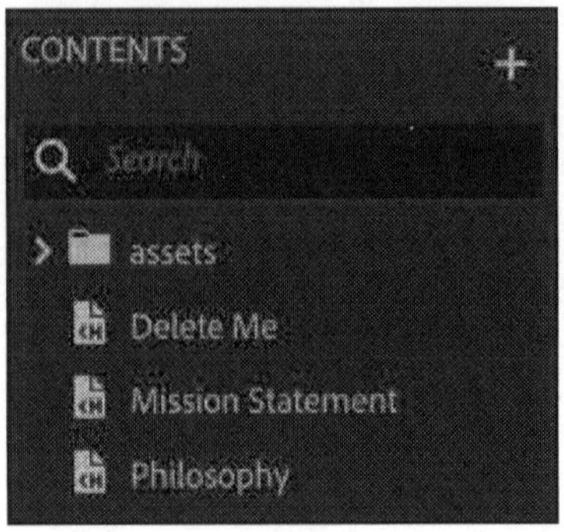

4. Delete a topic.

   ❐ from the Contents area, right-click the **Delete Me** topic and choose **Delete**

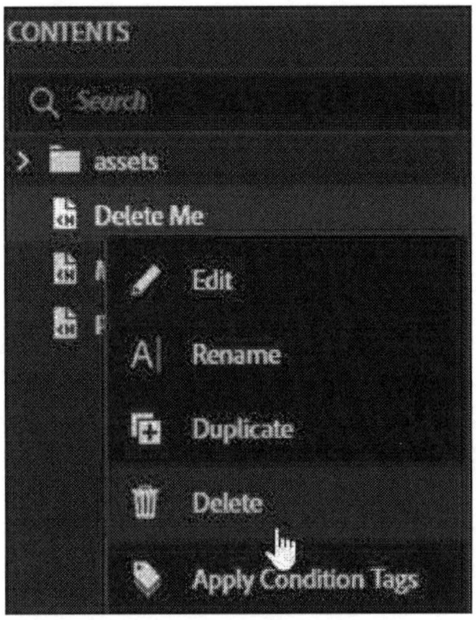

You will be asked to confirm the deletion.

❐ click the **Yes** button

Importing Content

You can import several types of existing documents into a RoboHelp project including HTML files, Microsoft Word documents (docx files), and Adobe FrameMaker documents. If the imported documents contain images or videos, those assets will also be imported.

Guided Activity 14: Import HTML Files as Topics

1. Ensure that the **Policies & Procedures** project is still open.

2. Import an HTML file.

   ❐ from the **Contents** area, right-click beneath the **Philosophy** topic and choose **Import > HTML Topic**

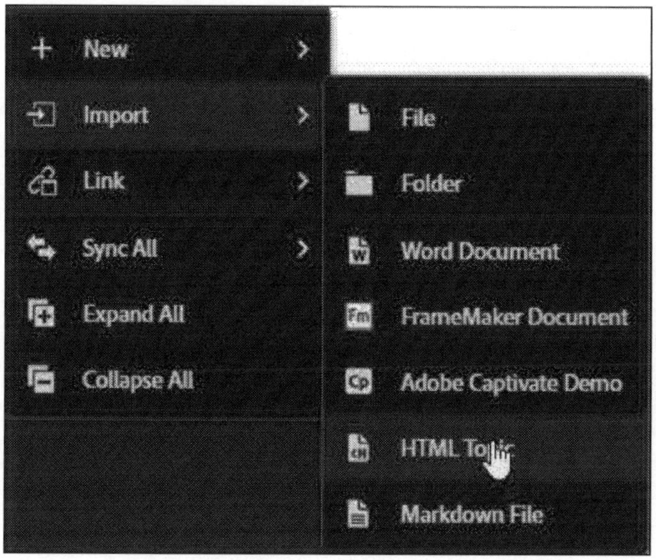

   ❐ from the **RoboHelp2022Data** folder, open the **topicContent** folder

   There are several HTML files in the folder.

   ❐ open **absence.htm**

   The **Absentee Policy** topic is imported and is listed with the other project topics.

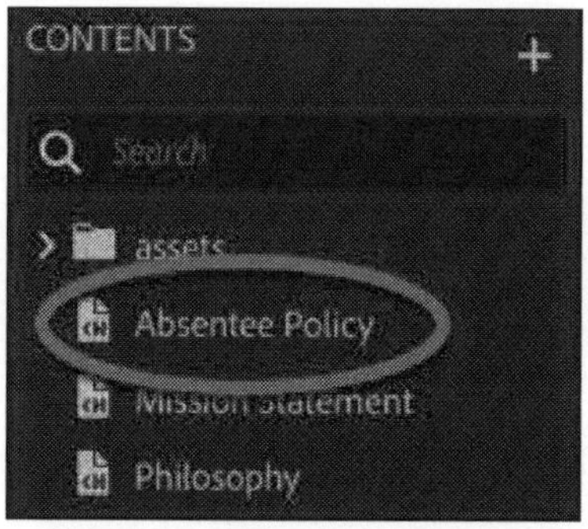

NOTES

Guided Activity 15: Import Word Documents

1. Ensure that the **Policies & Procedures** project is still open.

2. Import a Word document.

   ❒ click beneath the **Philosophy** topic to deselect any folders

   ❒ choose **File > Import > Word Document**

   The Word Import Settings dialog box opens.

   ❒ at the right of the **Word Document** area, click the **Select** icon

   ❒ from the **RoboHelp2022Data** folder, open the **topicContent** folder

   ❒ open **SubstanceAbuse.docx**

3. Control how the imported Word content will create new topics.

   ❒ from the **Start new topic from style** area, **Word Style** drop-down menu, choose **Heading 1**

   The document you are importing contains two paragraphs that are using Word's Heading1 style. By selecting Heading1 from the **Start new topic from style** area, the Word document will lead to two RoboHelp topics.

   ❒ click the **Import** button

   Two new topics, Alcohol Policy and Drug Policy, are added to the Contents area.

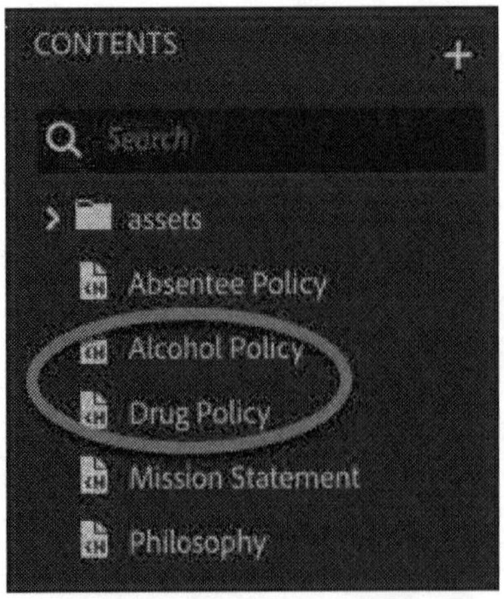

Importing Content Confidence Check

1. Import the following **HTML Topics** into your project. (You can import several HTML files at one time by [**shift**]-clicking to select contiguous files or [**ctrl**]-clicking (PC) or [**command**-clicking (Mac) to select noncontiguous files and then clicking **Open**.)

   conflict.htm, **overtime.htm**, **payroll.htm**, **pets.htm, purpose.htm**, **special.htm**, and **term.htm**

2. Import each of the following Word documents into your project. (While importing, use **Heading 1** to create new topics.)

   Electronic, Leave, Nondiscrimination, and **Vacation**

   You should now have 16 topics in your project.

3. Change the Title of the **Leave** topic to **Leave Policy**. (You learned how to change a topic's Title on page 27.)
4. Change the Title of the **General Office Information** topic to **Overtime Policy**.
5. Change the Title of the **Payroll** topic to **Payroll Policy**.
6. Change the Title of the **PURPOSE** topic to **About This Guide**.
7. Change the Title of **401(k) Plan** topic to **Special Benefits**.
8. Change the Title of the **Termination of Employment** topic to **Termination Policy**.
9. Save the project.

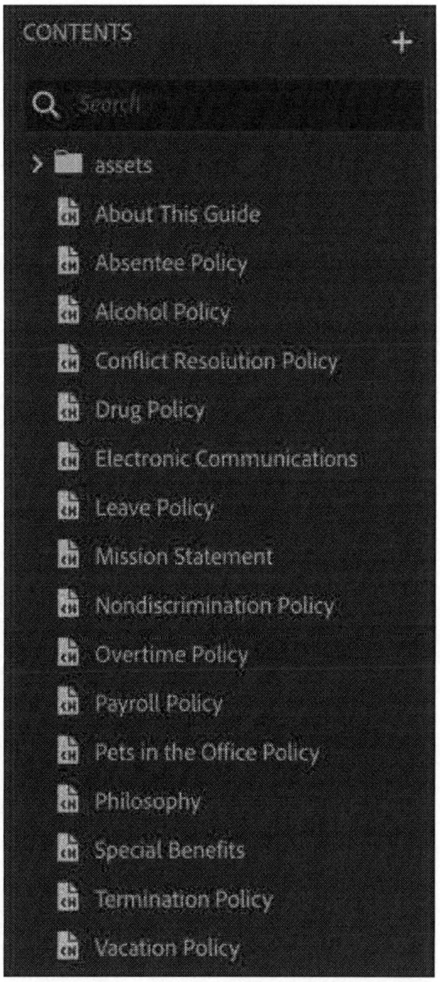

NOTES

NOTES

Source View

Although it is not necessary for you to know HTML to create RoboHelp projects, knowing a little HTML can pay off when imported content causes trouble because of misplaced or missing HTML tags. During the steps that follow, you will import a topic and use RoboHelp's Source View to edit the appearance of topic text.

Guided Activity 16: Edit Text Formatting in Source View

1. Ensure that the **Policies & Procedures** project is still open.

2. Open the **Conflict Resolution Policy** topic for editing.

   Notice that several words, such as Conflict Resolution, have been made bold.

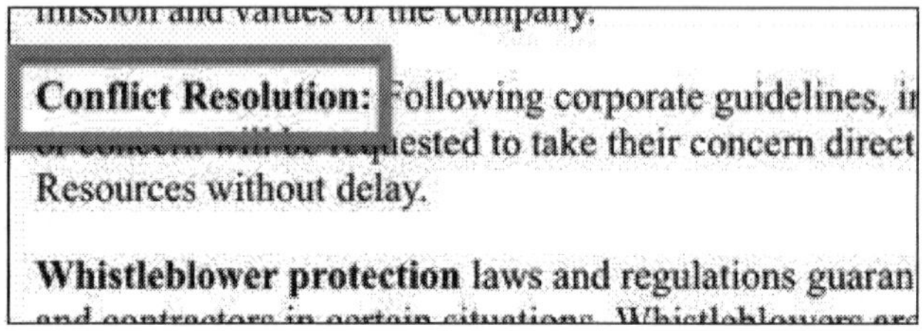

3. Use Source View to change the appearance of text from bold to italic.

   ❒ from the upper right of the RoboHelp window, click the **Source** icon </>

   ❒ in line **12**, replace the **<b>** with **<i>**

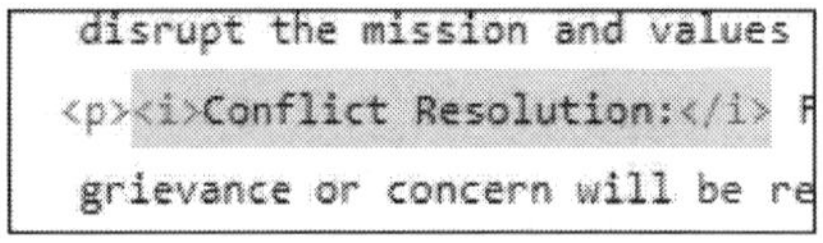

   The <i> is the HTML tag for the *italic* style.

   ❒ from the upper right of the RoboHelp window, click the **Author** icon

   In the fourth paragraph, the phrase **Conflict Resolution**, which was bold, is now italicized.

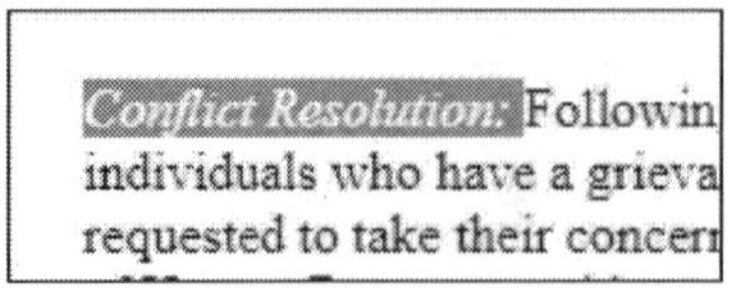

Source View Confidence Check

1. Using Source View, change the appearance of the phrase **Healthy Conflict** to **bold**, *italic* and <u>underline</u>.

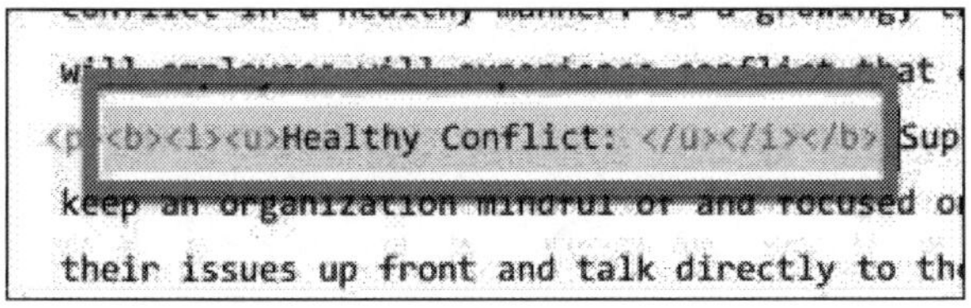

2. Using Source View, change the appearance of the phrase **Healthy Conflict** back to just bold.
3. Using Source View, change the appearance of the phrase **Conflict Resolution** back to just bold.

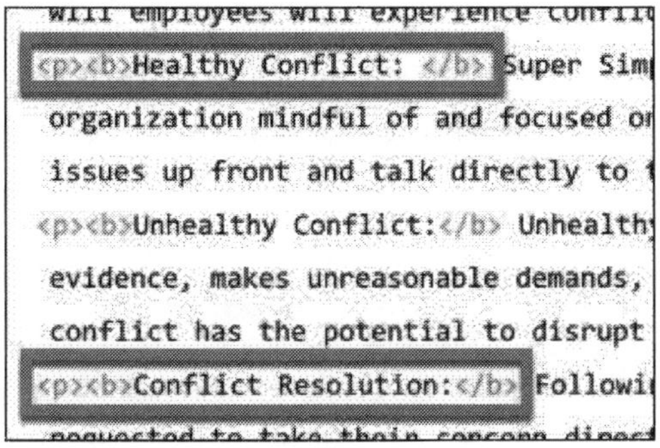

4. Save and close the Conflict Resolution Policy topic.
5. Close the project by choosing **File > Close Project**.

NOTES

Notes

iCONLOGIC

"Skills and Drills" Learning

Module 3: Project Structure, TOCs, and Styles

In This Module You Will Learn About:

And You Will Learn To:

NOTES

Project Structure

Creating folders and subfolders in the Contents area can help you organize your project's topics, images, and other assets. Folders make it easier to access and edit your content as your Help project grows and becomes more sophisticated. As an added bonus, the folder structure you create can be re-purposed and used to automatically create a Table of Contents. It's a nifty process you'll come to appreciate later in this module.

Guided Activity 17: Create Project Folders

1. Open an existing RoboHelp project.

   ❒ choose **File > Open Project**

   ❒ from the **RoboHelp2022Data** folder, open the **RoboHelpProjects** folder

   ❒ open the **project_structure_css** folder

   ❒ open **project_structure_css.rhpj**

   Note: If prompted to Upgrade the project, click the **Upgrade** button.

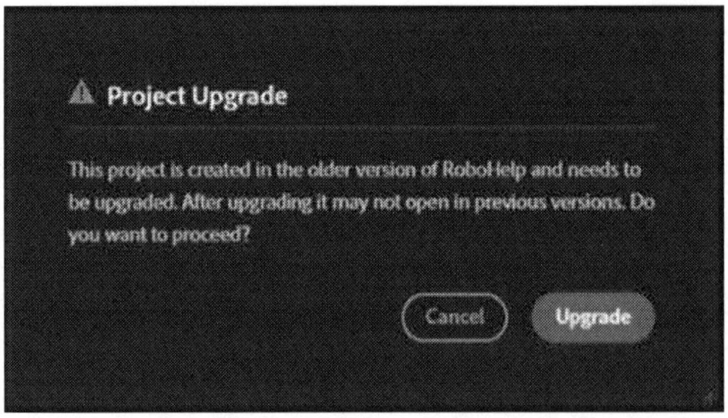

   This project is similar to the project you created during the last module.

2. Create a folder.

   ❒ from the **Contents** area, click the **New File/Folder** icon and choose **Folder**

   The New Folder dialog box opens.

   ❒ type **General Office Information** into the **Name** area

Because folder names cannot contain spaces, the spaces you typed are automatically replaced with underscores.

❐ click the **Done** button

The folder is added to your list of Contents.

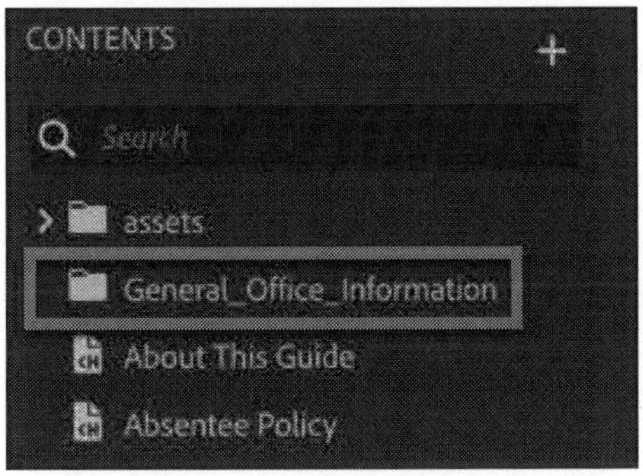

3. Move a topic into a project folder.

   ❐ from the list of **Contents**, drag the **About This Guide** topic into the **General_Office_Information** folder

   ❐ when prompted to **Confirm** the move, click the **Yes** button

   To see the moved topic, expand the **General_Office_Information** folder.

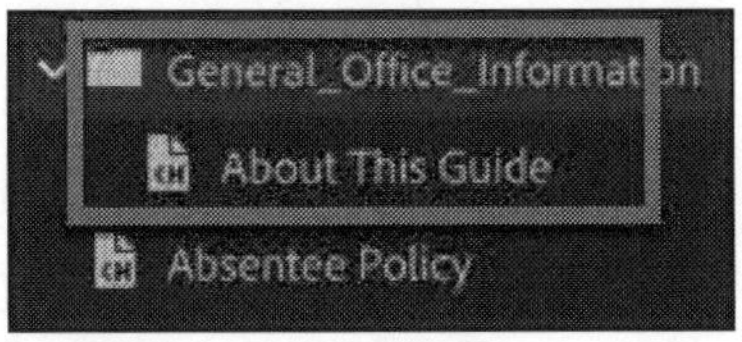

4. Save the project.

NOTES

Project Structure Confidence Check

1. Create a new folder named **Drugs and Alcohol**.
2. Create a new folder named **Leave and Vacation**.
3. Move topics to the project folders as necessary to match the project structure shown below.

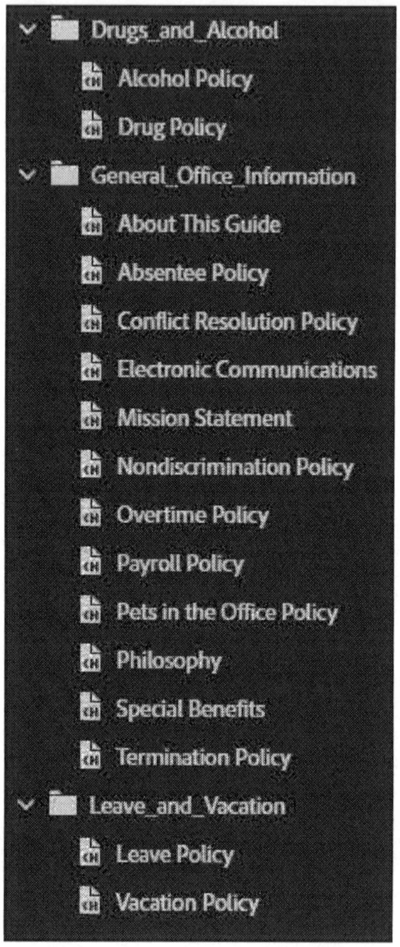

Table of Contents

When a Help System is output, it's common to include a Table of Contents. A typical TOC consists of sections and topics but can also include links to other TOCs or projects. Sections can contain topics or other sections.

Guided Activity 18: Create a TOC Section

1. Ensure that you are still working in the **project_structure_css** project.

2. Open a Table of Contents.

   ❒ from the left of the RoboHelp window, click **Table of Contents**

   There is a default Table of Contents in the project called **Default**. You can edit the default or create your own. You will work with new TOCs later in this book (page 168). For now, let's edit the default.

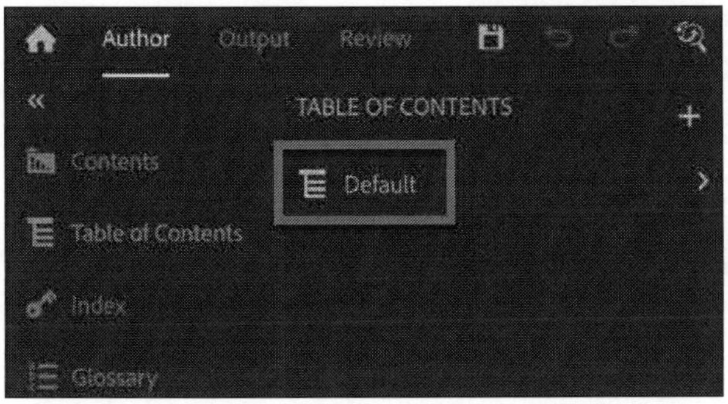

3. Remove a topic reference from the Default TOC.

   ❒ from within the **Table of Contents** area, double-click the **Default TOC** to open it for editing

   ❒ right-click the existing **First Topic** reference and choose **Delete**

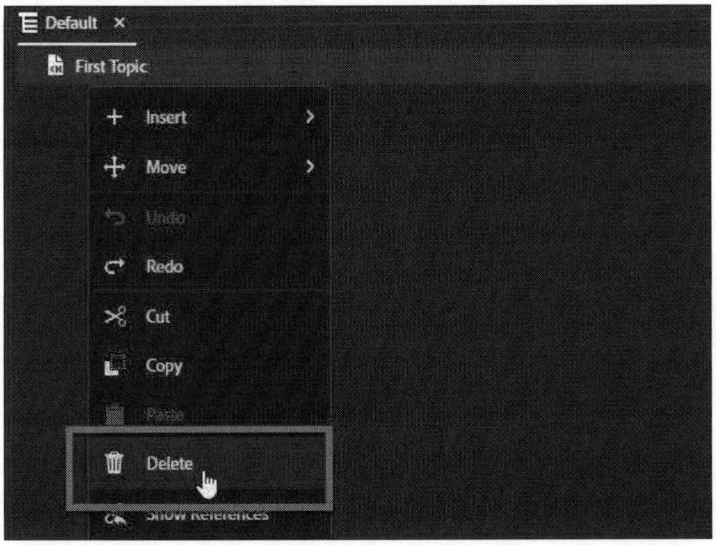

   Because you are not deleting content from the project but simply removing a reference that is pointing to existing content, you are not prompted to confirm the deletion.

NOTES

4. Add a section to the default Table of Contents.

   ❒ from the toolbar above of the **Default TOC**, click **Insert Section**

The Insert Section dialog box opens.

   ❒ in the **Title** area, type **Section 1**

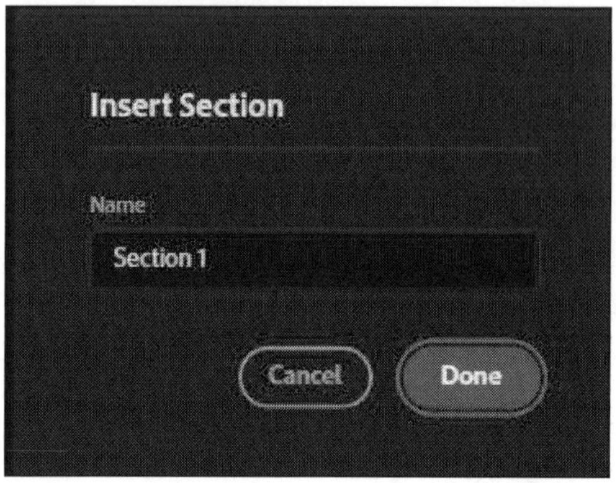

   ❒ click the **Done** button

The **Default TOC** now contains a single section. The section is not currently pointing toward any project content.

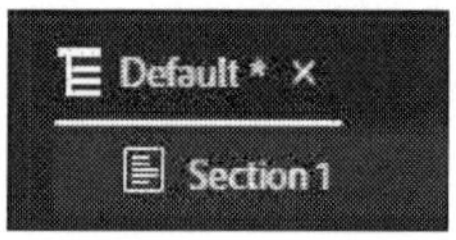

5. Add two topics to Section 1 on the TOC.

   ❒ from the left of the RoboHelp window, click **Contents**

   ❒ from the **Contents** area, open the **Drugs and Alcohol** folder

   ❒ drag the **Alcohol Policy** topic directly on top of **Section 1**

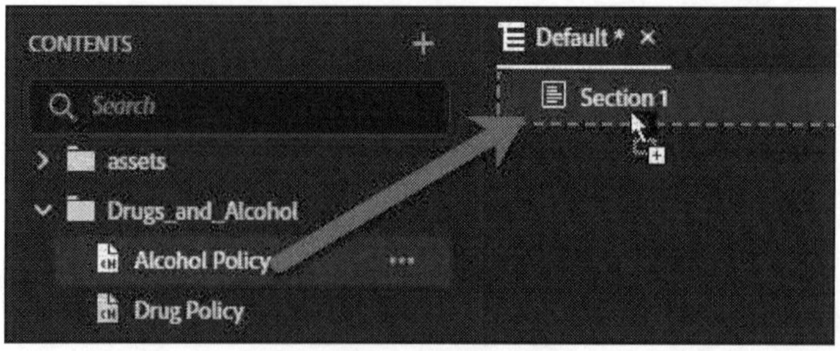

The Alcohol Policy topic is added to Section 1

❒ drag the **Drug Policy** topic directly on top of **Section 1**

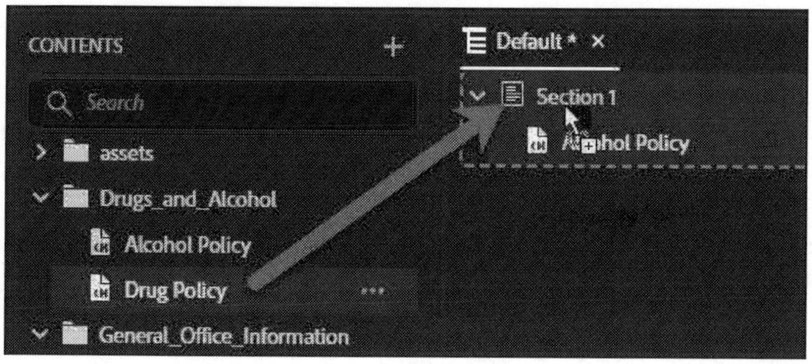

Section 1 now contains two topics: Alcohol Policy and Drug Policy.

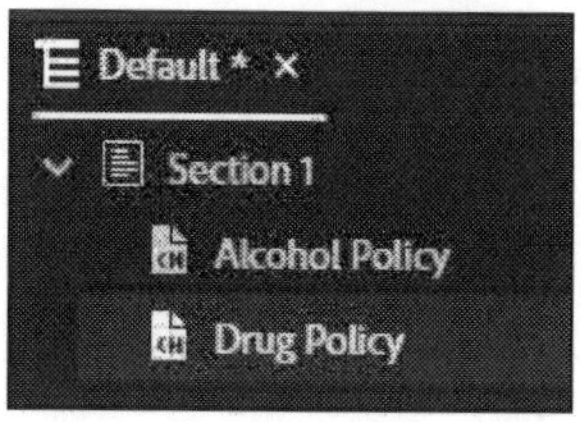

6. Save the project.

TOC Sections Confidence Check

1. Add three more sections to the TOC named **Section 2**, **Section 3**, and **Section 4**.
2. Add a few topics to each of the sections.

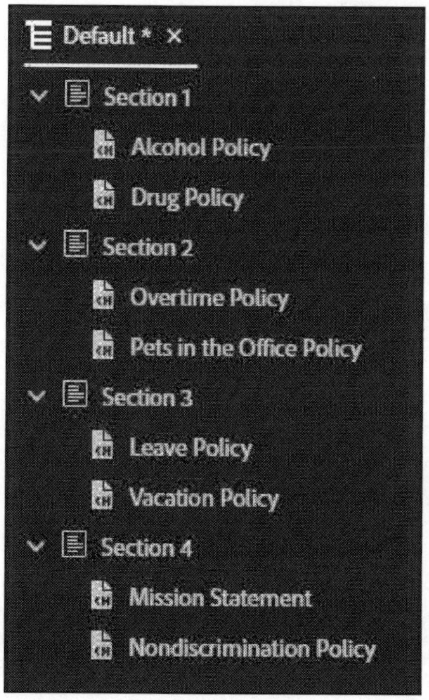

Note: You can use the Move icons located above the TOC to reposition Sections and Topics within the TOC.

NOTES

NOTES

Automatic TOCs

During the last activity, you learned how to build a TOC from scratch. However, if you have already spent time creating a folder structure for the project in the Contents area (which you did at the beginning of this module when you created folders for the topics), you can leverage RoboHelp's ability to automatically create a TOC based on that existing folder structure.

Guided Activity 19: Auto-Create a TOC

1. Ensure that the **Default TOC** is still **open**.

2. Auto-create a TOC based on existing folders.

   ❒ from above the **TOC**, click the **Auto-create TOC** icon

   The Confirm dialog box opens.

   ❒ select **Delete current TOC before creating new**

   Delete current TOC before creating new removes the existing TOC you created. **Create TOC pages for mid-topic links (bookmarks)** is an optional setting (you will learn about bookmarks during the activity on page 72).

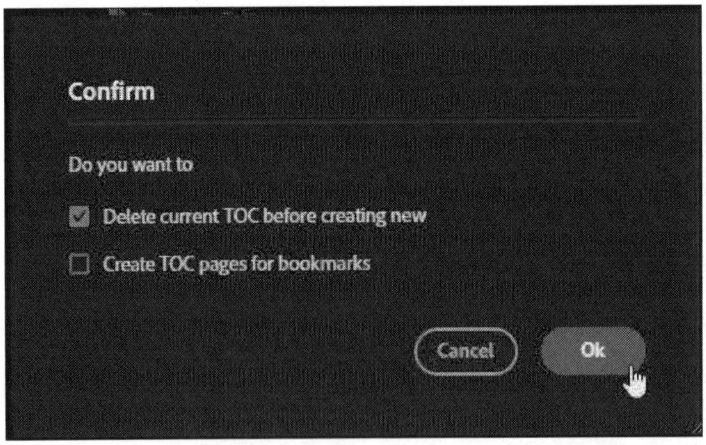

   ❒ click the **OK** button

   The content you originally added to the policies TOC is replaced by sections and topics that match the structure you set up in the Contents area earlier.

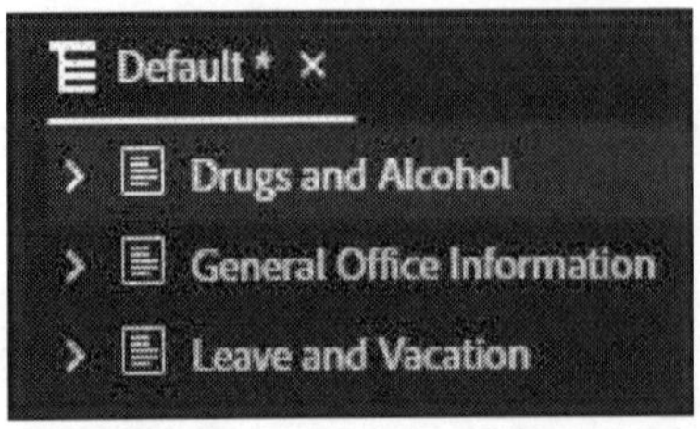

Guided Activity 20: Reorder TOC Section Topics

1. Ensure that the **Default TOC** is still **open**.

2. Reorder some of the pages in the TOC.

   ❒ on the TOC, expand the **General Office Information** section

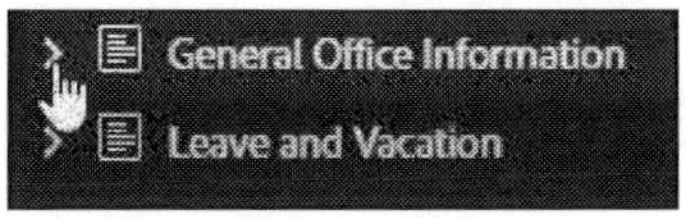

   ❒ select the **About This Guide** page

   ❒ from above the TOC, click the **Move Up** icon 

until the page is the first one listed in the **General Office Information** section

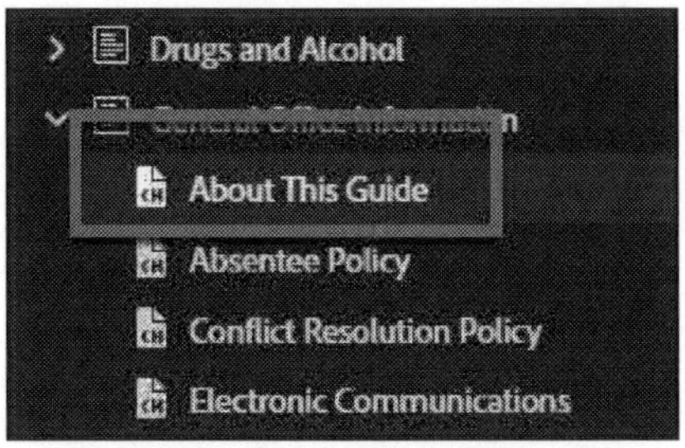

Note: When building a TOC, it is not necessary to list the topics alphabetically. Instead, topics should be named and structured in a logical, meaningful way that best meets the needs of your users.

Section Structure Confidence Check

1. Move the **About This Guide** page above the sections.

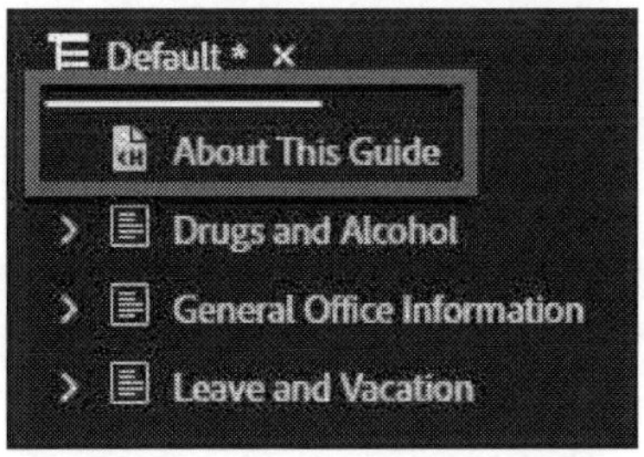

2. Change the order of a few of the topics within the sections as you see fit.
3. Save the project.

NOTES

NOTES

Style Sheets

Large RoboHelp project can contain thousands of topics. To ensure readability and help avoid visual distractions, the text should be readable and formatted consistently. Cascading Style Sheets (CSS) take the drudgery, and the work, out of formatting and updating the appearance of topics project-wide.

CSS files contain dozens of styles that can, in turn, contain hundreds of formatting options that you can assign to multiple topics. The beauty of a CSS file is that after it has been linked to a topic, future edits to styles contained with the CSS file immediately affect the appearance of associated topics project-wide.

Guided Activity 21: Attach a Style Sheet to a Topic

1. Ensure that you are still working in the **project_structure_css** project.

2. Open a topic and display the paragraph markers.

   ❒ from within the **Default TOC**, open the **About This Guide** topic

   ❒ choose **View > Show > Paragraph Markers**

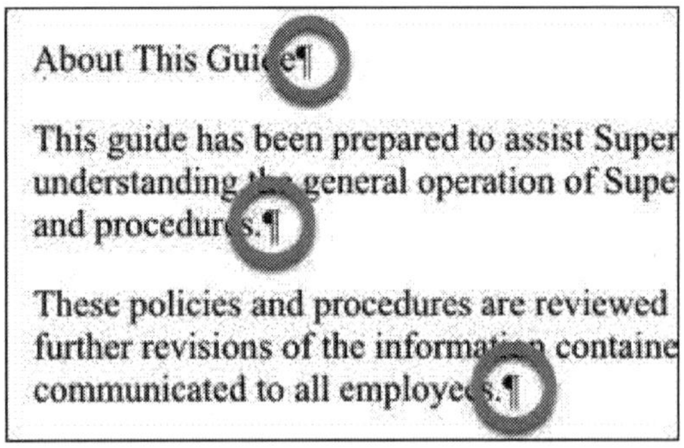

   The topic's "hidden" paragraph markers appear. In the next step, you will assign a style sheet to the topic which will dramatically change the appearance of the text. All style sheets can contain paragraph, character, and list styles. Because paragraph and list styles control the appearance of topic text up to the paragraph markers, it's nice to see where one paragraph ends and the next begins.

3. Apply a style to a single topic.

   ❒ from within the open topic, right-click the middle of the text and choose **Topic Properties**

   A Properties panel appears at the right of the RoboHelp window.

   ❒ select the **Topic Properties** icon

   ❒ expand **Style Sheets**

   ❒ click the **Style Sheets** drop-down menu

The Style Sheets you see in the menu were added by RoboHelp automatically when the project was created (default.css) or created when Word documents were imported into the project (vacation.css, for instance). All of the css files are stored in the Contents area within the **assets** folder.

❒ select **default.css** from the menu

Notice two things. First, if you collapse the Style Sheets menu, you will see that the applied Style Sheet is listed below the menu. Second, the appearance of the topic text changes dramatically to reflect the current attributes of default.css.

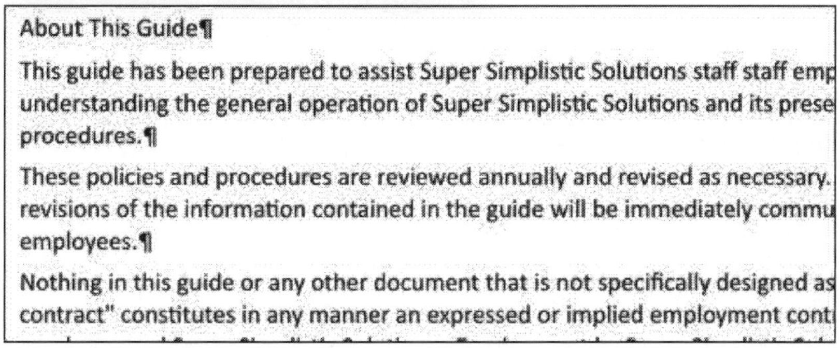
About This Guide¶

This guide has been prepared to assist Super Simplistic Solutions staff staff emp
understanding the general operation of Super Simplistic Solutions and its prese
procedures.¶

These policies and procedures are reviewed annually and revised as necessary.
revisions of the information contained in the guide will be immediately commu
employees.¶

Nothing in this guide or any other document that is not specifically designed as
contract" constitutes in any manner an expressed or implied employment cont

Note: On the **Topic Properties** of the **Properties** panel, you can click the **trash can icon** next to the Style Sheet name to remove the Style Sheet from the topic and return it to its previous formatting.

NOTES

NOTES

Guided Activity 22: Apply Paragraph Styles

1. Ensure that you are still working in the **project_structure_css** project and that the **About This Guide** topic is open.

   There are four icons on the Topic Properties panel: Content Properties, Topic Properties, Styles, and Spell Check

2. Display the paragraph styles.

   ❒ on the **Topic Properties** panel, click the **Styles** icon

3. Apply the Heading 1 paragraph style to a paragraph.

   ❒ in the **About This Guide** topic, click in the topic's first line of text (**About This Guide**)

   ❒ from the list of styles, click **Heading 1**

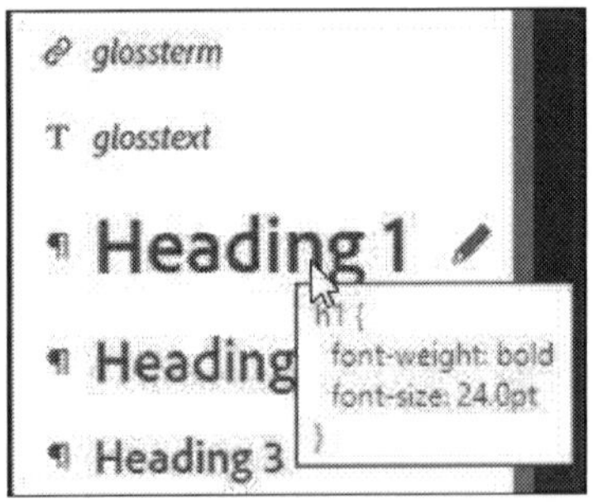

   The first paragraph in the topic is larger, and white space has been added below the paragraph.

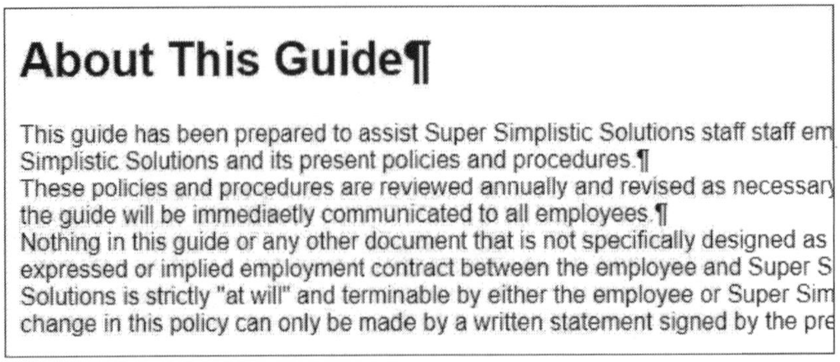

4. Assign a cascading style sheet to a topic and paragraph style to topic text.

❒ on the **Default TOC**, **General Office Information** folder, open the **Overtime Policy** topic

❒ on the **Topic Properties** panel, click the **Styles** icon 

Notice that there aren't any styles listed because you have not yet applied a Style Sheet to the topic.

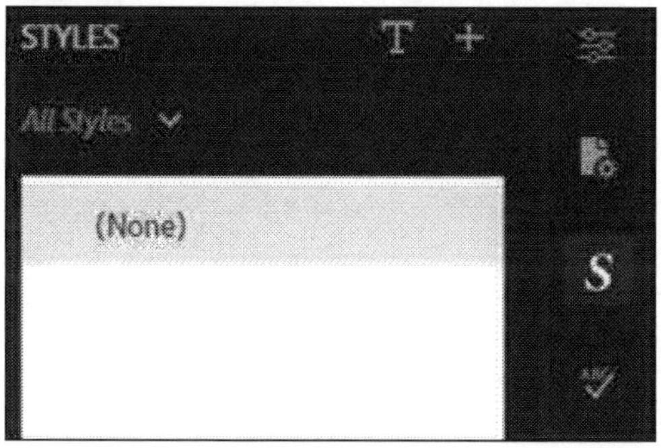

❒ on the **Topic Properties** panel, click the **Topic Properties** icon 

❒ from the **Style Sheet** drop-down menu, choose **default.css**

❒ on the **Topic Properties** panel, select the **Styles** icon 

Because the default.css file contains several styles, those styles are now available for use in the topic.

❒ click within the topic's main heading at the top of the topic (within the phrase **Overtime Policy**)

❒ from the list of styles, select **Heading 1**

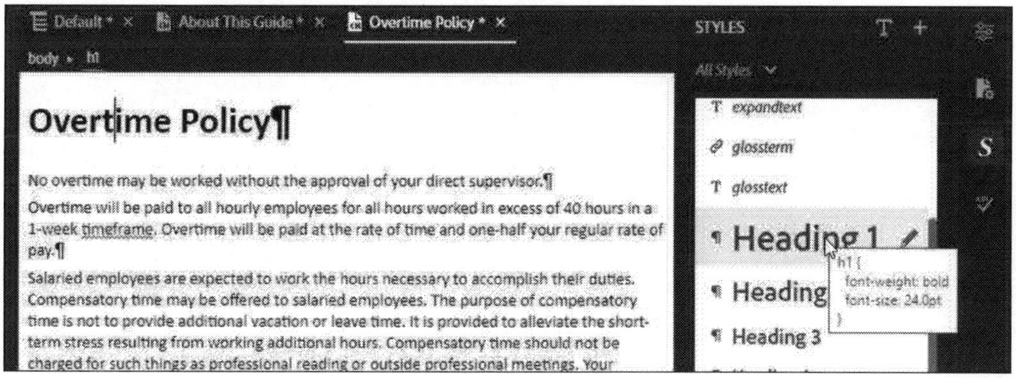

NOTES

Styles Confidence Check

1. Assign **default.css** to every topic in the project.
2. Assign the **Heading 1** style to the paragraph in each topic as necessary.
3. Open the **Termination Policy** topic and assign the **Heading 2** style to the following paragraphs:
   - ❒ Resignation
   - ❒ Disciplinary Policies and Procedures
   - ❒ Unemployment Insurance
4. In the **Special Benefits** topic, assign the Heading 2 style to the following paragraphs:
   - ❒ 401(k) Plan
   - ❒ Workers Compensation Insurance
   - ❒ Employee Assistance Program
5. In the **Electronic Communications Policy** topic, remove the extra paragraph breaks.

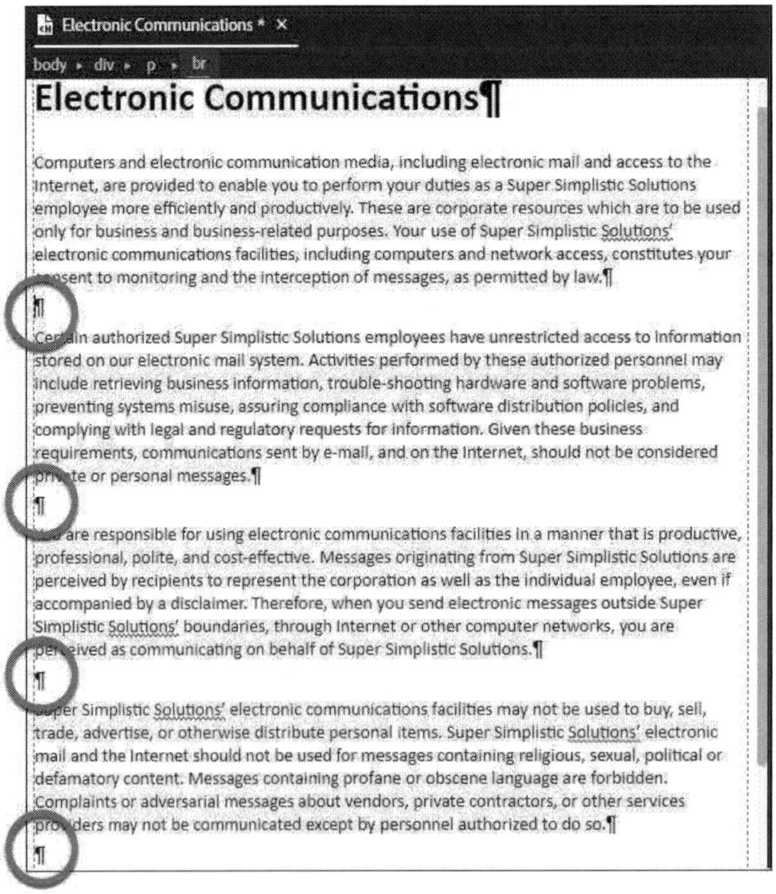

6. Save and close all of the open topics.
7. Save the project.

Custom Cascading Style Sheets

You can create your own cascading style sheets and define your own paragraph styles complete with specific fonts, sizes, colors, spacing, and much more. The CSS you create is an external file and can be assigned to any topic, imported into other RoboHelp projects and edited within RoboHelp or using a text editor such as Notepad (PC) or TextEdit (Mac).

Font Usage

Although there are thousands of fonts you can use in your Help System, there are only **two** main font categories: *serif* (fonts with feet) and *sans serif* (fonts without feet). Two popular fonts are Times New Roman (serif) and Arial (sans serif). Below is an example of each.

This is an example of Times New Roman, a serif font.

This is an example of Arial, a sans-serif font.

Serif fonts like Times Roman are generally considered easier to read on printed paper. Sans serif fonts like Arial are generally considered easier to read on a computer screen or mobile device than serif fonts. You can learn more about fonts at **https://www.w3schools.com/csSref/css_websafe_fonts.asp**.

Guided Activity 23: Create a Style Sheet

1. Ensure that you are still working in the **project_structure_css** project.

2. Create a style sheet.

   ❒ from the **Contents**, expand the **assets** folder

   ❒ select the **css** folder and then click **Options** (the three dots)

   ❒ choose **New > Stylesheet**

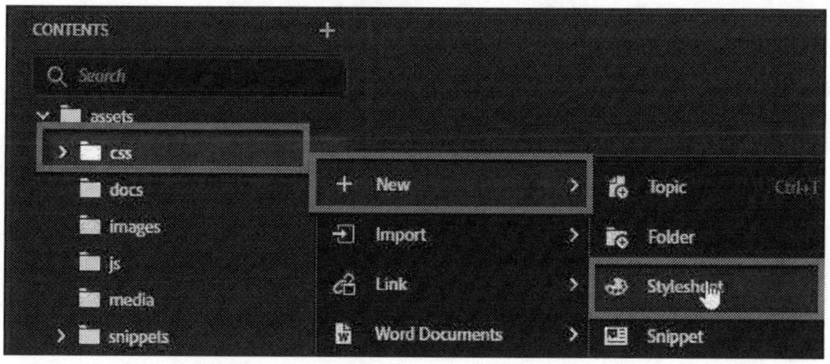

   The New Stylesheet dialog box opens.

   ❒ name the style sheet **policies**

   ❒ click the **Done** button

   Expand the css folder and notice that the new cascading style sheet file, **polices.css**, is added to the **css** folder. The style sheet also opens for editing. (If the policies.css file does not open on its own, double-click the file to open it).

NOTES

NOTES

3. Add a paragraph style to the policies cascading style sheet.

❒ from the list of **Styles**, select **Paragraph Styles**

Notice that there is a small toolbar at the top of the RoboHelp window.

❒ click the **New Style** icon

The **Add Style** dialog box opens.

❒ from the **Tag** menu, scroll down and review the available styles

I've mentioned in this book that you do not need to know HTML to use RoboHelp. While I'm standing by that statement, it cannot hurt to understand the role of cascading style sheets and how Tags, Classes, and Pseudo Classes work. I suggest spending time at **W3Schools.com** and reviewing the **CSS Tutorial**. Because much of RoboHelp's higher-end page and paragraph formatting depends upon CSS, the more you know, the better. Here's a link to the CSS Tutorial: **https://www.w3schools.com/css/default.asp**.

❒ from the **Tag** menu, select the **p** tag

The **p** tag is used to control the appearance of standard paragraph text.

❒ click the **Done** button

The paragraph tag is added to the Paragraph group.

4. Set the font properties for the paragraph style.

❒ expand the style's **Font** category

❒ from the **Font Family** drop-down menu, choose **Verdana** and then change the **Font Size** to **10 pt**

Note: The RoboHelp default unit of measurement is pixels. Ensure that you add the **pt** after the Font Size to represent points.

5. Change the paragraph spacing for the paragraph style.

   ❒ from within the style Properties area, scroll down and then expand the **Layout** options

   ❒ from the **Margin** area, click the **lock icon** to disable it

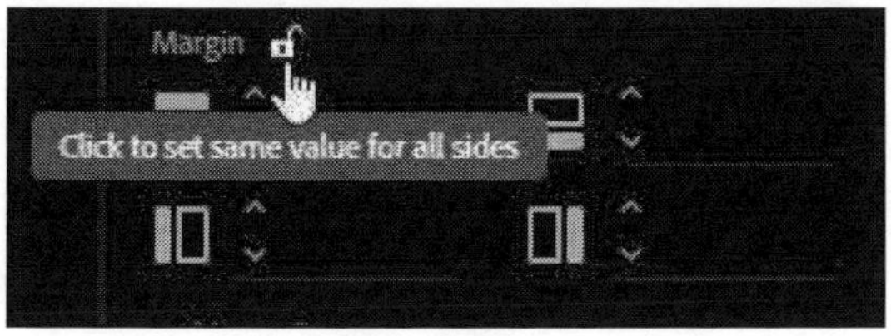

   ❒ change the **Bottom Margin** to **12 px**

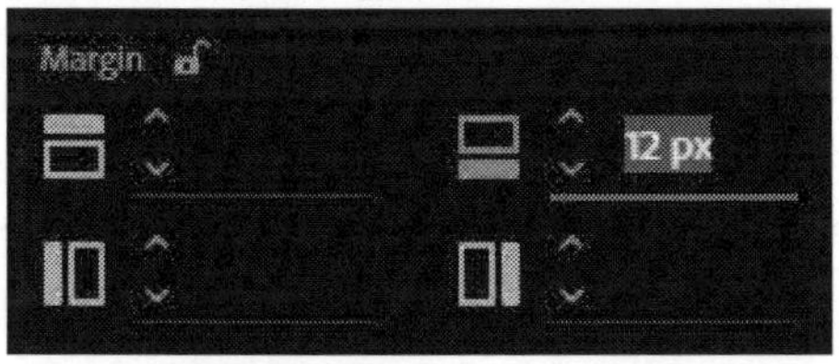

6. Add a heading 1 style to the policies style sheet.

   ❒ on the toolbar just above Properties, click the **New Style** icon

   The Add Style dialog box reopens.

   ❒ from the Tag list, scroll down and select **h1**

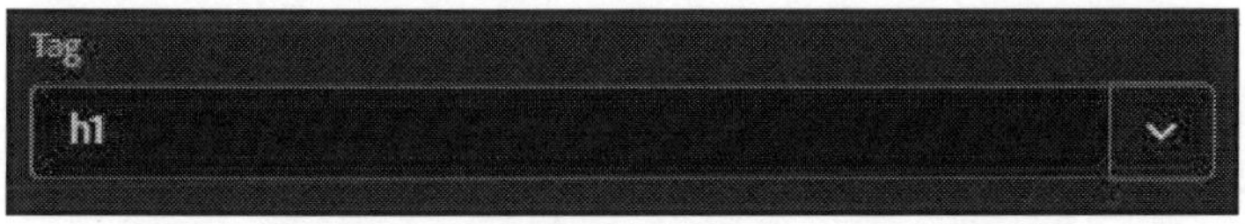

   The h1 tag is used to control the appearance of the Heading 1 style.

   ❒ click the **Done** button

7. Set the font properties for the heading style.

   ❒ from the list of policies.css Heading Styles, select **h1**

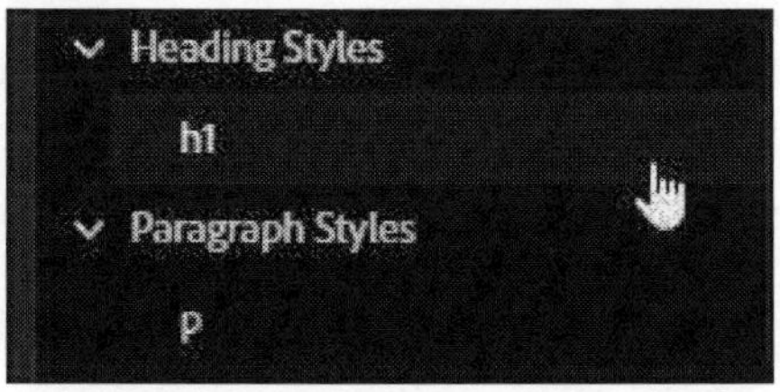

NOTES

NOTES

- ❐ from the style's **Properties** area, change the **Font** to **Verdana**
- ❐ change the **Font Size** to **14 pt**

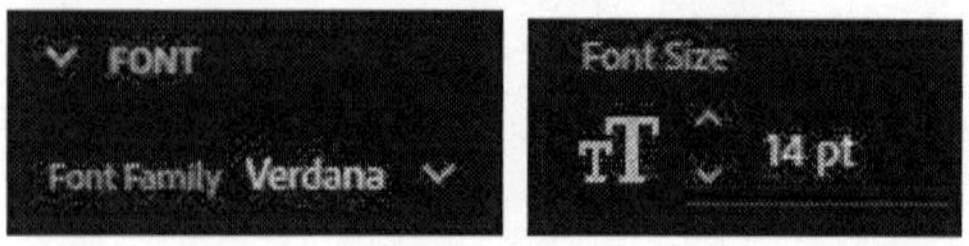

8. Add paragraph spacing below the h1 style.

- ❐ scroll down on the Properties panel to the **Layout** area
- ❐ unlock the **Margins** (click the lock icon)
- ❐ change the **Bottom Margin** to **12 px**

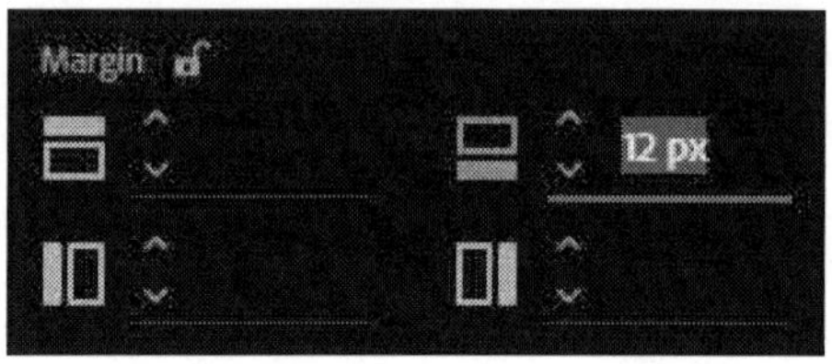

9. Save and close the **policies** cascading style sheet (CSS).

10. Remove a style sheet reference from a topic.

- ❐ from the **General Office Information** folder, open the **Special Benefits** topic

The topic is still using the default.css. Next, you'll remove the reference to the style sheet from the topic and apply your new **policies** style sheet.

- ❐ on the **Properties** panel, select the **Topic Properties** icon 
- ❐ from the **Style Sheets** area, click the **Trash can** icon next to the default.css reference

The style sheet file was not deleted from the project, just disconnected from the topic. Without the styles from the CSS, the text in the Special Benefit is formatted using default fonts, sizes, and colors.

11. Connect a different CSS to a topic.

- ❐ still working on the **Topic Properties** panel, from the **Style Sheets** drop-down menu, choose **policies.css**

The main heading and the paragraph text take on the attributes of the **h1** and **p** styles in the policies CSS. Because you have not added a style for the h2 paragraphs, the formatting of the subheads still needs work.

Tag Confidence Check

1. From the **assets** folder, open **policies.css** for editing.
2. Add an **h2** Style (the h2 tag controls the second level headings).
3. Format the **h2** tag as follows:

   Font: Verdana

   Font Size: 11 pt

   Bottom Margin: 12 px

4. Save and close the style sheet.

   In the Special Benefits topic, the second level headings should all be formatted to match the h2 tag you just created.

5. Reopen the **policies.css** file.
6. Edit the **h1** tag, changing the **Color** to a **dark red**.

7. Save and close the style sheet.

   The color for the topic's Special Benefits main heading should now be dark red.

NOTES

Character Styles

When you format selected text, you are using a technique known as **inline formatting**. Have you ever used the Bold tool on selected text in programs like Microsoft Word or PowerPoint? Ever changed plain text to *italic*? If so, then you've applied an inline format. Using inline formatting is easy, but it can be a bad habit because inline formatting is as stubborn. If you attach a different Style Sheet to a topic, the inline formatting can be stubborn and not go away.

Imagine having to manually move through a project and change every occurrence of text that is bold and maroon to italic and navy. That would be a tough task if there were just a few dozen such instances. But a few hundred? Ouch!

Much like Paragraph styles, Character styles allow you to quickly format selected text. Unlike Paragraph styles (such as the Heading styles you used earlier in this module), Character styles can be applied only to selected text. Once applied, Character styles are easy to update (just like Paragraph styles).

Guided Activity 24: Create a Character Style

1. Ensure that you are still working in the **project_structure_css** project.

2. If necessary, open the **policies.css** style sheet for editing.

3. Add a Character style.

   ❒ on the toolbar just above Properties, click the **New Style** icon

   The Add Style dialog box opens.

   ❒ in the **Tag** text field, type **span.emphasis**

   Typing the word "span" is the same as choosing the span tag from the Tag menu. In HTML, the span tag is a generic inline container element. Span tags usually wrap sections of text for styling purposes or for adding attributes to a section of text without creating a new line of content. By adding the word "emphasis," you're naming the new style **emphasis**. This is the Character Style name that will appear in the Styles panel later.

   ❒ click the **Done** button

   The Character Style is added to the Character category.

   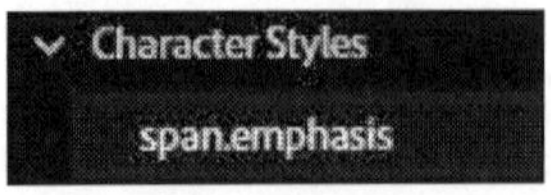

4. Change the font color for the character style.

   ❒ with the new **span.emphasis** tag selected, change the **Font Color** to **a dark red**

5. Save and close the policies style sheet.

6. Apply a Character Style to selected topic text.

   ❒ if necessary, open the **Special Benefits** topic

   ❒ in the first paragraph of the topic, highlight the phrase **21 years or older**

   ❒ at the right of the Topic Properties panel, select the **Styles** icon 

   ❒ from the **Styles** drop-down menu, choose **Character Styles**

   The emphasis style is the Character Style you just created.

   ❒ click the **emphasis** style

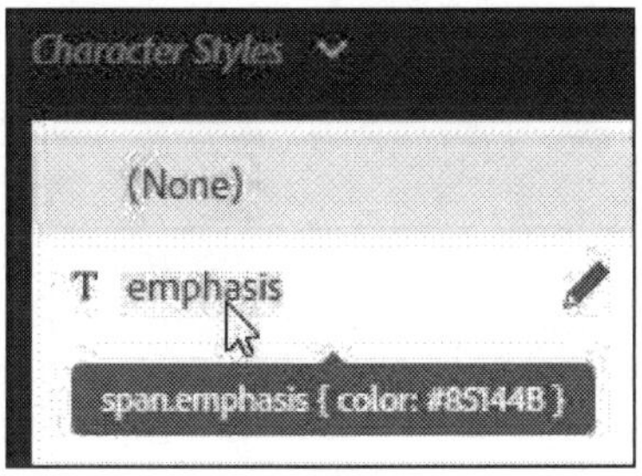

   Only the selected text in the topic takes on the appearance of the **emphasis** tag—the text should now be dark red.

7. Save your work.

NOTES

Character Style Confidence Check

1. In the **Employee Assistance Program** section, highlight the phrase **resolve your problems** in the second paragraph and apply the **emphasis** style to the text.
2. Go through the entire project and remove the references to the **default**.css. In its place, apply **policies**.css.

   Note: If any topics are referencing other/multiple CSS files, remove the references.

3. Open the **Termination Policy** topic and apply the **emphasis** style to the following phrases:

   First Notice

   Second Notice

   Final Notice

   Discharge

4. Open the **policies.css** file for editing.
5. Change the color of the **span.emphasis** style to **any color you like.**

   Reminder: The **span.emphasis** style is located in the **Character Styles** section of the **policies.css** file.

6. After closing and saving the style sheet, confirm that all instances of the emphasis style, across any topics where you've applied it, display the new color. (As a reminder, you used the emphasis style within the Special Benefits and Termination Policy topics.)
7. Save the project.

List Styles

There are two main types of lists used in HTML (and in RoboHelp): numbered lists, also known as ordered lists, and bulleted lists, also known as unordered lists. The formatting for both types of lists is controlled by tags that can be added to a style sheet.

Guided Activity 25: Format a Bulleted List

1. Ensure that you are still working in the **project_structure_css** project.

2. Open the **Pets in the Office Policy** topic for editing.

   During the last Confidence Check, you were instructed to apply the **policies** style sheet to all of the topics in the project. You may have noticed after doing so that the formatting of the bulleted list in the Pets policy did not update along with the rest of the topic. The reason? There isn't a style in the policies style sheet that instructs the topic how to format the bulleted list, so the text uses the default formatting (Times New Roman).

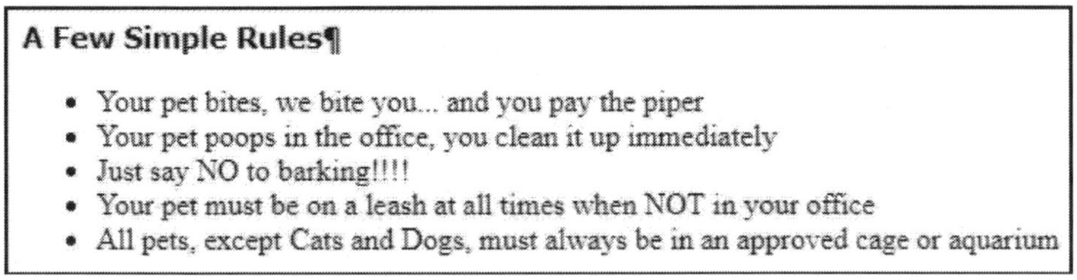

3. Open the **policies.css** style sheet for editing.

4. Create a new style to be used on the bulleted list.

   ❒ from the list of Styles, select **List Styles**

   ❒ click the **New Style** icon

   By default, the tag that appears in the tag list is the **ol** tag. The **ol** tag controls the formatting of numbered lists. Although it's worth setting up the formatting for this tag, let's focus instead on the tag that controls bulleted lists: the **ul** tag.

   ❒ replace the **ol** tag with the **ul** tag

   ❒ click the **Done** button

NOTES

NOTES

5. Format the bullets.

❒ from the top of the screen, select **Advanced Formatting**

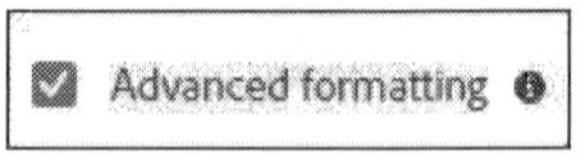

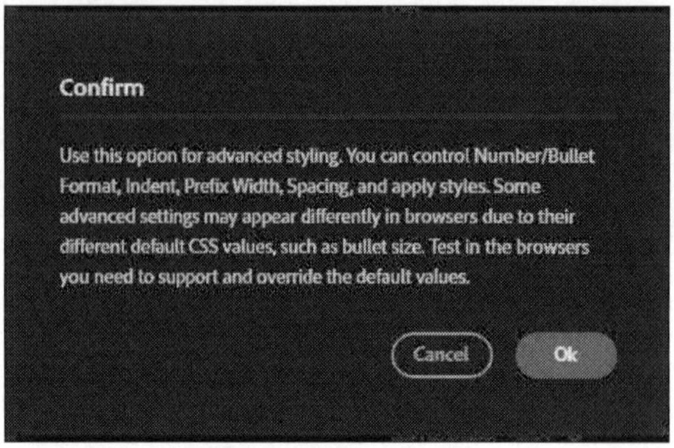

❒ click the **OK** button

❒ from the **Apply Styling to** drop-down menu, choose **Bullets** (if necessary)

❒ from the **Font** area, change the **Font Family** to **Verdana**

❒ change the **Font Size** to **10 pt**

6. Format the content used in a bulleted list.

❒ from the **Apply Styling to** drop-down menu, choose **Content**

❒ from the **Font** area, change the **Font Family** to **Verdana**

❒ change the **Font Size** to **10 pt**

7. Save and close the style sheet.

In the Pets in the Office Policy topic, the bulleted list matches the **ul** tag you just set up.

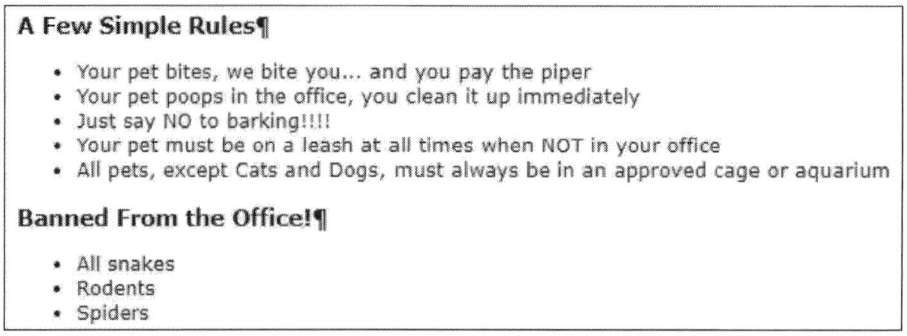

A Few Simple Rules¶

- Your pet bites, we bite you... and you pay the piper
- Your pet poops in the office, you clean it up immediately
- Just say NO to barking!!!!
- Your pet must be on a leash at all times when NOT in your office
- All pets, except Cats and Dogs, must always be in an approved cage or aquarium

Banned From the Office!¶

- All snakes
- Rodents
- Spiders

List Style Confidence Check

1. Open the **policies** style sheet for editing.
2. Select the **ul** list style.
3. Change **Apply Styling to Bullets**.

4. Change the **List Style Type** to **circle** and then save the css file.

The bullets in the bulleted list should now look like circles.

5. Change the **style** of the bullets used in the bulleted list to **square**.
6. Change the **style** of the bullets used in the bulleted list back to the original style: **disc**.
7. Save and close the project.

NOTES

Notes

iCONLOGIC
"Skills and Drills" Learning

Module 4: Links

In This Module You Will Learn About:

And You Will Learn To:

NOTES

Linking to External Content

You learned earlier how to import Microsoft Word documents into your project (see page 30). After the import process, the original source document has little value in RoboHelp because its contents have been copied into the RoboHelp project as one or more topics. Any changes you make to the imported content from within RoboHelp will not appear in the original Word document; changes to the original Word document will not appear in RoboHelp. If changes have been made to the original Word document and you want those changes to appear in the RoboHelp project, you'll need to make the identical changes to the content within RoboHelp. Otherwise, you can delete the imported content from the RoboHelp project and re-import the updated Word content. Neither of these two scenarios is ideal.

If the Word content you need to use in your RoboHelp project is a "moving target" and is constantly being updated by an author or subject matter expert, consider linking to the Word document instead of importing the content.

Guided Activity 26: Link to a Word Document

1. Open a source document using Microsoft Word.

   ❒ start **Microsoft Word**

   ❒ from **RoboHelp2022Data > topicContent**, use Microsoft Word to open **Holiday Schedule.docx**

   The first paragraph has been formatted using Word's Heading 1 style. The rest of the document is using Word's Normal style.

   Super Simplistic Solutions Holiday Schedule

   Super Simplistic Solutions celebrates the following holidays:

   2022

   January 1: New Year's Day
   January 18: Martin Luther King Day
   March 6: Biff's Birthday!
   May 31: Memorial Day
   July 4: Independence Day
   September 6: Labor Day
   October 11: Columbus Day
   November 11: Veterans Day
   November 25: Thanksgiving Day
   December 25: Christmas Day

   2023

   January 1: New Year's Day
   January 17: Martin Luther King Day
   March 6: Biff's Birthday!
   May 30: Memorial Day
   July 4: Independence Day
   September 5: Labor Day
   October 10: Columbus Day
   November 11: Veterans Day
   November 24: Thanksgiving Day
   December 25: Christmas Day

2. Close Microsoft Word and return to RoboHelp.

3. Open an existing RoboHelp project.

   ❒ using RoboHelp, choose **File > Open Project**

   ❒ from the **RoboHelp2022Data** folder, open the **RoboHelpProjects** folder

   ❒ open the **linking** folder

   ❒ open **linking.rhpj**

   Note: Click the **Upgrade** button if prompted.

4. Create a folder for linked content.

   ❒ from the **Contents** area, right-click below the **Leave and Vacation** folder and choose **New > Folder**

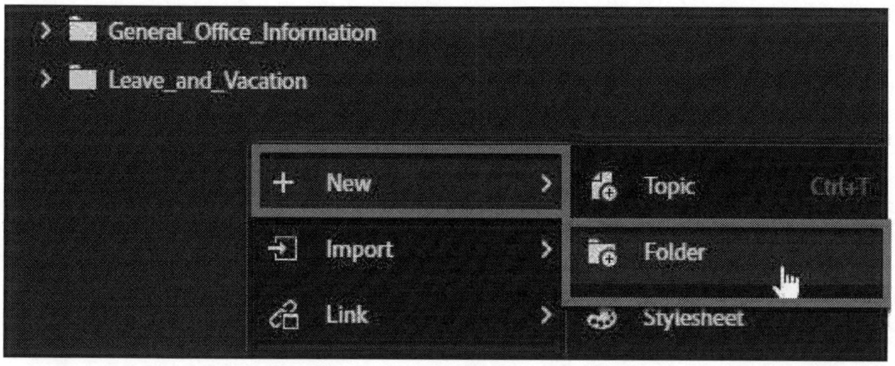

   The New Folder dialog box opens.

   ❒ name the new folder **Linked Documents** (RoboHelp will automatically add an underscore to the name)

   ❒ click the **Done** button

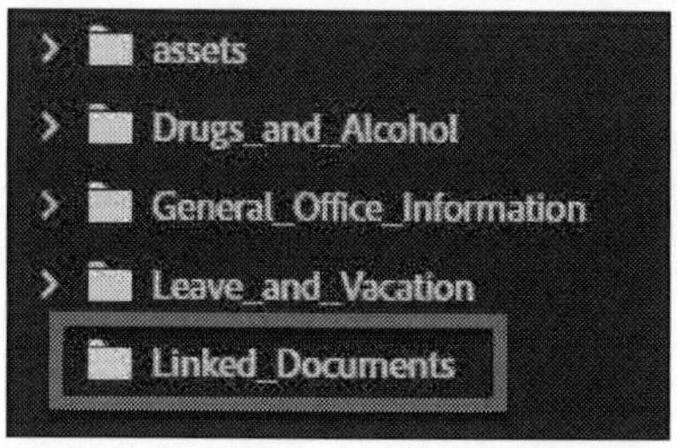

NOTES

NOTES

5. Link to a Word document.

❒ right-click the **Linked_Documents** folder and choose **Link > Link File**

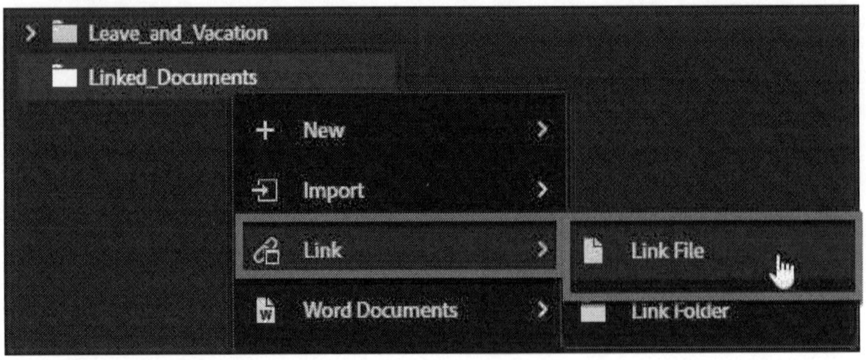

❒ from **RoboHelp2022Data > topicContent** open **Holiday Schedule.docx**

You'll see a confirmation of the link in the lower right of the RoboHelp window.

The Holiday Schedule document appears in the Linked_Documents folder. Notice the green icon to the left of the file name. The green icon indicates that the document in RoboHelp and its source back in **RoboHelp2022Data > topicContent** are synchronized.

6. Create a topic from the linked Word document.

❒ right-click the linked document and choose **Create/Update Topics**

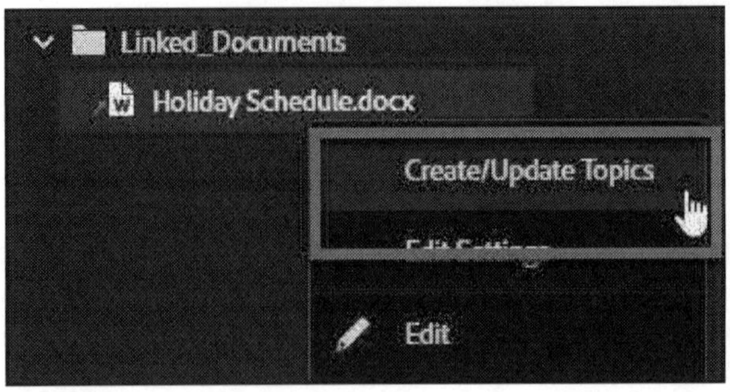

You'll see a confirmation that content was created from the linked document.

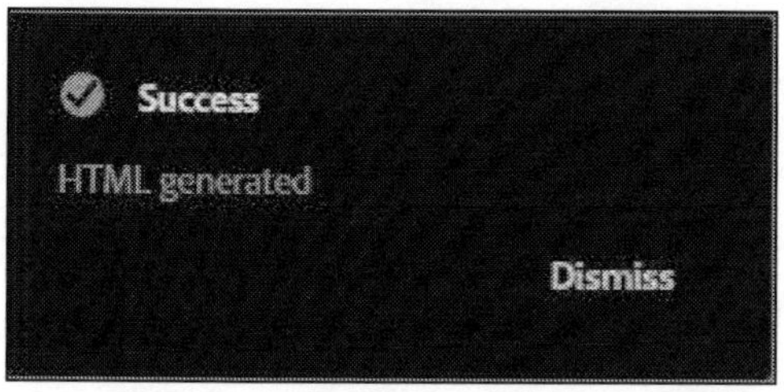

7. Explore the new topic.

   ❐ from the **Linked_Documents** folder, open the **Holiday Schedule** folder

   Notice that in addition to a new topic named **Holiday Schedule**, the process of creating topics from the linked Holiday Schedule.docx file has created a new style sheet named **Holiday Schedule.css**.

   ❐ open the **Holiday Schedule** topic

Thanks to the Holiday Schedule.css file, the content in the RoboHelp topic matches the content in the linked Word document.

NOTES

8. Close the Holiday Schedule topic.

9. Edit the source document.

   ❒ start **Microsoft Word**

   ❒ from **RoboHelp2022Data > topicContent**, use Word to open **Holiday Schedule.docx**

   ❒ in the **2023** dates, click after Martin Luther King Day and press [**enter**] to create a new line

   ❒ add the following holiday: **February 14: Valentine's Day**

2022
January 1: New Year's Day
January 18: Martin Luther King Day
March 6: Biff's Birthday!
May 31: Memorial Day
July 4: Independence Day
September 6: Labor Day
October 11: Columbus Day
November 11: Veterans Day
November 25: Thanksgiving Day
December 25: Christmas Day

2023
January 1: New Year's Day
January 17: Martin Luther King Day
February 14: Valentine's Day
March 6: Biff's Birthday!
May 30: Memorial Day
July 4: Independence Day
September 5: Labor Day
October 10: Columbus Day

10. Add the same holiday to **2024.**

11. Save and close the Word document.

12. Return to the RoboHelp project.

13. In the **Linked_Documents** folder, notice that the reference to the source Word document is **red**, an indication that the content in your project is not in sync with the source document.

14. Sync the topic content in RoboHelp with the linked Word document.

❒ from the **Linked_Documents** folder, right-click **Holiday Schedule.docx**

❒ choose **Sync > From Source to Project**

❒ click **Yes** to confirm the action

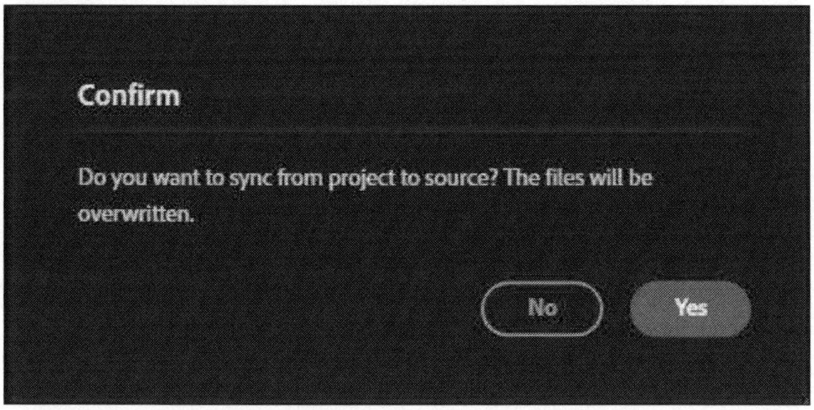

A Success message appears in the bottom-right of the RoboHelp window.

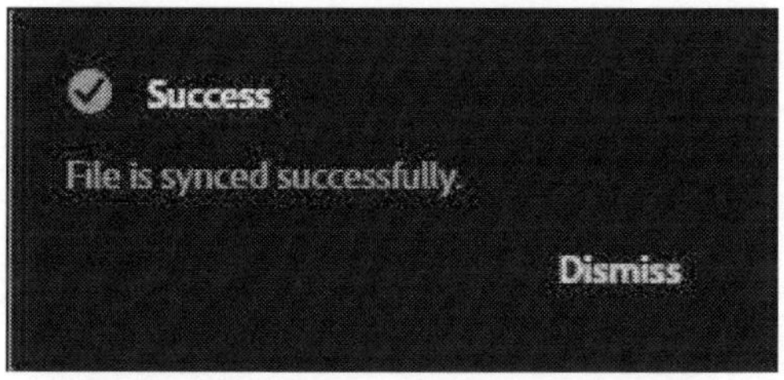

The icon color to the left of the Word document reference is once again green.

❒ right-click **Holiday Schedule.docx** and choose **Create/Update Topics**

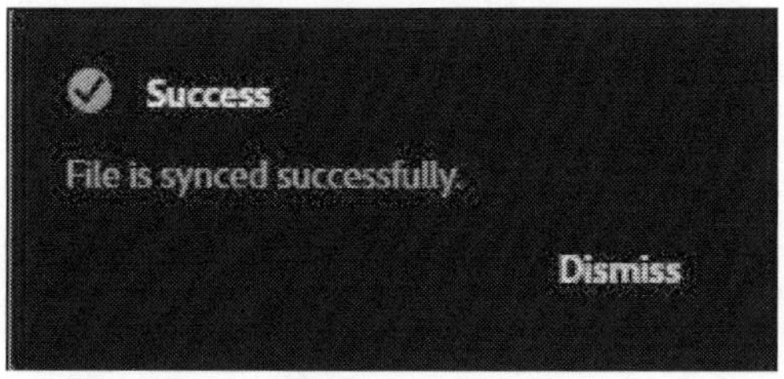

15. Explore the updated topic.

❒ from the **Linked_Documents** folder, open the **Holiday Schedule** folder

❒ open the **Holiday Schedule** topic

Notice that the changes made to the topic in Word appear in the RoboHelp topic.

NOTES

NOTES

External Content Links Confidence Check

1. Using **Microsoft Word**, reopen the source **Holiday Schedule.docx** document.

2. Using Word, apply **bullets** to all of the vacation dates.

Super Simplistic Solutions Holiday Schedule

Super Simplistic Solutions celebrates the following holidays:

2022

- January 1: New Year's Day
- January 18: Martin Luther King Day
- March 6: Biff's Birthday!
- May 31: Memorial Day
- July 4: Independence Day
- September 6: Labor Day
- October 11: Columbus Day
- November 11: Veterans Day
- November 25: Thanksgiving Day
- December 25: Christmas Day

2023

- January 1: New Year's Day
- January 17: Martin Luther King Day
- February 14: Valentine's Day
- March 6: Biff's Birthday!

3. Save and close the Word document.

4. Back in RoboHelp, right-click **Holiday Schedule.docx** and choose **Create/Update Topics**.

5. Open the **Holiday Schedule** topic.

   The changes made in Word appear in RoboHelp. However, the topic is not using the same style sheet as the other topics in the project so the bulleted lists are not formatted like the other topics.

6. From the **Properties** area, **Topic Properties**, **Style Sheets** area, **remove** Holiday Schedule.css.

7. Apply **policies.css** to the **Holiday Schedule** topic.

Note: Changes made to a linked topic from within RoboHelp are reverted whenever you Sync to the Source document. Because the **Holiday Schedule** topic is linked to the **Holiday Schedule.docx** Word document, the edit you just made would be undone should you again Sync to the source document.

Hyperlinks

Hyperlinks allow your users to jump from one project location to another. There are several types of hyperlinks you can create including standard links (links that typically jump from one Help topic to another), web address links (links that open a website or resource), email links (links that send an email to a recipient you specify), and links to local files.

Guided Activity 27: Insert Hyperlinks

1. Ensure that the **linking** project is still open.

2. From the **Drugs and Alcohol** folder, open the **Drug Policy** topic.

3. Add text to a topic.

   ❒ in the second paragraph ("If you are having difficulties resulting..."), click after the word **drug**

   ❒ press [**spacebar**] and then type **or alcohol**

   The sentence should now read "If you are having difficulties resulting from drug or alcohol use, Super Simplistic Solutions may request that you enter a rehabilitation program."

4. Insert a hyperlink to another topic in the project.

   ❒ double-click the word **alcohol** that you just typed (to highlight the word)

   ❒ from the top of the RoboHelp window, click the **Insert Link** icon and choose **Hyperlink**

   The **Link to** dialog box opens.

   ❒ from the **Link to** area, ensure that **Project Files** is selected

   ❒ from the **Drugs and Alcohol** folder, select **Alcohol Policy**

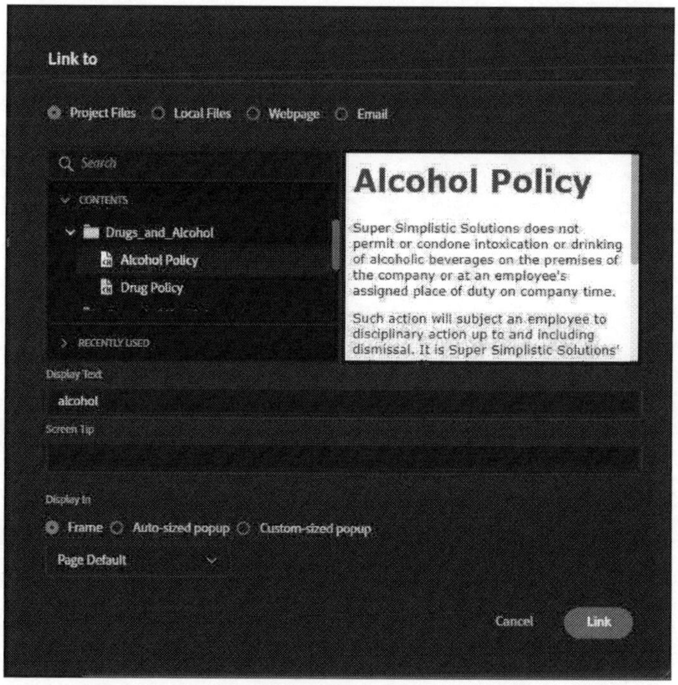

NOTES

❒ click the **Link** button

Now that you have changed the word "alcohol" to a hyperlink, the text takes on the traditional appearance of linked text (**blue** with an **underline**).

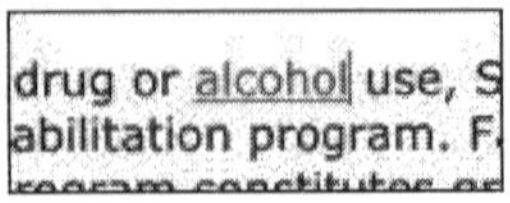

5. Insert a hyperlink in another topic by dragging and dropping.

❒ open the **Alcohol Policy** topic

❒ at the end of the topic text, click after the last word and press [**enter**] to add a new paragraph

❒ type **See also:**

❒ from the **Contents** area, drag the **Drug policy** topic to the right of the **See also:** text that you just typed

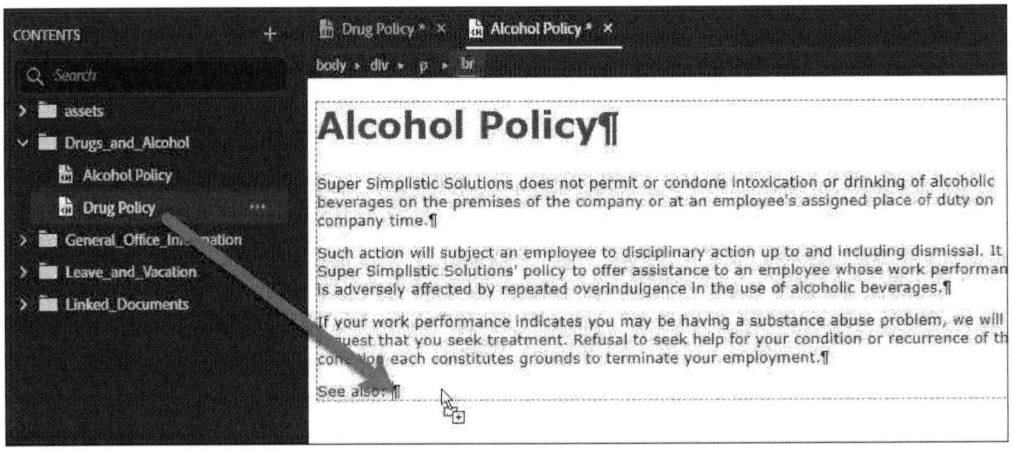

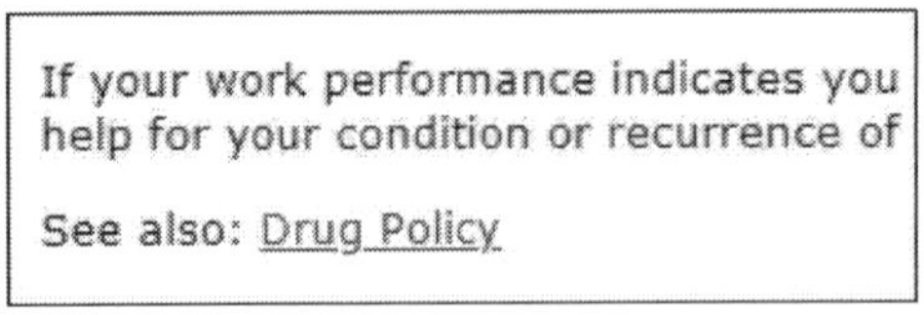

Your project now has two hyperlinks to existing topics.

6. Save the project.

7. Preview a topic and test the hyperlinks.

❒ ensure that the Alcohol Policy topic is still open

❒ at the far right of the RoboHelp window, click the **Preview** icon

While you're in preview mode, notice that the editing tools at the top of the topic window disappear.

❒ click the **Drug Policy** hyperlink

The Drug Policy topic opens in its own window.

❒ click the word **alcohol** in the open Drug Policy window

The Alcohol Policy topic opens.

8. Close the preview window and then click the **Author** icon to exit Preview mode.

Links Confidence Check

1. Open the **Payroll Policy** topic.
2. Add the following new paragraph at the end of the topic:
   See also: Overtime Policy.
3. Highlight the phrase **Overtime Policy** and link the text to the **Overtime Policy** topic.
4. Open the **Overtime Policy** topic and add the following new paragraph at the end of the topic: **See also: Payroll Policy**.
5. Link the phrase **Payroll Policy** to the Payroll Policy topic.

   Note: You can remove an unwanted link by right-clicking any link and choosing **Remove Hyperlink.**

6. Open the **Payroll Policy** topic.
7. Click after the hyperlink to **Overtime Policy** and press [**spacebar**].
8. Type **or Vacation Policy**.
9. Hyperlink the words **Vacation Policy** to the **Vacation Policy** topic.
10. Save the project.
11. Preview the topics and test your new links.
12. Close the Preview window.
13. Open the **Drug Policy** Topic.
14. Notice that there's a misspelled word in the last paragraph ("ditribute").
15. Right-click the word and replace it with **distribute**.

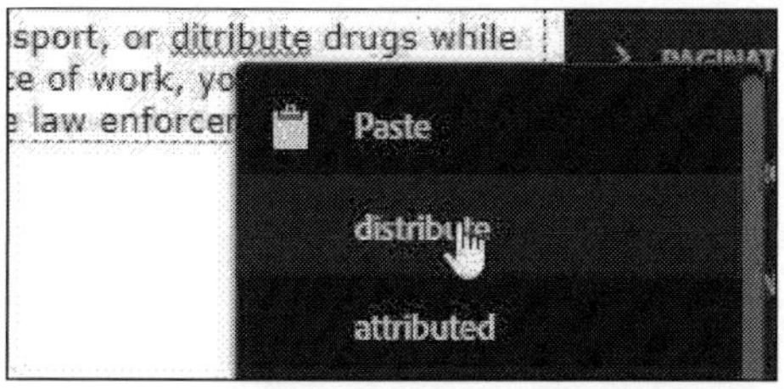

Note: RoboHelp allows you to correct spelling errors on-the-fly as you've just seen. You can also run a traditional Spell Check by choosing **Edit > Spell Check**. You can Spell Check a single topic, all topics, or All Project Files. Although choosing **All Project Files** makes it longer to run the spell check, I suggest going with this option at least once every so often to ensure you've checked for spelling errors within all topics, the TOC, and the Index.

NOTES

NOTES

Bookmarks

You learned how to create hyperlinks that take users from one topic to another on page 69. Bookmarks allow you to create hyperlink targets within topics. One use for bookmarks would be navigating a large topic. The topic contains several subheadings. You can bookmark each of the topic's subheadings and then insert a hyperlink that takes a user not just to the topic but directly to the location or a bookmark.

Guided Activity 28: Insert Bookmarks

1. Ensure that the **linking** project is still open.

2. From the **General Office Information** folder, open the **Termination Policy** topic.

3. Insert a Bookmark.

   ❒ at the top of the topic, click to the left of the **Resignation** heading

   ❒ from the toolbar above the topic, click the **Insert Bookmark** icon

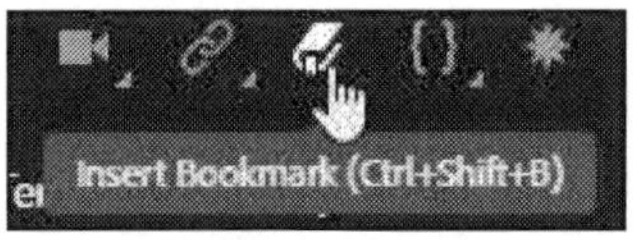

   The Bookmark dialog box opens.

   ❒ in the **ID** field, replace the placeholder text with **resignation**

   ❒ click the **Insert** button

   A bookmark icon appears to the left of the word Resignation. This is a visual indicator that a bookmark has been inserted.

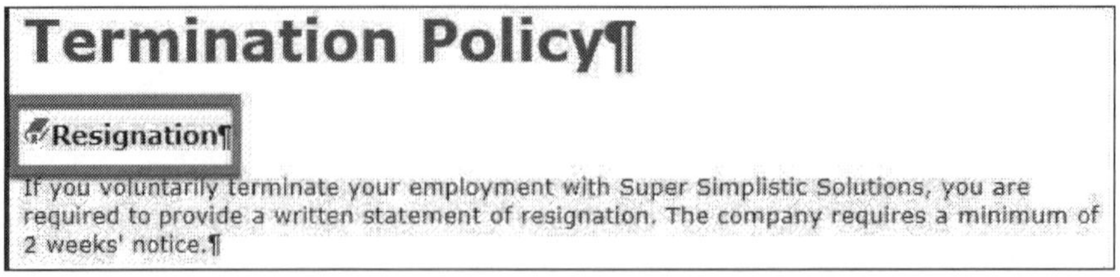

Bookmarks Confidence Check

1. Insert a second bookmark to the left of the second heading (**Disciplinary Policies and Procedures**) with the ID **disciplinary_policies_and_procedures**.
2. Add a third bookmark for the last heading in the topic with the ID **unemployment_insurance**.

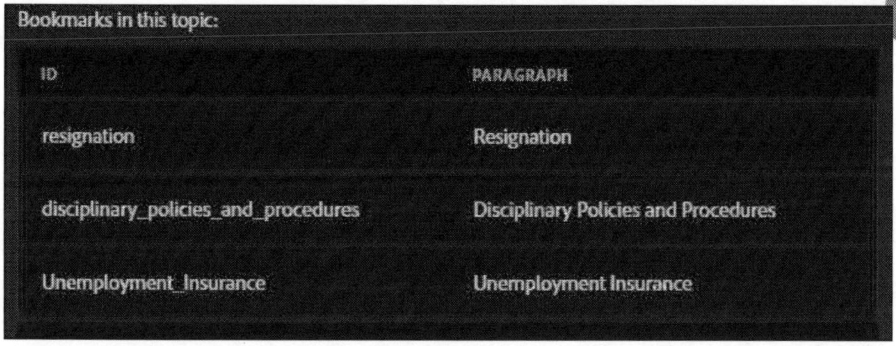
Bookmarks in this topic:

ID	PARAGRAPH
resignation	Resignation
disciplinary_policies_and_procedures	Disciplinary Policies and Procedures
Unemployment_Insurance	Unemployment Insurance

3. Still in the **Termination Policy** topic, click after the main heading (**Termination Policy**) and press [**enter**] to add a line between the main heading and subheading **Resignation**.
4. Type **Our Termination Policy consists of three main areas: Resignation, Disciplinary Policies and Procedures and Unemployment Insurance.**

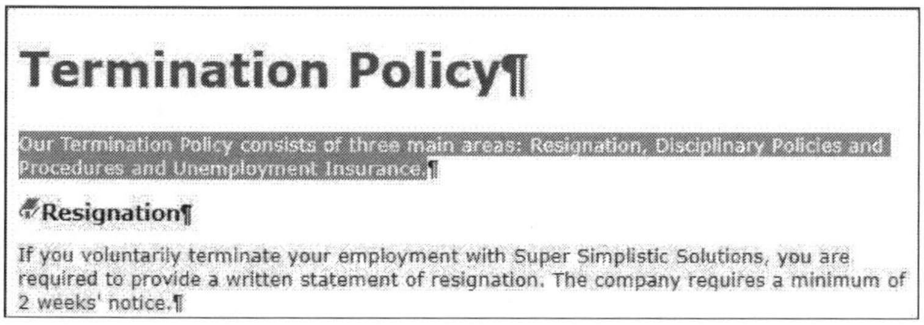
Termination Policy¶

Our Termination Policy consists of three main areas: Resignation, Disciplinary Policies and Procedures and Unemployment Insurance.¶

Resignation¶

If you voluntarily terminate your employment with Super Simplistic Solutions, you are required to provide a written statement of resignation. The company requires a minimum of 2 weeks' notice.¶

5. Save the project.
6. Highlight the word **Resignation** in the text that you just typed.
7. Display the **Link to Hyperlink** dialog box.

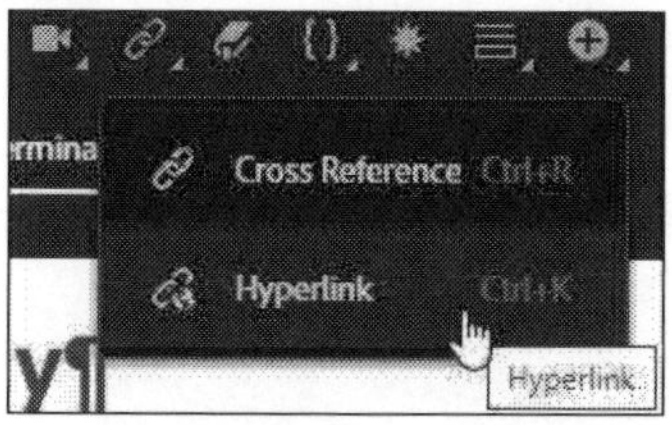

8. From the **General Office Information** folder, expand the **Termination Policy** topic to see the bookmarks you added.

NOTES

NOTES

9. Select the **resignation** bookmark and then click the **Link** button.
10. Link the text **Disciplinary Policies and Procedures** and **Unemployment Insurance** to their respective bookmarks.

11. **Preview** the topic. 
12. Test the bookmarks (by clicking any of the links at the top of the page).
13. When finished, return to **Author** mode. 

Popup Links

The hyperlinks you have added to topics have taken users from one topic to another. If you want users to link to a small window within a topic, popups are just the ticket. When users click the hyperlink, the content they link to can appear in either an auto-sizing popup (which is only as big as necessary to display the content) or a custom-sized popup (which appears in a window size that you control).

Guided Activity 29: Insert Auto-Sizing Popups

1. Ensure that the **linking** project is still open.

2. Add a new folder.

   ❒ in the **Contents** area, right-click beneath the last folder and choose **New > Folder**

   ❒ name the folder **Corporate_Officers**

   ❒ click the **Done** button

3. Create a new topic.

   ❒ right-click the **Corporate_Officers** folder and choose **New > Topic**

   ❒ change the **Title** to **Our President**

   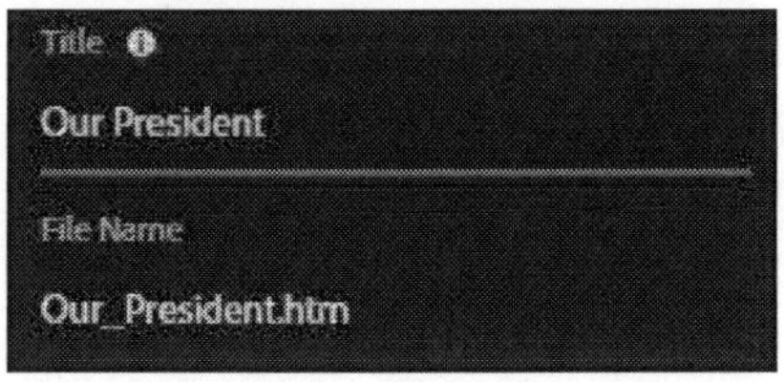

   ❒ click the **Create** button

4. Add the following text to the new topic: **The president of Super Simplistic Solutions is Biff Bifferson. Our tireless leader can be reached by dialing extension 123 or by sending an Email.**

   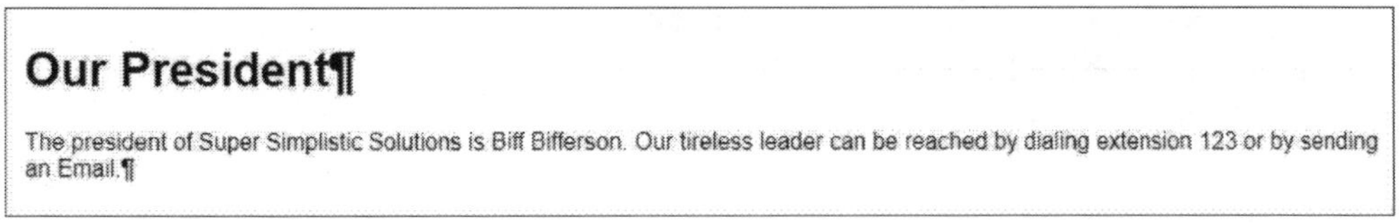

NOTES

5. Remove a reference to a style sheet.

   ❒ on the **Properties** panel, **Topic Properties**, **Style Sheets** area, click the **Delete** icon

6. Apply a different style sheet to a topic.

   ❒ on the **Properties** panel, **Topic Properties**, **Style Sheets** area, select **policies.css** from the drop-down menu

Note: You have been instructed to remove references to topic style sheets and apply different style sheets multiple times. From a teaching perspective, having you go through this process multiple times is great for reinforcing the process. However, if you choose **File > Project Settings**, you can select any style sheet as the Default Stylesheet. The Default Stylesheet will automatically be applied to new topics.

7. Save the project.

8. Insert an auto-sizing popup.

   ❒ open the **About This Guide** topic

   ❒ highlight the word **president** (it is the last word in the topic)

   ❒ from the top of the RoboHelp window, click the **Insert Link** icon and choose **Hyperlink**

   The **Link to** dialog box opens.

   ❒ from the **Contents** area, open the **Corporate Officers** folder

   ❒ select the **Our President** topic

   ❒ from the **Display In** area, select **Auto-sized popup**

   ❒ click the **Link** button

9. Preview the **About This Guide** topic and test the pop-up link by clicking the link to the **president** topic.

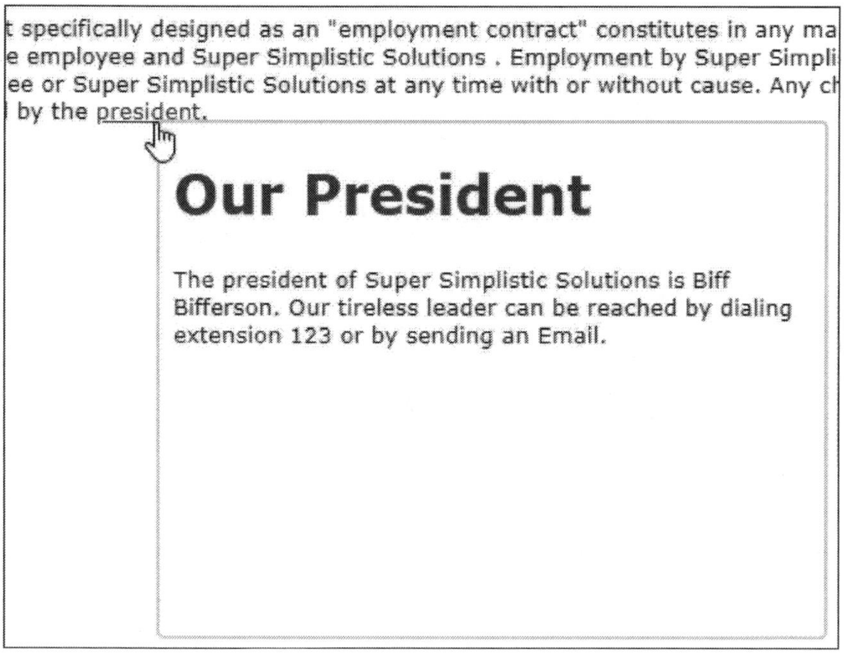

10. Return to **Author** mode.

11. Save the project.

Popup Hyperlink Confidence Check

1. Open the **Our President** topic and select the word **Email** that you typed.
2. Insert a Hyperlink and, from the **Link to** area, choose **Email**.
3. In the **To** field, type **biff.bifferson@supersimplisticsolutions.com** (click the **Link** button when finished to close the **Link to** dialog box).

   When clicked by your users, the Email link starts the user's email application and addresses the email to **biff.bifferson@supersimplisticsolutions.com**.

4. Create a new topic in the **Corporate_Officers** folder called **Human Resources**.
5. Add the following text to the new topic: **Our Human Resources Director is Brandy McNeill at extension 552.**
6. Create a new topic in the **Corporate_Officers** folder called **Information Services Director**.
7. Add the following text to the new topic: **Our Information Services Director is Travis DonBullian at extension 33.**
8. Create a new topic in the **Corporate_Officers** folder called **Webmaster**.
9. Add the following text to the new topic: **Our Webmaster is Sandra Stimson at extension 34.**
10. Open the **Overtime Policy** topic.
11. Highlight the words **Human Resources** (in the "Authorization for Employees' Earned Compensatory Time" paragraph near the end of the topic).
12. Link the phrase to the **Human Resources** topic in an **Auto-sized popup**.
13. Open the **Electronic Communications Policy** topic.
14. Add a blank paragraph at the end of the topic.
15. Type **See also: Information Services Director or Our Webmaster**.
16. Insert Auto-sized popup links for the phrases **Information Services Director** and **Our Webmaster** that link to the appropriate topics.
17. Save and close the project.

iCONLOGiC
"Skills and Drills" Learning

Module 5: Images and Multimedia

In This Module You Will Learn About:

And You Will Learn To:

Images

Given today's distractions and stress levels, most people who use your Help System will want to find information as quickly as possible. Unlike the old days, text-heavy topics are not effective. A modern approach to help documentation is to use a minimal amount of text and instead use visually appealing, relevant images as much as possible.

RoboHelp allows you to import such image formats as **GIFs, JPEGs, BMPs**, **ICOs, SVGs**, and **PNGs**. You can learn about the strengths and weaknesses of each image format at **https://www.w3.org/Graphics/**.

Guided Activity 30: Insert an Image

1. Open the **images_multimedia** RoboHelp project.
   (The project is in **RoboHelp2022Data > RoboHelpProjects**.)

   Note: Click the **Upgrade** button if prompted.

2. Display the Topic List panel and add a column.

   ❒ choose **View >Topic List**

   All of the topics in the project appear on a single screen. Although the list of topics includes topic file names, TOC assignment, and more, it's likely that topic titles aren't displayed. You'll add a Titles column next.

   ❒ from the right of the RoboHelp window, within the **Columns** area, click **Title**

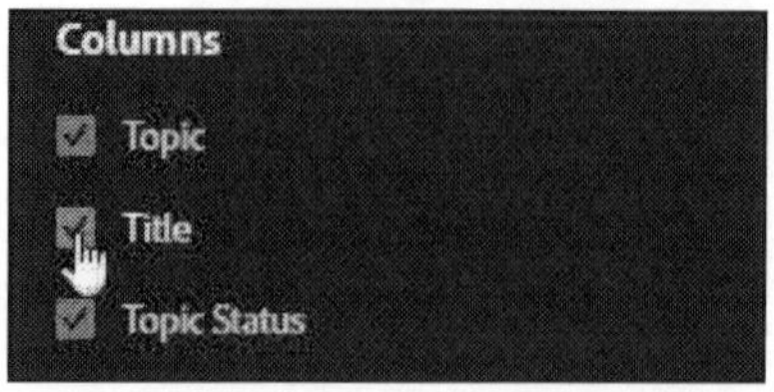

In the **Topic List**, notice that you can now see all of the topic Titles.

3. Use the Topic List to open a topic.

   ❒ from within the **Topic List**, right-click the **Mission Statement** topic and choose **Edit**

4. Insert an image.

   ❒ from within the **Mission Statement** topic, click at the end of the topic and press [**enter**] to insert a blank line

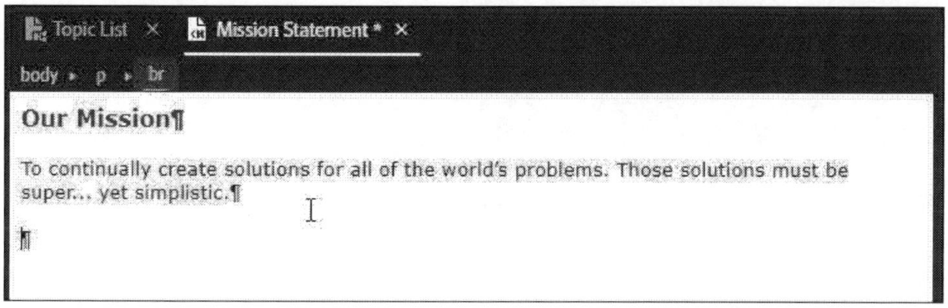

   ❒ from above the topic, click the **Insert Image** icon

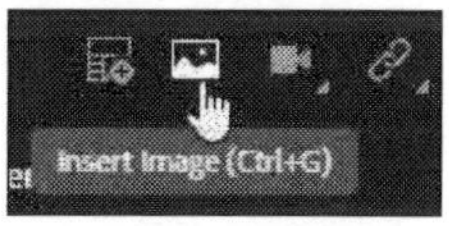

   The **Insert Image** dialog box opens.

   ❒ select **Local Files**

   ❒ click the **Browse** icon

   ❒ from the **RoboHelp2022Data** folder, open the **images** folder

   ❒ open the **puzzle.jpg** image file

   ❒ click the **Insert** button

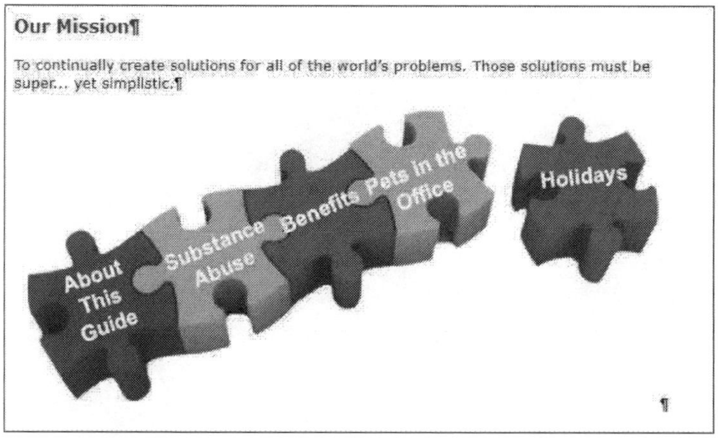

Note: If you want to use an imported image in another topic, you do not need to import it a second time. Instead, go to **Contents > assets > images** and drag the image into the topic.

NOTES

NOTES

Guided Activity 31: Add Alternate Text and an Image Title

1. Ensure that you're still working in the images_multimedia project.

2. Add Alternate Text to an image.

   ❒ still working in the **Mission Statement** topic, select the **puzzle image** you just inserted

   ❒ at the right of the RoboHelp window, click the **Content Properties** icon

   ❒ in the **Alternate Text** area, type **Image containing links to popular topics.**

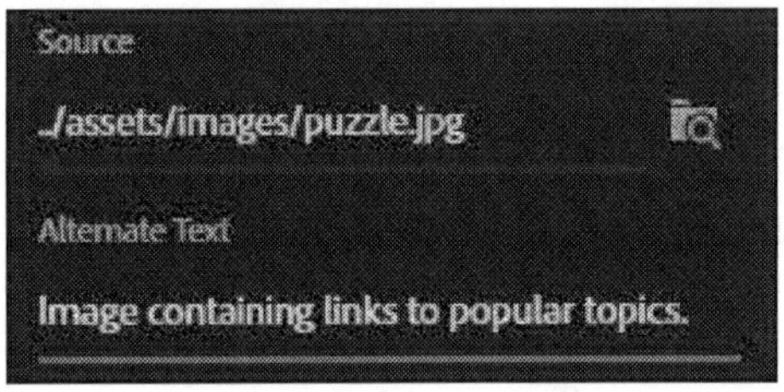

   Alternate Text is typically a brief description of the image. Alternate Text serves two purposes. It appears in published output if the image cannot be displayed for any reason. For visually impaired users, accessibility devices read the Alternate Text out loud.

3. Add an Image Title.

   ❒ in the **Image Title** area of the **Content Properties**, type **Image Map: Links to Popular Topics**

4. Preview the topic.

5. Move your mouse over the puzzle image. Notice that the Image Title appears as your mouse hovers over the puzzle image.

Images Confidence Check

1. Return to **Author mode** and save the project.
2. Open the **Our President** topic and click to the left of the text "The president of Super Simplistic Solutions is Biff Bifferson."
3. From **RoboHelp2022Data** > **images**, insert the **biff_baby.jpg** image.
4. Edit the Properties of the graphic you just inserted:
   - ❒ Add the following Alternate Text: **Image of Biff Bifferson.**
   - ❒ Add the following Image Title: **Our President, Biff Bifferson**
   - ❒ Change the **Width** to **64** and press [**tab**] or [**enter**].

   Because **Maintain Aspect Ratio** is enabled by default, the image's **Height** automatically changes to **91** (ensuring that the image is resized proportionally).

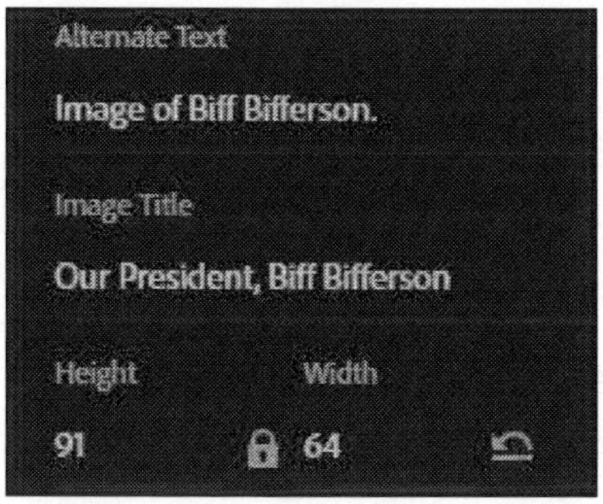

5. Change the **Text wrapping** to **Right**.

   Text wrapping will move the image to the right side of the screen and force the text to wrap around it. Depending upon how large your RoboHelp window is, you'll see the text wrapping without having to preview the topic.

6. Open the **Webmaster** topic.
7. Click to the left of the text "Our Webmaster is Sandra Stimson" and insert the following image: **sandra_baby.jpg**.

NOTES

NOTES

8. Edit the Properties for the image.
    - ❒ add the following **Image Title** and **Alternate Text** to the image: **Our Webmaster, Sandra Stimson**
    - ❒ change the **Width** of the image to **116**
    - ❒ change its **Text wrapping** to **Right**

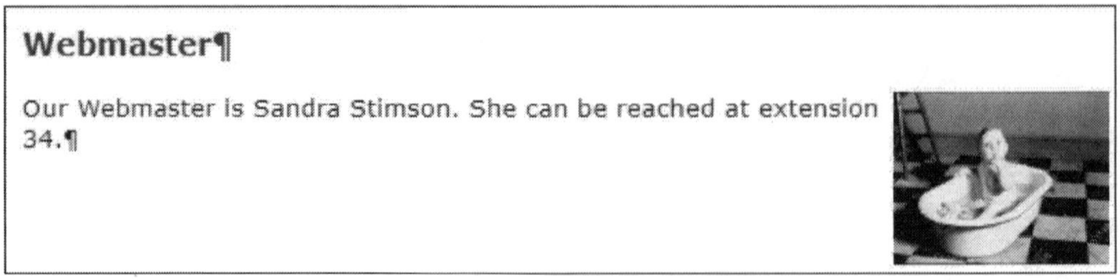

9. Open the **Human Resources** topic.
10. Click to the left of the text "Our Human Resources Director is Brandy McNeill at extension 552" and insert the following image: **brandy_baby.jpg**.
11. Edit the image Properties:
    - ❒ add the following **Image Title** and **Alternate Text**: **Our HR Director, Brandy McNeill**
    - ❒ change its **Width** to **120**
    - ❒ change its **Text wrapping** to **Right**

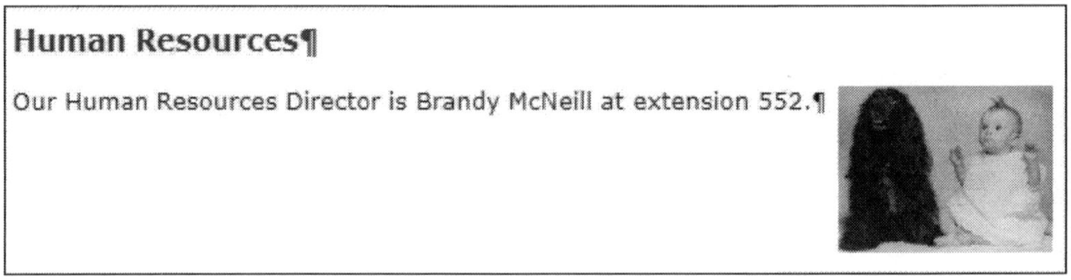

12. Open the **Information Services Director** topic.
13. Click to the left of the text "Our Information Services Director is Travis DonBullian at extension 33" and insert the following image: **travis_baby.jpg**.

14. Edit the image Properties:

    ❐ add the following **Image Title** and **Alternate Text** to the image: **Travis and his big sister, Matilda.**

    ❐ change its **Width** to **73**

    ❐ change its **Text wrapping** to **Right**

15. Save the project.

NOTES

Image Maps

Image Maps allow the user to click on a particular area (hotspot) of an image and jump to a different area of a Help System. Image Maps are made up of two elements: an image and multiple hotspots. Hotspots (also known as clickable regions) can target websites, topics, bookmarks, email addresses, or files. You can create circles, polygons, or rectangular clickable regions.

Guided Activity 32: Add Hotspots to a Graphic

1. Ensure that the **images_multimedia** project is still open.

2. Insert an image within a topic to be used as the image map.

   ❒ open the **Mission Statement** topic

   ❒ click at the end of the text **yet simplistic.**

   ❒ press [**enter**] to create a new paragraph

   ❒ type **Use the image below to move around this Help System.**

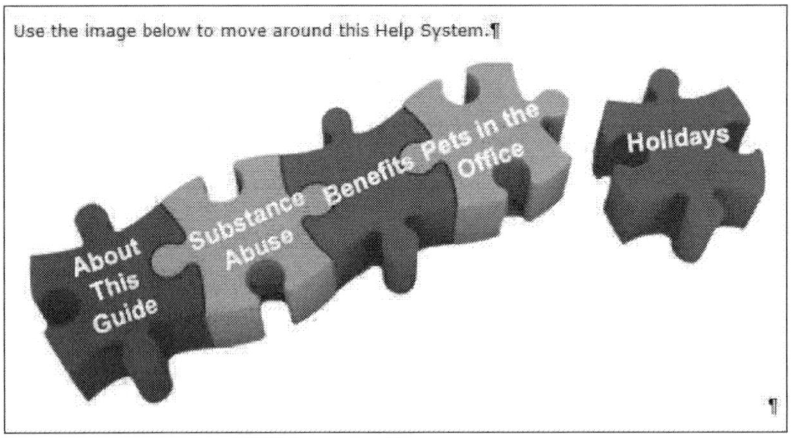

3. Insert an image map on the puzzle image.

   ❒ right-click the **puzzle** graphic and choose **Insert Image Map**

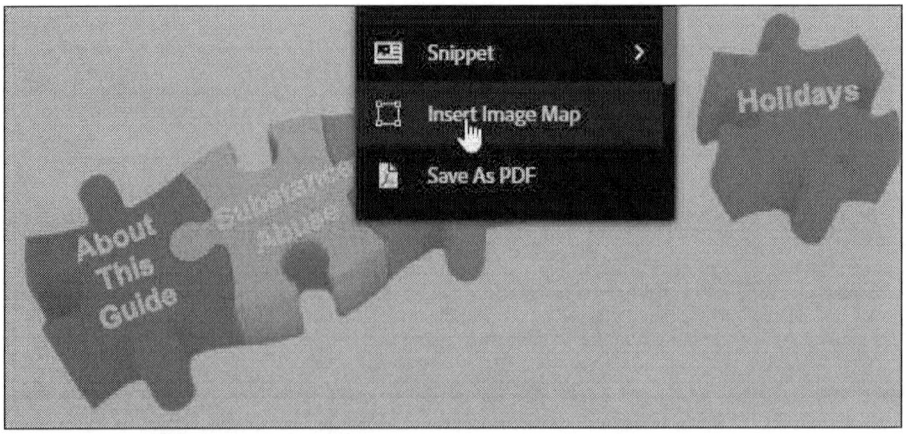

The Image Map dialog box opens.

4. Add a hotspot to the image map.

   ❒ select the **Insert Rectangle** icon (shown highlighted in the image below)

   ❒ draw a box over the **About This Guide** puzzle piece

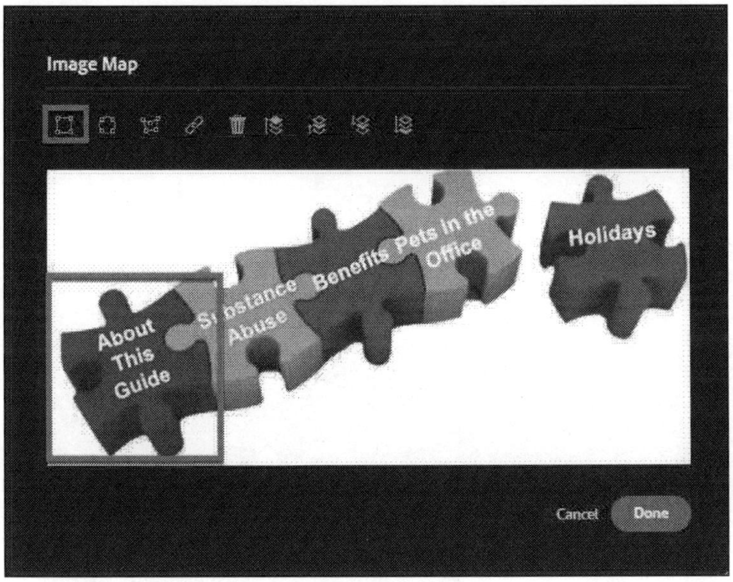

A red box (a hotspot) surrounds the **About This Guide** puzzle piece of the image map. You can move the red box, resize it, or delete it (using the Trash icon). Next, you'll link the hotspot to an existing topic.

5. Link a hotspot to a topic.

   ❒ double-click the rectangle hotspot

   The **Link to** dialog box opens.

   ❒ ensure **Project Files** is selected

   ❒ from the **General Office Information** folder, select **About This Guide**

   ❒ click the **Link** button

   ❒ click the **Done** button

   Although nothing appears to change, when you hover your mouse over the hotspot, a popup lets you know that you've linked the hotspot to the About This Guide topic (purpose.htm).

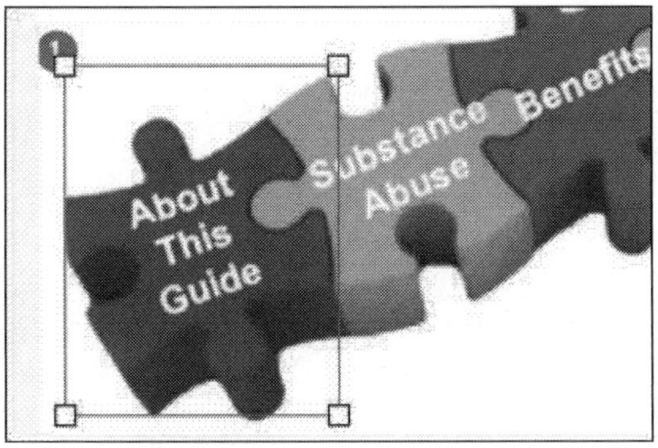

NOTES

NOTES

Image Map Confidence Check

1. Insert a rectangular hotspot that links the words **Substance Abuse** on the image map to the **Drug Policy** topic.

   Note: If you accidentally select the wrong target topic, double-click the hotspot and select a different topic.

2. Create a hotspot for **Benefits** that links to the **Special Benefits** topic.
3. Create a hotspot for **Pets in the Office** that links to the **Pets in the Office** topic.
4. Create a hotspot for **Holidays** that links to the **Holiday Schedule** topic.
5. Move and/or resize the hotspots similar to what is shown in the image below.

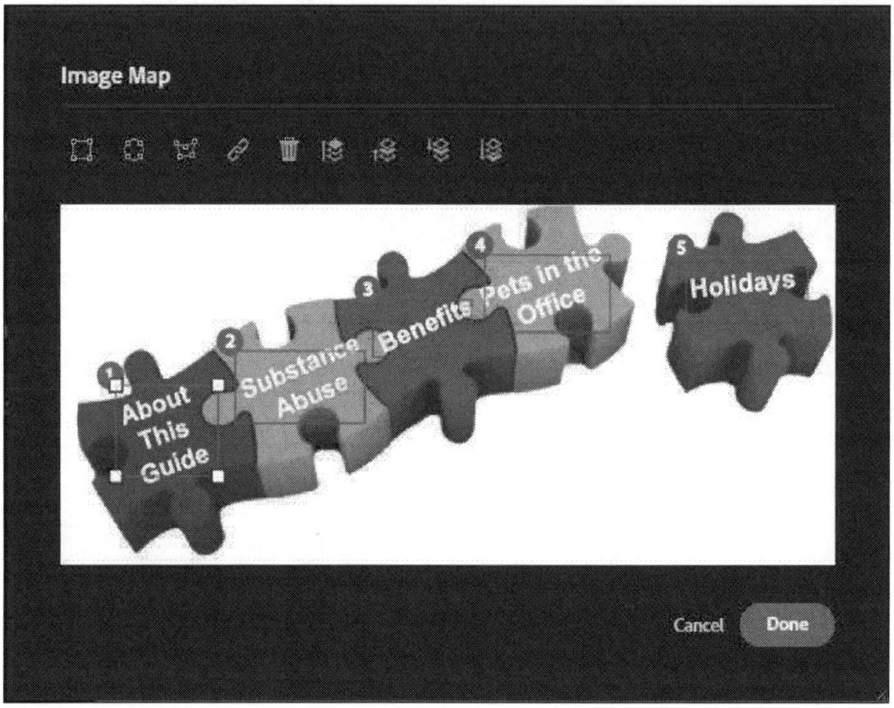

6. When finished, click the **Done** button.
7. Preview the Mission Statement topic and test the image map links.

   When you click any of the blocks in the image map, the topic you targeted for each hotspot opens.

8. Close the topic's preview window.
9. Return to **Author** mode.
10. Save the project.

eLearning Integration

If you have created eLearning courses using tools such as Adobe Captivate, TechSmith Camtasia, or Articulate Storyline, you can import published content into RoboHelp. During the lessons that follow, you will import Adobe Captivate Demos into a project and then insert the imported interactive eLearning content into a topic.

Guided Activity 33: Import Captivate Demos into a Project

1. Ensure that the **images_multimedia** project is still open.

2. Create a folder for the eLearning content.

   ❒ right-click beneath the last folder in the **Contents** area and choose **New > Folder**

   ❒ name the new folder **eLearning**

   ❒ click the **Done** button

3. Import an Adobe Captivate Demo.

   ❒ right-click the **eLearning** folder and choose **Import > Adobe Captivate Demo**

   ❒ navigate to **RoboHelp2022Data > eLearning**

   ❒ open the **StartAnApplication** folder

   ❒ open **index.html**

4. Import a second Adobe Captivate Demo.

   ❒ right-click the **eLearning** folder and choose **Import > Adobe Captivate Demo**

   ❒ from the **eLearning** folder, open the **SaveFile** folder

   ❒ open **index.html**

5. Import a third and final Adobe Captivate Demo.

   ❒ right-click the **eLearning** folder and choose **Import > Adobe Captivate Demo**

   ❒ from the **eLearning** folder, open the **CopyPasteBetweenApps** folder

   ❒ open **index.html**

NOTES

Guided Activity 34: Insert Captivate Demos into Topics

1. Ensure that the **images_multimedia** project is still open.

2. Insert an Adobe Captivate demo into a topic.

   ❒ from the **General Office Information** folder, open the **The Learning Center** topic

   ❒ click after the **Start an Application** heading and press [**enter**] to add a blank line

   ❒ from the toolbar above the topic, click the **Insert Multimedia** icon

   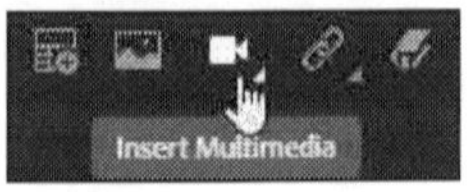

   ❒ choose **Adobe Captivate Demo** from the drop-down menu

   The Adobe Captivate Demo dialog box opens.

   ❒ from the **eLearning** folder, select **StartAnApplication**

   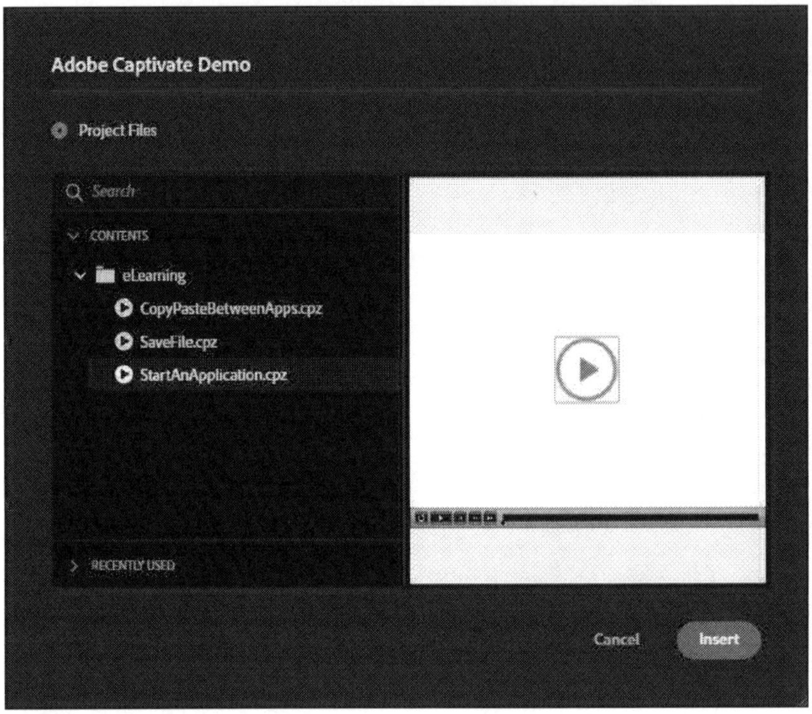

   ❒ click the **Insert** button

   A placeholder for the Captivate Demo appears. Next, you'll resize the video.

3. Resize a Captivate Demo.

   ❒ with the video placeholder selected, go to the **Content Properties** panel

   ❒ from the **Width** and **Height** area, disable **Maintain Aspect Ratio** (the option is disabled when the lock icon appears open)

   ❒ change the **Height** of the demo to **480** and the **Width** to **640**

eLearning Confidence Check

1. Still working within The Learning Center topic, add a paragraph after the **Save a File** subhead.
2. Insert the **SaveFile** Adobe Captivate Demo.
3. Add a paragraph after the **Copy and Paste Content Between Applications** subhead.
4. Insert the **CopyPasteBetweenApps** Adobe Captivate Demo.
5. Resize both of the Adobe Captivate demos to **480 x 640**.

6. Save the project.
7. Preview **The Learning Center** topic and interact with the Adobe Captivate Demos as prompted onscreen.

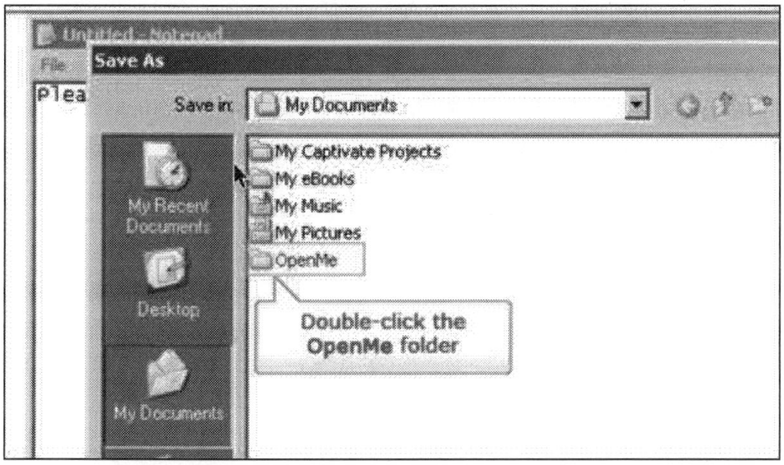

8. Return to Author mode.

NOTES

Drop-down Text

Using RoboHelp's Drop-down Text feature, you can quickly take a long, overwhelming topic and make it manageable for your users.

Consider The Learning Center topic. The topic contains three interactive eLearning modules that appear on the screen at the same time. There is so much going on within the topic, users are likely to become overpowered by the content. Using Drop-down Text, you can effectively hide the eLearning within each of the three subheads. As users click the appropriate subhead, the eLearning lesson appears.

Guided Activity 35: Create Drop-Down Text

1. Ensure that the **images_multimedia** project is still open.

2. If necessary, open the **The Learning Center** topic and ensure that you're in Author mode.

3. Insert Drop-down Text.

   ❒ right-click the first demo (Start an Application) and choose **Cut**

   The video has not been deleted. Instead, it's hanging out on the clipboard. You'll paste it back within the topic shortly.

   ❒ highlight the **Start an Application** heading

   ❒ on the toolbar above the topic, click the **Create Drop-down Text** icon

   Placeholder text appears beneath the heading ("Type your drop-down text here.").

   ❒ highlight the placeholder text and **paste** the demo on the clipboard in place of the text

   The selected heading text becomes a link with the demo beneath.

4. Preview the topic.

   Notice that your first Captivate demo is not currently visible.

5. Click the **Start an Application** heading.

   The demo appears.

6. Click the **Start an Application** heading again.

   The demo disappears. How slick is that? Using this feature, you can quickly make some of your longer topics more manageable for users.

7. Return to **Author** mode.

Drop-Down Text and Images Confidence Check

1. Use Drop-Down Text for the other two headings (**Save a File** and **Copy and Paste Content Between Applications**) and the two remaining Adobe Captivate Demos
2. Preview the topic and test the Drop-Down Text links.
3. When finished, return to Author mode.
4. Open the **Pets in the Office Policy** topic.
5. At the end of the first paragraph, press [enter] to add an empty paragraph.
6. Insert the **dog.jpg** image into the topic.
7. Add the following **Alternate Text** and **Title** to the dog image: **Dogs are allowed in the office.**
8. Ensure that **Maintain Aspect Ratio** is enabled and change the **Width** of the dog image to **500**.

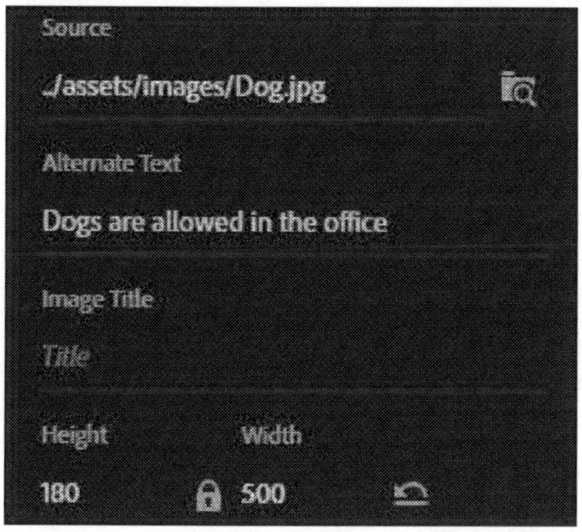

9. Preview the topic.

Pets in the Office Policy

Pets... we love them. As a Super Simplistic Solutions employee, you are permitted to bring your pet to work every Friday, provided your pet is not on the banned list below and you follow a few, simple rules.

A Few Simple Rules

- Your pet bites, we bite you... and you pay the piper

10. Save and then close the project.

Notes

iCONLOGIC
"Skills and Drills" Learning

Module 6: Tags, Expressions, and Variables

In This Module You Will Learn About:

And You Will Learn To:

Condition Tags

A project can easily contain thousands of topics. But what if you want to exclude specific topics from being generated? Using conditions, you can *tag* topics or selected topic content (such as words, phrases, images... even table rows). You can then create conditions that control which tagged content is generated. Using conditions, you can maintain one project but generate multiple outputs; each output can have unconditional content (content that was not tagged and potentially appears in every output) or unique content that was tagged and associated with a specific output.

Guided Activity 36: Create a Condition Tag

1. Open the **reuse_content** project. (The project is in the **RoboHelpProjects** folder.)

   Note: Click the **Upgrade** button if prompted.

2. View the Condition Tag area.

   ❒ select the **Author** panel

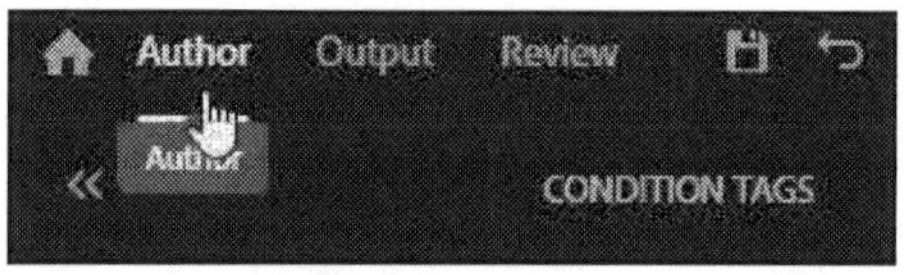

   ❒ click **Condition Tags**

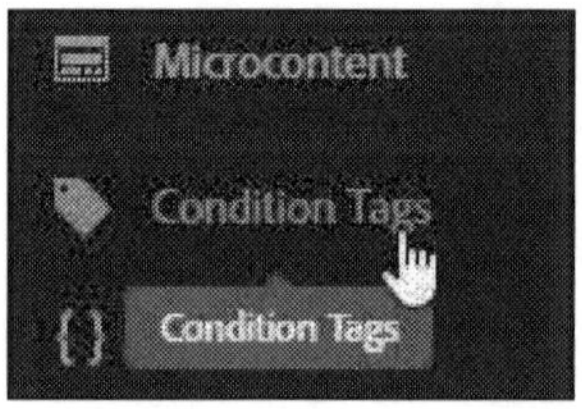

   In the Condition Tags area, notice there are already two build tags (Online and Print). These tags are default tags that appear in every new RoboHelp project. You can elect to use the existing tags, delete them, or ignore them. For this project, you'll be ignoring the default tags and creating your own.

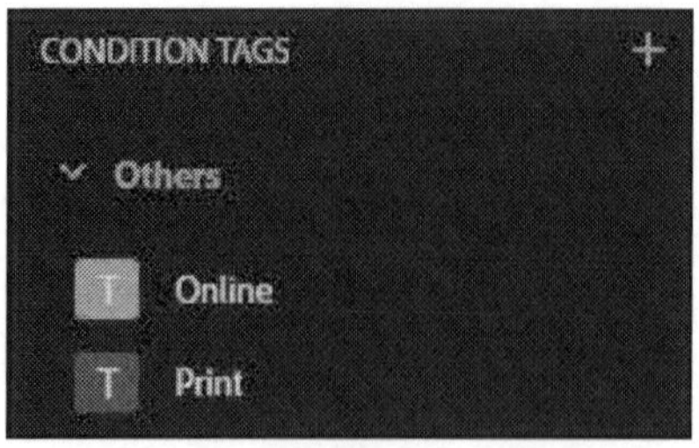

3. Create a new Condition Tag.

   ❒ at the top of the **Condition Tags** area, click the **New Tag** icon

The **Define Condition Tag** dialog box opens.

❒ from the **Group** drop-down menu, choose **Audience**

❒ name the new tag **East Coast**

❒ choose any color you like as the **Background** and **Text**

Note: After you apply a tag to topic text and/or images (you'll do so very soon), you'll see the Background and Text colors. These colors allow you to quickly identify the tag that has been applied.

❒ click the **Done** button

The new Condition Tag is listed in the Condition Tags area within the Audience group.

4. Create another Tag.

   ❒ at the top of the **Condition Tags** area, click the **New Tag** icon

   The Define Condition Tag dialog box reopens.

   ❒ from the **Group** drop-down menu, choose **Audience**

   ❒ name the new tag **West Coast**

   ❒ choose any color you like as the **Background** and **Text**

   ❒ click the **Done** button

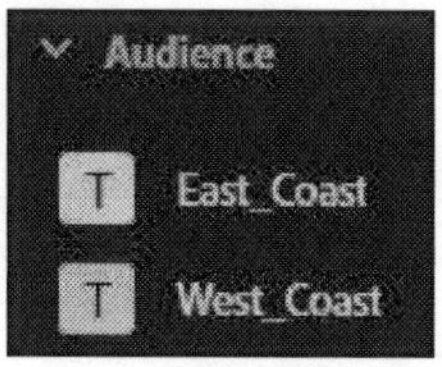

5. Save the project.

Guided Activity 37: Apply a Condition Tag to Topic Content

1. Ensure that the **reuse_content** project is still open.

2. Apply a Condition Tag to text within a topic.

   ❒ open the **Our President** topic

   Because the topic contains information about two presidents (AJ and Biff), it's difficult to read.

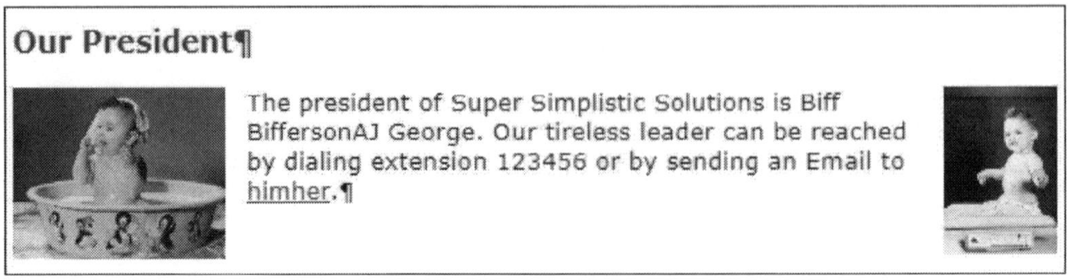

   Here's the scenario for the upcoming use of conditional text: Super Simplistic Solutions has grown so large that the company has been split into two independent divisions: **East** and **West**. The two divisions have different presidents (Biff in the East; AJ in the West) but share much of the same policies and procedures. Beyond personnel, the differences between the two companies are largely regional. For instance, the Eastern office isn't near the water; the Western office is near a beach, and employees routinely take their surfboards out during the lunch hour. Western management has recently installed surfboard racks. Information about the surfboard racks is relevant to those who work for the Western division but not to those who work for the Eastern division. You will use Condition Tags and Expressions to ensure that employees in the East see only information relevant to them, likewise for the employees in the West.

   ❒ in the **Our President** topic, highlight the phrase **Biff Bifferson**

   ❒ from the **Author** area at the left, select **Condition Tags**

   ❒ drag the **East_Coast** Condition Tag onto the selected text

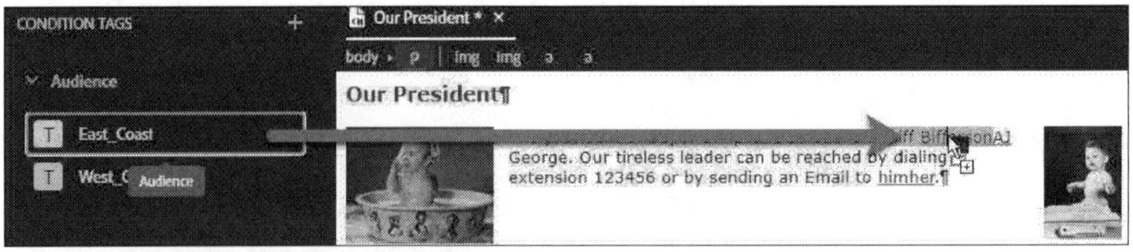

   The Background and Text colors you selected when you created the condition appear on the selected text.

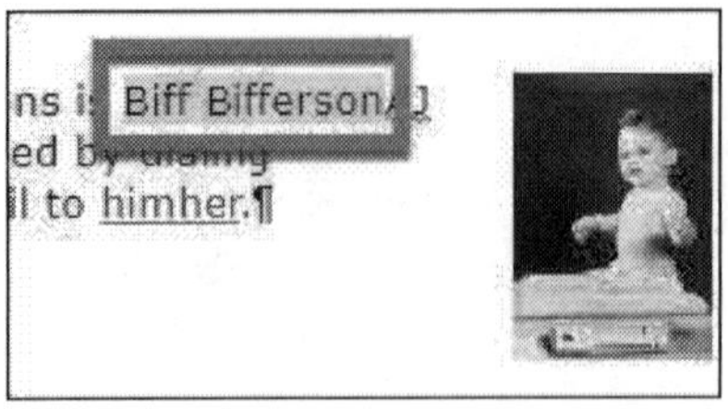

3. Apply a Condition Tag to more text within a topic.

   ❒ highlight the **Email** link for **him**

   ❒ from the **Condition Tags** area, drag the **East_Coast** Condition Tag onto the text

4. Save the project.

   Note: If you don't see the condition colors, choose **View > Show > Condition Tags** to make them appear. If you do not like the condition colors, double-click the tag in the Condition Tag area and change the **Identify with** colors at any time.

NOTES

Condition Tags Confidence Check

1. Select the picture at the right and apply the **East_Coast** Condition Tag to the picture.
2. Apply the **East_Coast** Condition Tag to the numbers **123**.
3. Apply the **West_Coast** Condition Tag to the following:

   AJ George

   456

   the word **her** (the email link)

   the picture at the **left**.

   Note: You can remove a condition by right-clicking anything that has been tagged and choosing **Remove Condition Tags**.

4. Save the project and then Preview the topic.
5. From the **Filters** area at the right, select **Condition Tags**
6. From the **Audience** area, select **East Coast**.

   Information pertaining to AJ, who heads up the West Coast offices, disappears.

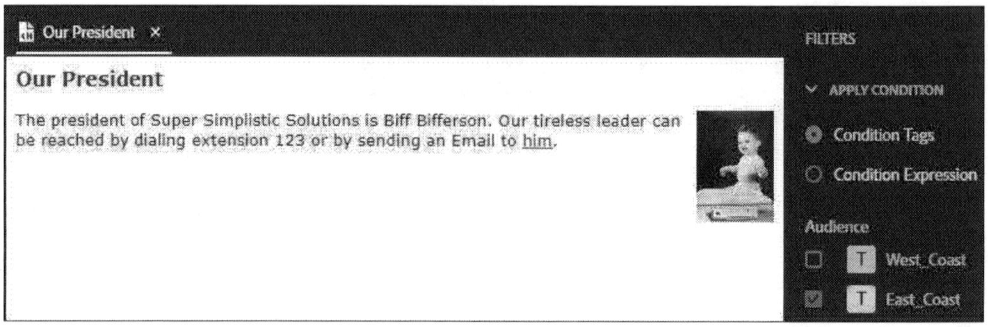

7. From the **Audience** area, deselect **East Coast**.

   Information pertaining to both presidents reappears.

8. From the **Audience** area, select **West Coast**.

   Information pertaining to Biff, who heads up the East Coast offices, disappears.

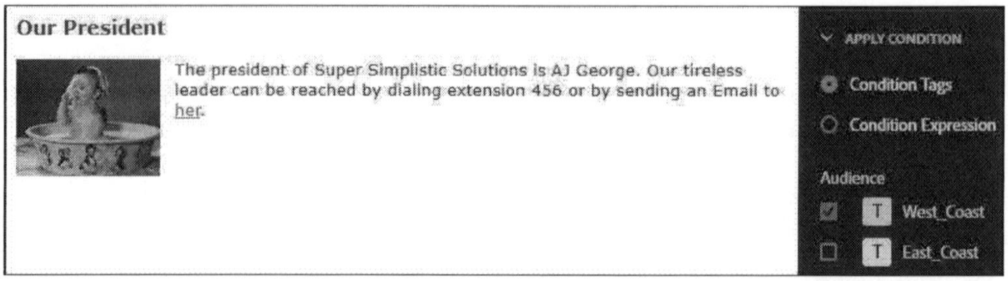

9. Return to Author mode.

Condition Expressions

You have created two Condition Tags, applied them to topic text and images, and used the Preview feature to ensure the Filters are displaying/hiding topic content correctly.

To ensure that you can generate outputs that use the correct Condition Tags, you need to create condition expressions. An expression is a set of instructions that specify topics to include or exclude from an output. You can define a basic expression that excludes tags or a complex expression with Boolean operators, such as AND, OR, and NOT.

Guided Activity 38: Create a Condition Expression

1. Ensure that the **reuse_content** project is still open.

2. Create a Condition Expression to be used for the West Coast output.

   ❒ select the **Output** panel

   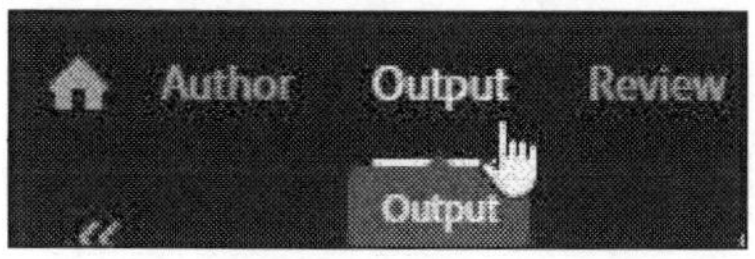

   ❒ from the list of tools on the left, select **Condition Expressions**

   ❒ click the **New Condition Expression** icon

   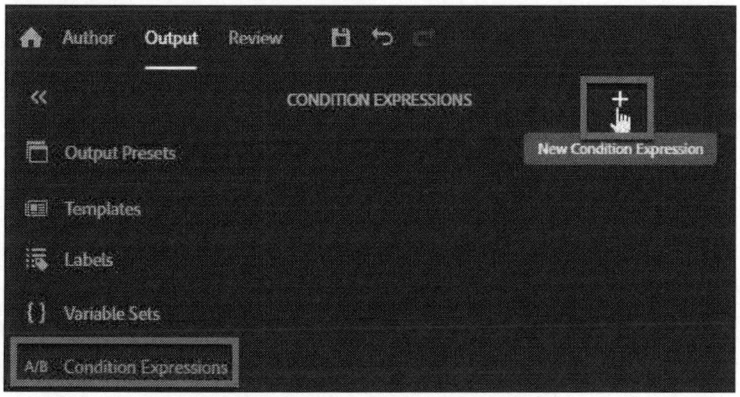

   The **New Condition Expression** dialog box opens.

   ❒ name the expression **West Coast**

   ❒ click the **Done** button

3. Define a condition.

   ❒ from the **A/B West Coast, Condition Tags** area, drag **West Coast** into the empty space at the right

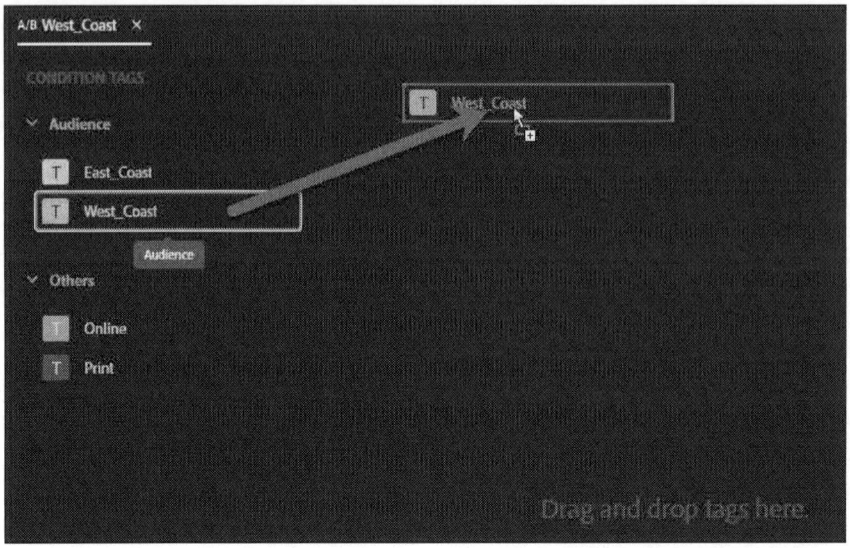

Congratulations, you've just defined your first build expression. Programmers, beware! Okay, fine, there wasn't any programming skill required to define the expression. Nevertheless, if you review the expression, you'll see that the West_Coast content will be excluded in the output. You'll edit the expression so that the West_Coast content is included in the output.

4. Edit a condition expression.

   ❒ from the drop-down menu, choose **Include**

Notice that the expression is now set so that any output that relies on this condition will include West coast content.

Expressions Confidence Check

1. Create a new Condition Expression named **East Coast** with content that will be **included** if the audience is made up of **East Coast** users.

2. On the **Output** panel, select **Output Presets**.

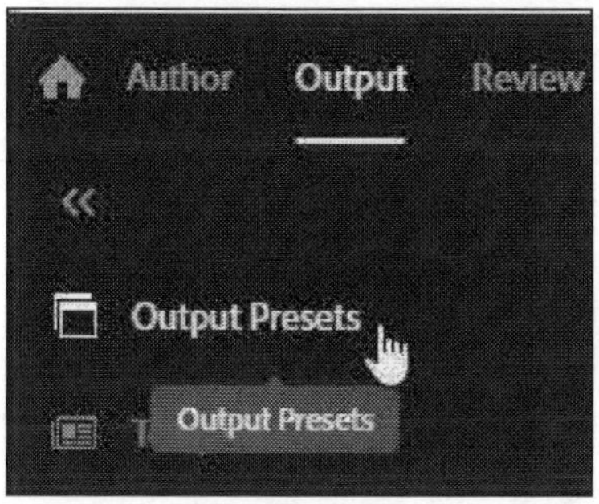

3. Create a new **Frameless** Preset named **West Coast**.

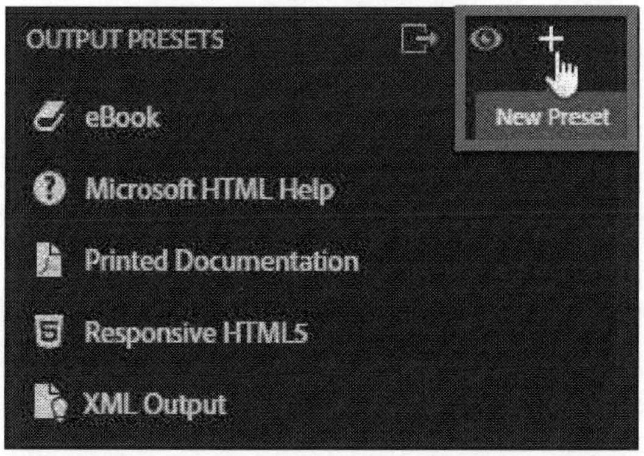

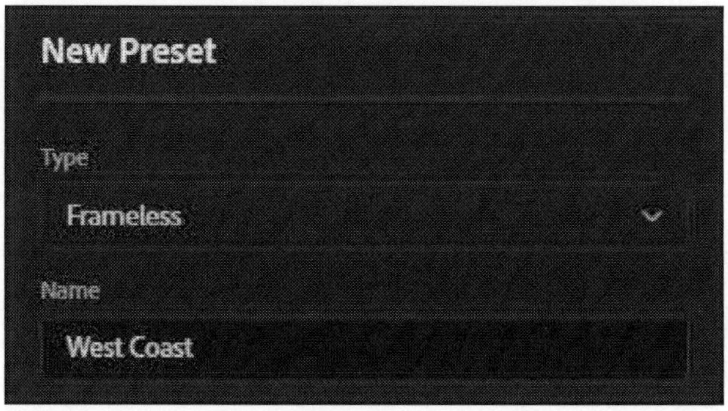

NOTES

4. Change the **Title** of the West Coast output to **West Coast Policies**.

5. Change the Output path for the West Coast output to **RoboHelp2022Data > output > SSS West**.

6. Select the **Content** category from the list at the left.
7. From the **Condition Expression** drop-down menu, choose **West Coast**.

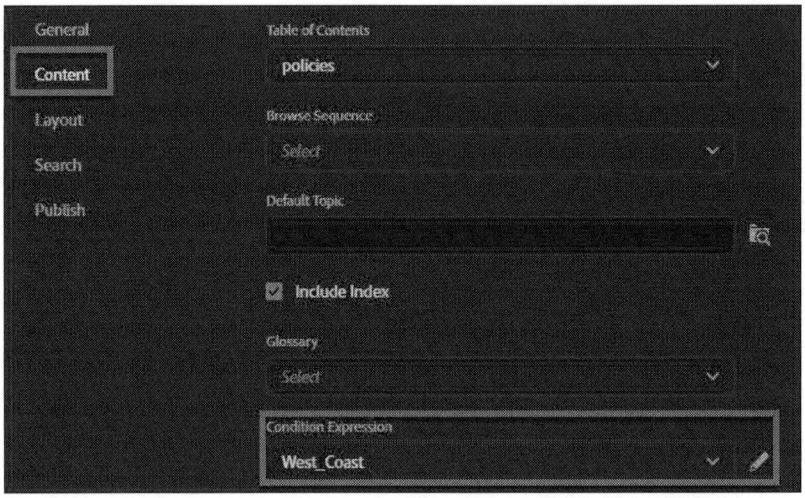

8. Save the project.
9. Generate the **West Coast** output. (Right-click the output and choose **Generate**.)
10. **View** the output. (Right-click the output and choose **View Output**.)
11. Open the **About This Guide** topic.
12. Click the **president** link.

    Because you selected **West Coast** as the **Condition Expression**, Biff does not appear, and AJ is shown as the president.

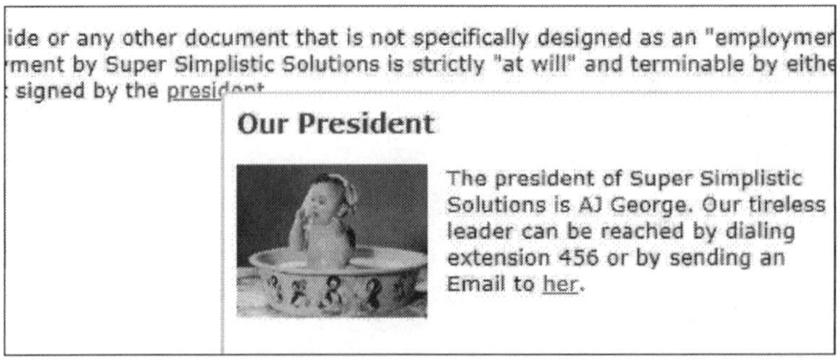

13. Close the web browser and return to the RoboHelp project.
14. Create a new **Frameless** Preset named **East Coast**.
15. Change the **Title** of the East Coast output to **East Coast Policies**.

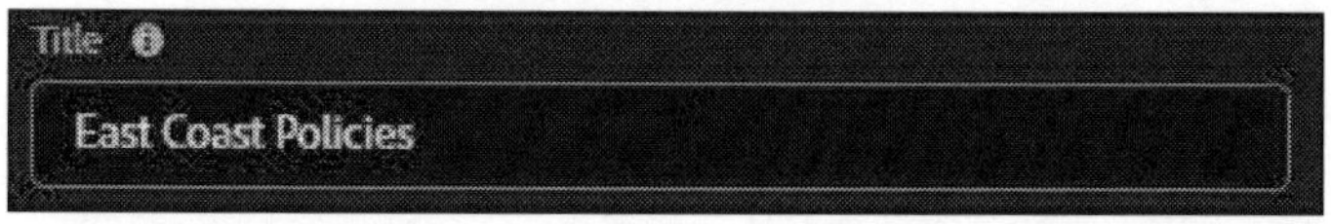

16. Change the Output path for the West Coast output to **RoboHelp2022Data > output > SSS East**

17. From the Content category, **Condition Expression** drop-down menu, choose **East Coast**.

18. Save the project.
19. Generate the **East Coast** output.
20. **View** the output.
21. Open the **About This Guide** topic.
22. Click the **president** link.

    Because you selected **East Coast** as the **Condition Expression** for the output, AJ does not appear, and Biff is shown as the president.

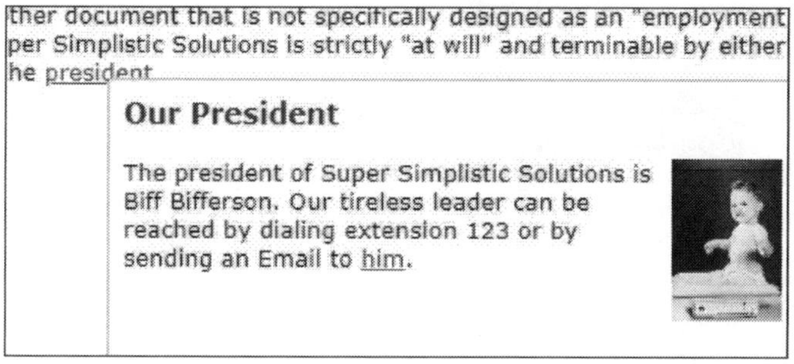

23. Close the web browser and return to the RoboHelp project.

NOTES

Guided Activity 39: Apply a Condition Tag to a Topic

1. Ensure that the **reuse_content** project is still open.

2. Apply a Condition Tag to a topic.

   ❒ select the **Author** panel

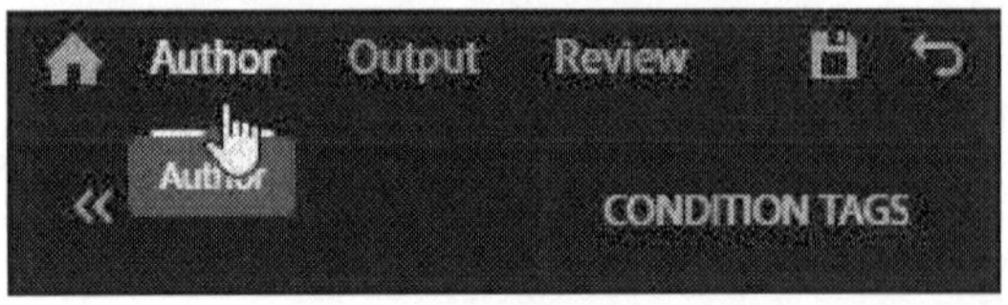

   ❒ from the **Contents**, open the **General Office Information** folder

   ❒ right-click the **Surfboards** topic and choose **Properties**

   ❒ scroll down and expand **Condition Tags**

   ❒ from beneath **Topic Level**, click **Apply Tags**

   The Apply Condition Tags dialog box opens.

   ❒ from the **Audience** area, click **West Coast**

   The topic is added to the Audience list at the right.

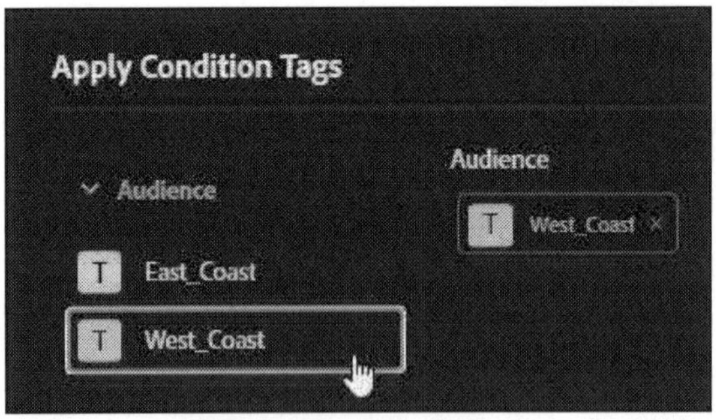

   ❒ click the **Apply** button

   By assigning the West Coast tag to the Surfboards topic, the topic will appear *only* in the West Coast output. Because surfing is not a relevant topic for East Coasters, the topic does not need to appear in the East Coast output.

❒ click the **Apply** button again

It's a subtle thing, but if you look at the Surfboards topic (in the General Office Information folder), a circle has been added to the right of the topic title indicating that a condition tag has been applied to the topic. (The circle's color is the one specific when the tag was first created.)

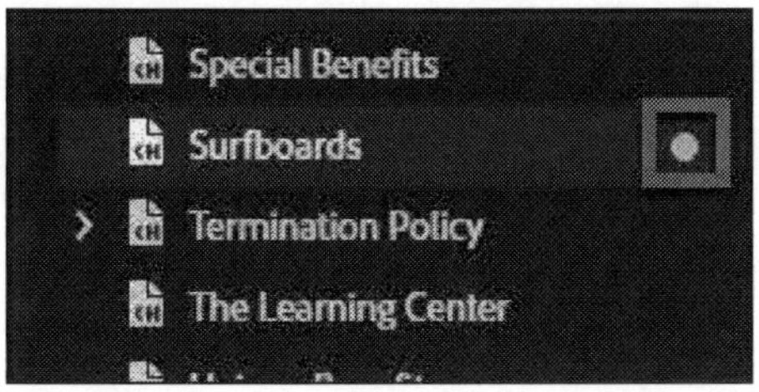

NOTES

Dynamic Content Filters

You have learned how to create multiple Condition Tags and Condition Expressions and how to generate multiple outputs from one project (each containing potentially unique content). But what if you want to generate both outputs, combine them into one, and then let the users decide which output they want? During the activities that follow, you will create Dynamic Filters and then generate one output that contains information for both corporate locations. A user is then able to pick the appropriate content from a drop-down menu.

Guided Activity 40: Create Dynamic Content Filters

1. Ensure that the **reuse_content** project is still open.

2. Create a Dynamic Filter.

   ❒ select the **Output** panel

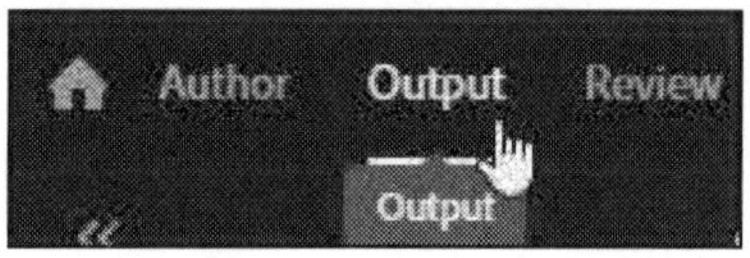

   ❒ select **Dynamic Content Filters**

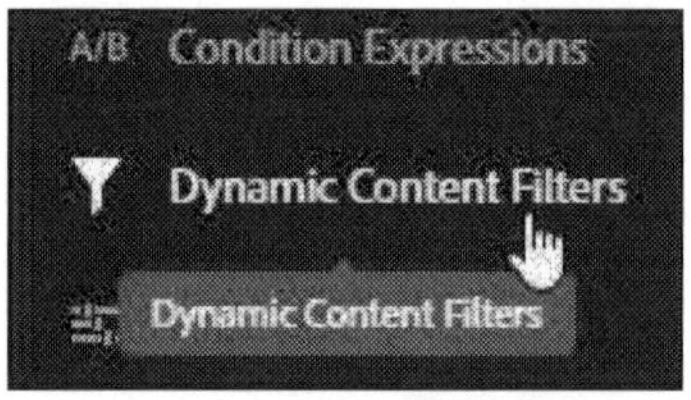

   ❒ click the **New Filter** icon

   The New Filter dialog box opens.

   ❒ name the filter **Regions**

❒ click the **Done** button

3. Set Filter properties.

   ❒ at the right of the RoboHelp window, in the **Title** area, replace the placeholder text ("Select the options") with **Choose Your Region**

   ❒ deselect **Allow multiple selection in groups**

4. Add a Condition tag to the Filter.

   ❒ from the **Condition Tags** area, drag the **East_Coast** tag to where it says **Drag and drop tags here**.

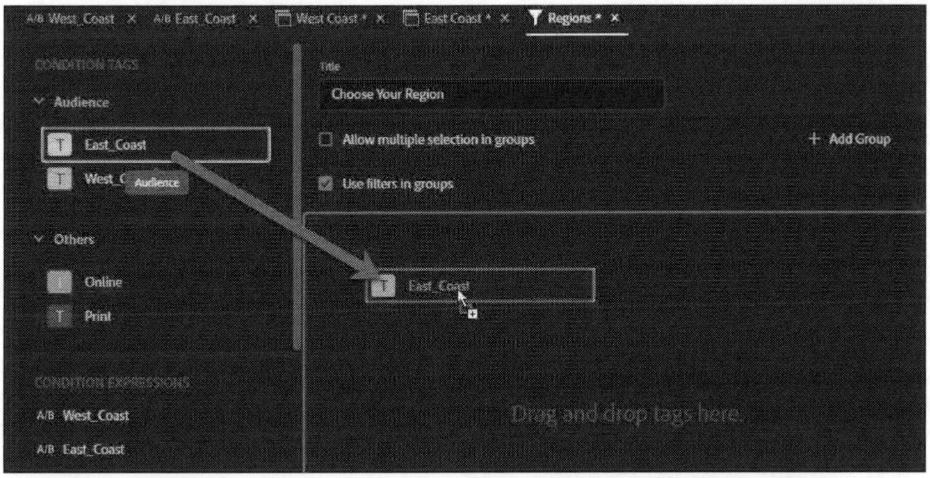

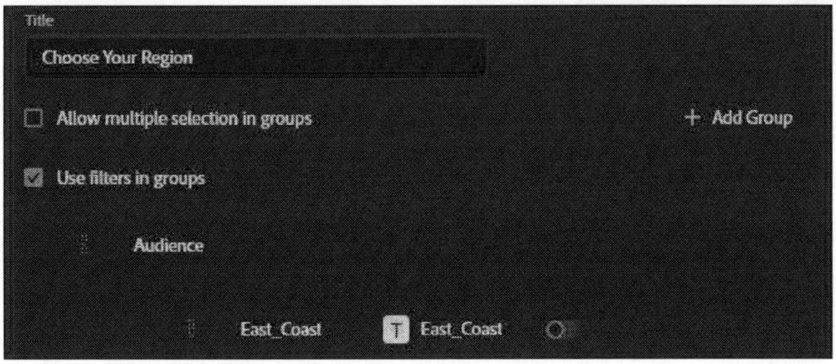

NOTES

NOTES

Dynamic Filters Confidence Check

1. Drag the **West_Coast** tag beneath the **East_Coast** tag.

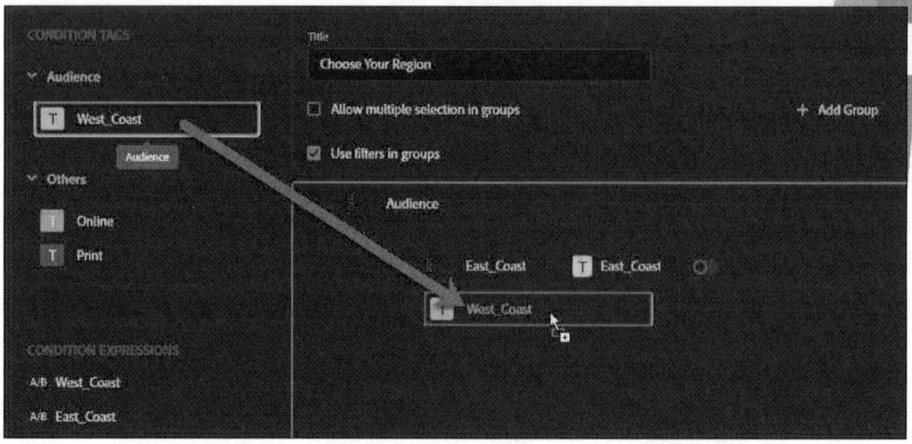

2. Select the **East_Coast** tag and then click **Select by default**.

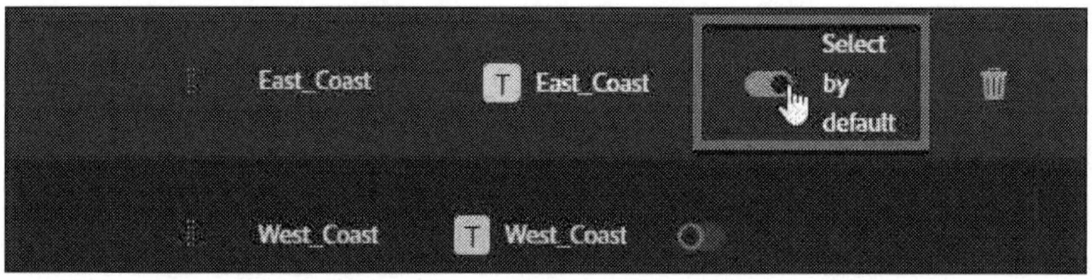

   There are more employees working at the East Coast division than at the West Coast. By making the East_Coast filter the default, users will see the East Coast content by default but be able to quickly switch to the West Coast content.

3. Select the **Output presets**.
4. Right-click **Responsive HTML5** and choose **Duplicate**.
5. Change the name of the new layout to **Dynamic** and then click the **Done** button.

6. If necessary, open the **Dynamic** output for editing and, on the **General** tab, ensure that the **Output path** is **RoboHelp2022Data > output > Responsive_HTML5/** (browse to and Select/Open that folder now if necessary).

7. Still in the **Dynamic** output, select the **Content** tab.

8. From the **Condition Expression** drop-down menu, choose **<None>**.
9. From the **Dynamic Content Filter** drop-down menu, choose **Regions** (this is the Filter you created a moment ago)

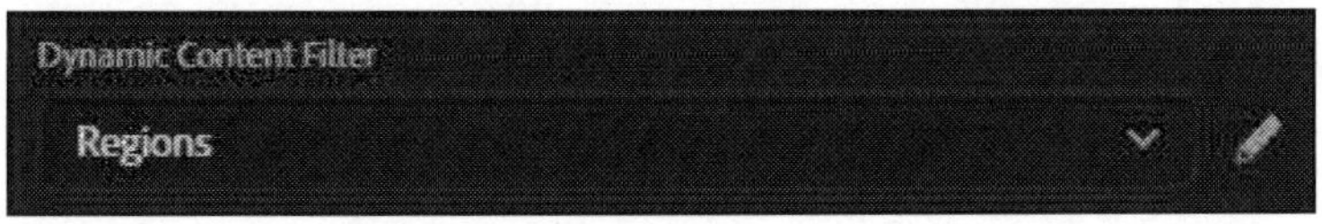

10. Save the **Dynamic** output, **Generate** the output and then **View** it.
11. On the TOC, open **General Office Information**.

    The East Coast content is the default. Because you made the **Surf Boards** topic conditional to the West Coast output, the Surf Boards topic is hidden from view because it is not relevant to East Coast employees. (The Surf Boards topic would appear just below The Learning Center.)

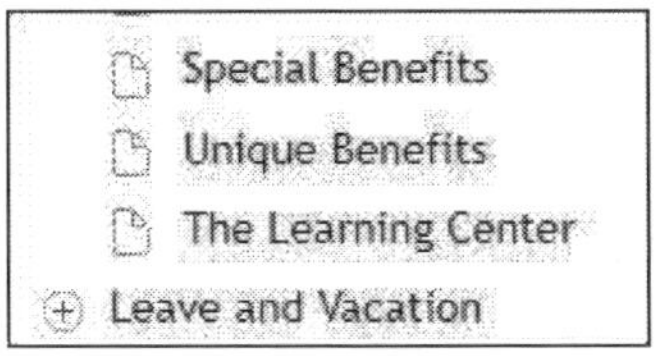

12. On the TOC, click the **About This Guide** topic and then click the link for the **president**.

    Because this is the East Coast content and Biff is the president, Biff's information appears.

13. From the top of the window, click the **Filter** icon  and then select the **West Coast** Audience.

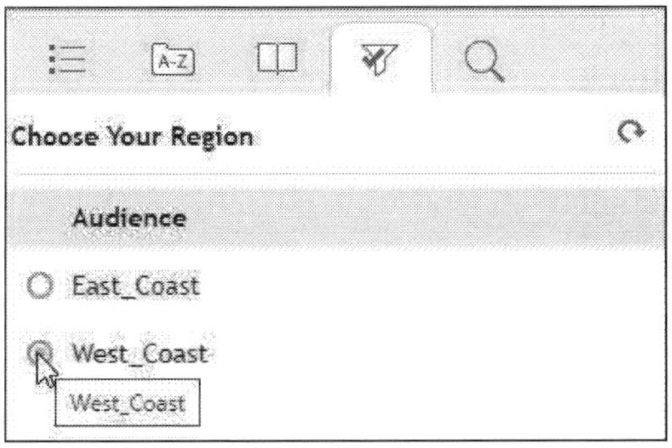

    The change to the displayed content is as immediate as it is awesome. The link to the Our President topic is now all about AJ, who is the President in the West Coast. And the TOC includes the Surf Boards topic (in the General Office Information book.)

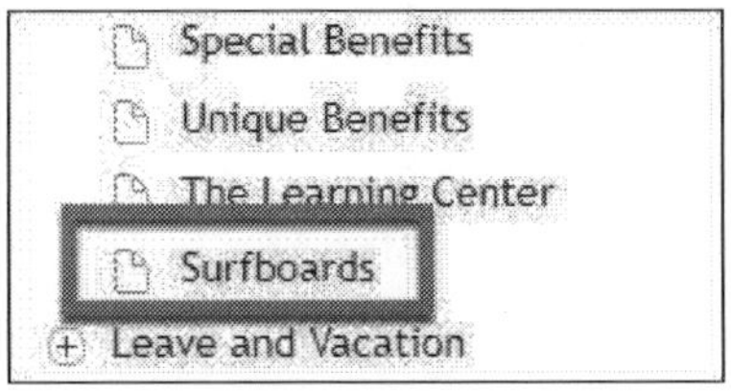

14. Close the browser window and return to the RoboHelp project.

Variables

Let's say you want to have your company name appear throughout a project. You could accomplish the task the old-fashioned way by typing the company name over and over again. Or you can create a Variable called CompanyName, whose definition is your actual company name. After creating the Variable, it's a simple matter of dragging the CompanyName Variable into any topic.

Now here's the cool part. Assume your company name appears throughout your project and you need to change it. Without the Variable, you would have to use the Find/Replace feature or manually find and edit every instance. Thanks to Variables, all you'll need to do is update the definition of the CompanyName Variable one time to change the displayed company name throughout the project.

Guided Activity 41: Create, Insert, and Edit a Variable

1. Ensure that the **reuse_content** project is still open.

2. Create a Variable for the company name.

   ❒ from the **Author** area, click **Variables**

   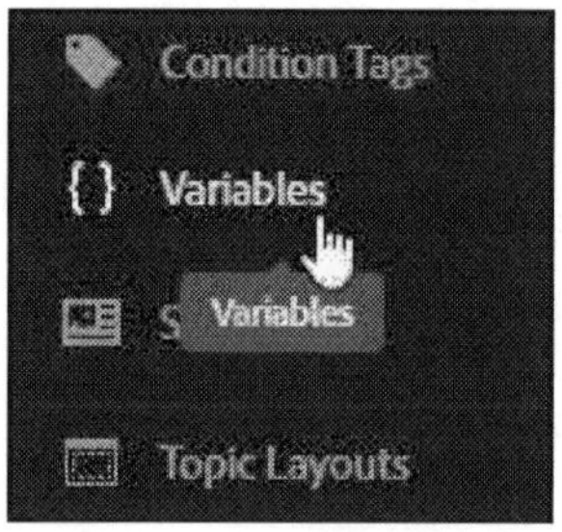

   ❒ click the **New Variable** icon

   The Define Variable dialog box opens.

   ❒ in the **Name** field, type **CompanyName**

   ❒ in the **Value** field, type **Sup. Simplistic Solutions**

   ❒ click the **Done** button

The new variable is listed in the Variables area.

3. Insert the CompanyName Variable into a topic.

   ❒ from the **Author** area, click **Contents**

   ❒ from the **General Office Information** folder, open the **Nondiscrimination Policy** topic

   ❒ from the **Author** area, click **Variables**

   ❒ from the **Variables** area, drag the **CompanyName** variable into the **Nondiscrimination Policy** topic (in front of the first word in the topic: **believes**)

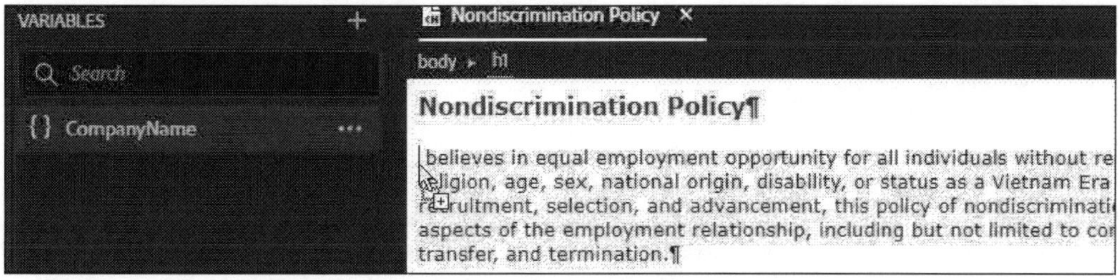

The CompanyName's variable value, **Sup. Simplistic Solutions**, appears in the topic. The green color indicates that the text is actually a variable, not text. The text is seen by users in the output, the green color is not.

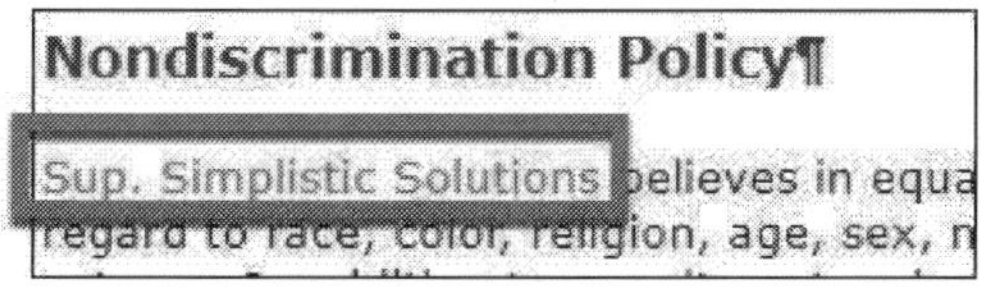

4. Insert the CompanyName Variable into another topic.

   ❒ from the **Author** area, click **Contents**

   ❒ from the **General Office Information** folder, open the **Absentee Policy** topic

   ❒ from the **Author** area, click **Variables**

   ❒ from the **Variables** area, drag the **CompanyName** variable into the topic (in the first sentence in front of the phrase **will permit**) and then press **[spacebar]**

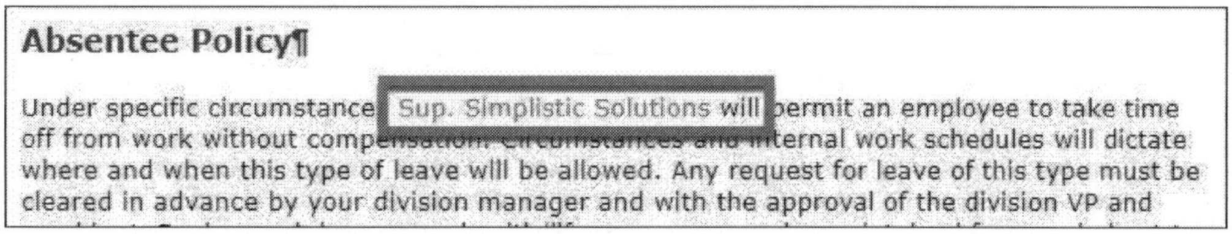

5. Edit a Variable value.

   ❒ from the **Variables** area, double-click the **CompanyName** variable

   The Edit Variable dialog box opens.

   ❒ replace the word **Sup.** with **Super**

   ❒ click the **Done** button

6. Review either the **Nondiscrimination Policy** or **Absentee Policy** topic.

   The updated Variable value appears.

   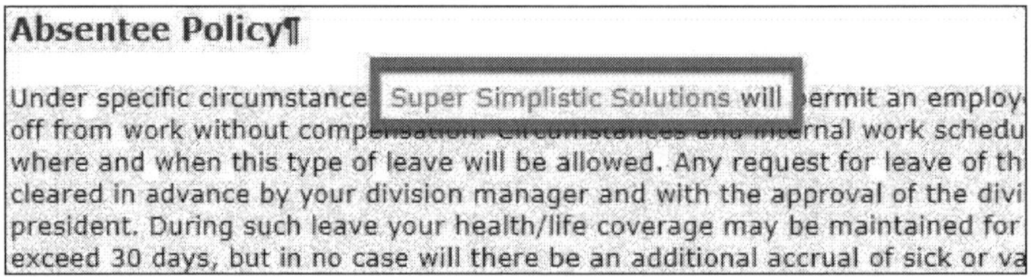

7. Save the project.

8. Close all open topics.

Snippets

Snippets are similar to variables but can contain multiple paragraphs (variable values can contain multiple lines, but not paragraphs), tables, and more complex HTML code.

You can add Snippets to a project and later insert them into a desired topic. Like Variables, when you edit a Snippet shared by different topics, the changes to the Snippet are reflected in all the associated topics.

Guided Activity 42: Insert and Edit Snippets

1. Ensure that the **reuse_content** project is still open.

2. Create a Snippet.

   ❒ from the **Author** area, click **Snippets**

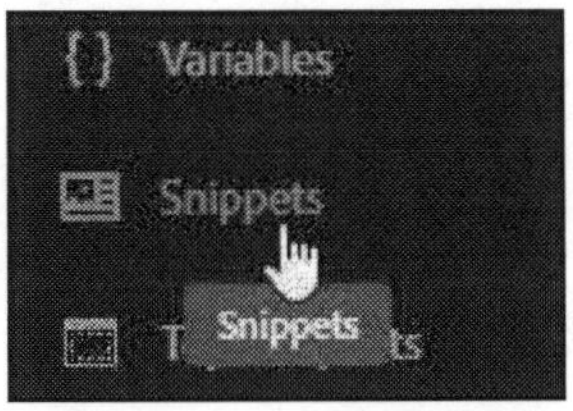

   ❒ click the **New Snippet** icon

   The New Snippet dialog box opens.

   ❒ type **AbuseInfo** into the **Name** field

   ❒ in the **Description** field, type **Encourages employees to seek treatment.**

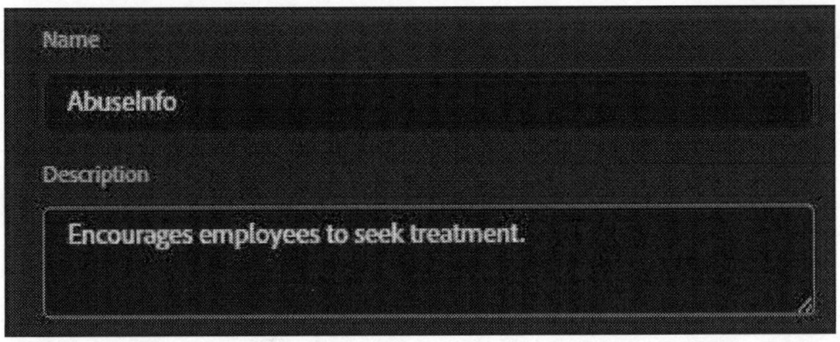

   ❒ click the **Create** button

   The Snippet opens in its own window, similar to creating a new topic.

NOTES

NOTES

❒ type the following into the Snippet window: **SSS recognizes that alcoholism and drug abuse are treatable illnesses, and encourages employees who may have alcohol or drug abuse problems to seek treatment for them. Any individual afflicted by alcoholism or drug dependency will have the same options as employees with other illnesses have to participate in prescribed treatment programs, including the use of paid leave and unpaid leave of absence.**

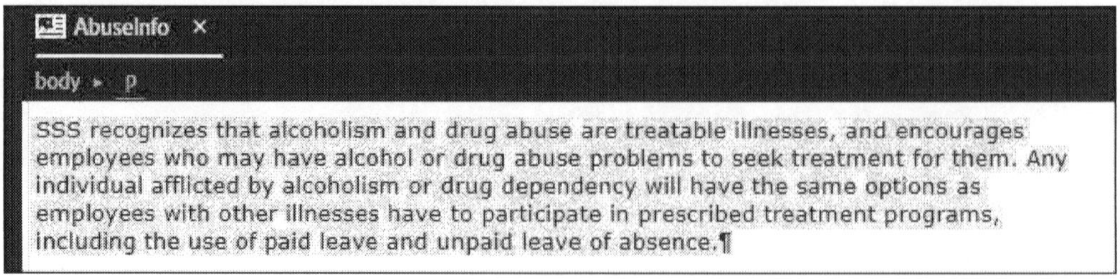

3. Save the project.

Snippets Confidence Check

1. Open the **Alcohol Policy** topic.
2. Add a new paragraph after the word **beverages** in the second paragraph.
3. From the **Snippets** panel, drag the **AbuseInfo** Snippet into empty space you added to the topic.

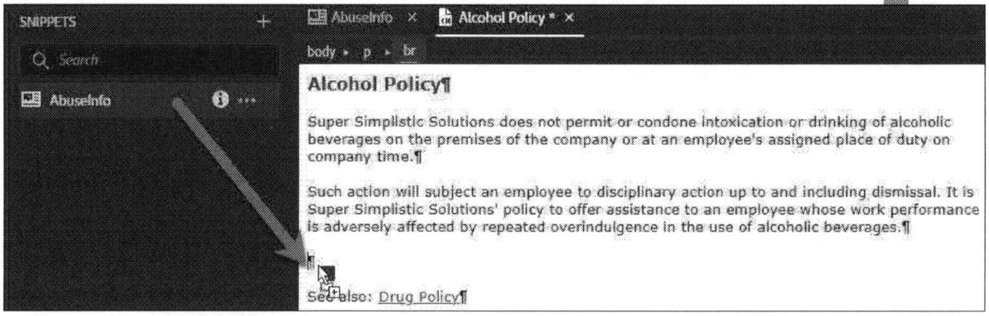

The text you typed into the Snippet appears within the topic.

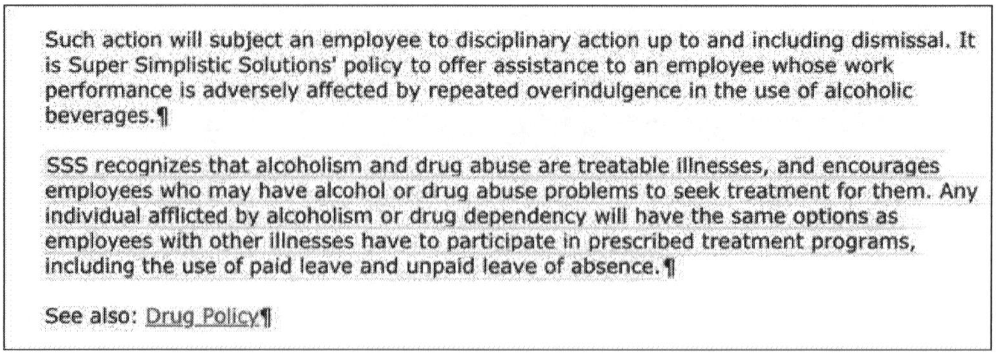

4. Open the Drug Policy topic.
5. Insert a new paragraph at the end of the topic text.

6. Insert the **AbuseInfo** Snippet at the end of the **Drug Policy** topic.

> If you are apprehended while selling or attempting to sell, transport, or distribute drugs while on Super Simplistic Solutions property or at your assigned place of work, your employment will be terminated and your actions reported to the appropriate law enforcement authorities.¶
>
> SSS recognizes that alcoholism and drug abuse are treatable illnesses, and encourages employees who may have alcohol or drug abuse problems to seek treatment for them. Any individual afflicted by alcoholism or drug dependency will have the same options as employees with other illnesses have to participate in prescribed treatment programs, including the use of paid leave and unpaid leave of absence.¶

7. On the Snippets panel, double-click the **AbuseInfo** Snippet to open the Snippet.
8. From the middle of the Snippet, add the word "a" in front of the phrase **drug dependency**.
9. From near the end of the Snippet text, remove "**have to participate in prescribed treatment programs,**".
10. From the beginning of the Snippet text, replace the letters **SSS** with the Variable **CompanyName**.

> Super Simplistic Solutions recognizes that alcoholism and drug abuse are treatable illnesses, and encourages employees who may have alcohol or drug abuse problems to seek treatment for them. Any individual afflicted by alcoholism or a drug dependency will have the same options as employees with other illnesses including the use of paid leave and unpaid leave of absence.¶

11. Save and close the Snippet.
12. Open both topics that are using the Snippet (Alcohol Policy and Drug Policy).

    Notice that the Snippet text has been automatically updated in both topics. And how cool is it that you can combine Variables with Snippets and further enhance your editing efficiency power? I love these two features!

13. Save and then close the project.

NOTES

Notes

iCONLOGiC

"Skills and Drills" Learning

Module 7: Tables, Indexes, Search, and Glossaries

In This Module You Will Learn About:

And You Will Learn To:

NOTES

Tables

Tables, which are made up of cells, columns, and rows, allow you to organize data in an easy-to-read format. During the activities that follow, you will learn how to insert and edit tables—and how to work with table styles that make table formatting a breeze.

Guided Activity 43: Insert a Table

1. Using RoboHelp, open the **tables_index** project file.

   Note: Click the **Upgrade** button if prompted.

2. Insert a table into the Vacation Policy topic.

   ❒ from the **Contents** area, **Leave_and_Vacation** folder, open the **Vacation Policy** topic

   ❒ click after the topic text **10,001 + 20 days** and press [**enter**] to create a new paragraph

   ❒ from the toolbar above the topic, click the **Insert Table** icon

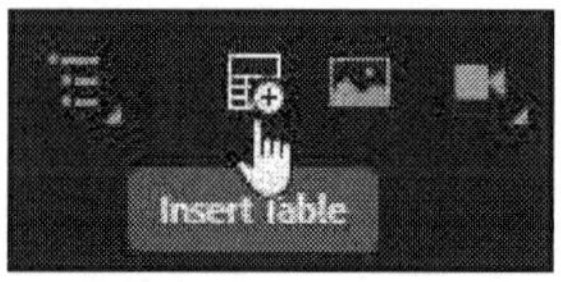

   ❒ choose **4 rows** and **2 columns**

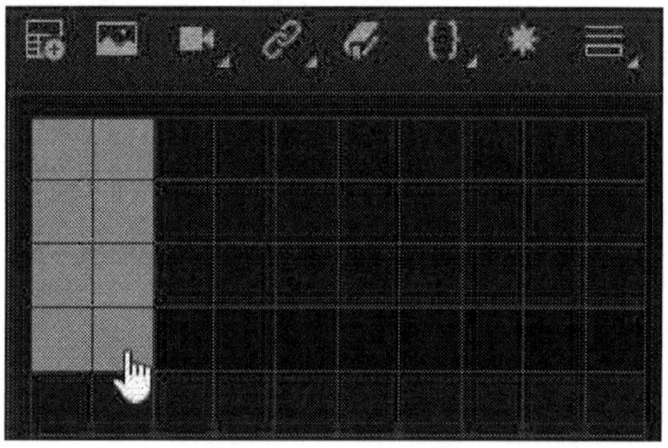

There is now an empty table just above the last paragraph in the topic.

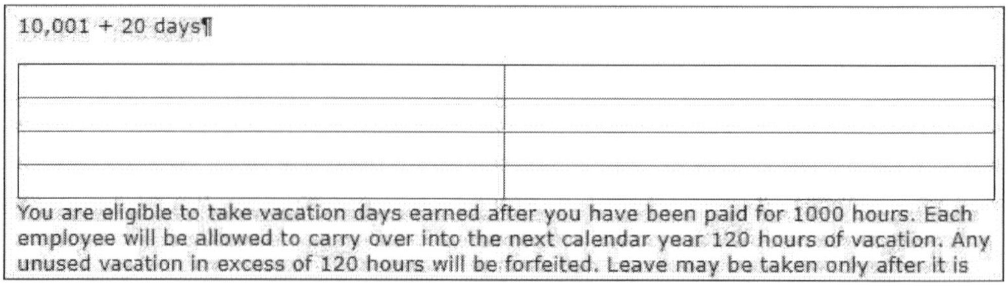

Tables Confidence Check

1. From above the table, drag the phrase **Hours Worked i**nto the **first** cell in the **first** row

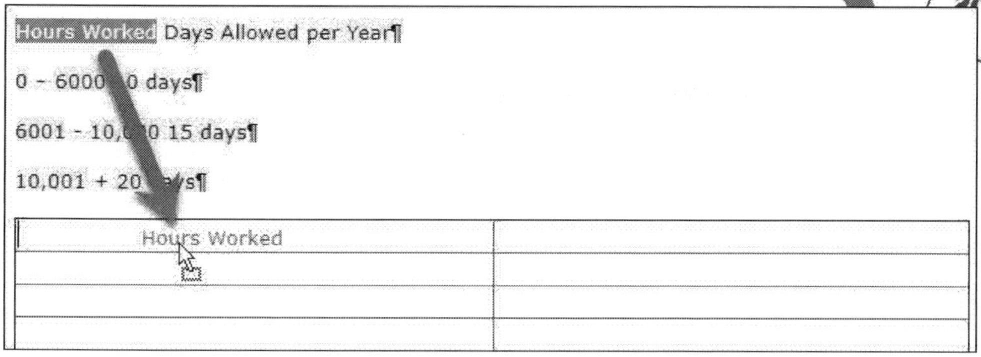

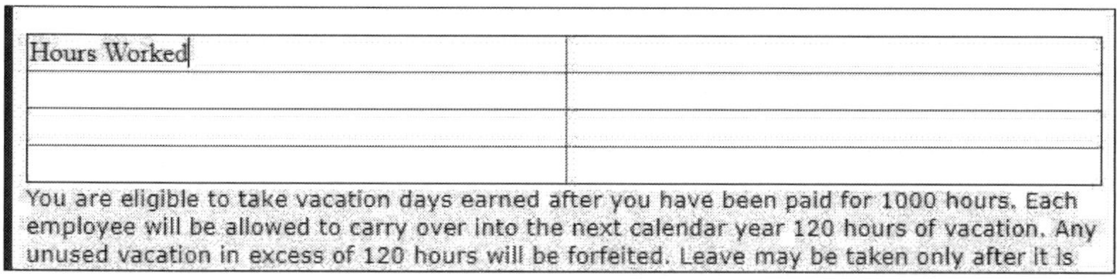

Hours Worked	

You are eligible to take vacation days earned after you have been paid for 1000 hours. Each employee will be allowed to carry over into the next calendar year 120 hours of vacation. Any unused vacation in excess of 120 hours will be forfeited. Leave may be taken only after it is

2. Continue dragging topic content (the hours worked and the days allowed per year) into the table until your table looks like the picture below.

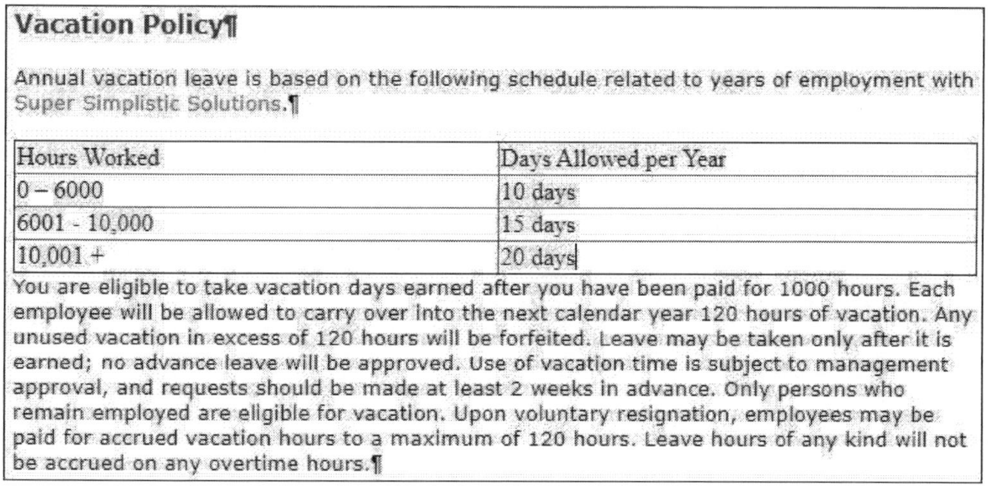

Vacation Policy¶

Annual vacation leave is based on the following schedule related to years of employment with Super Simplistic Solutions.¶

Hours Worked	Days Allowed per Year
0 – 6000	10 days
6001 - 10,000	15 days
10,001 +	20 days

You are eligible to take vacation days earned after you have been paid for 1000 hours. Each employee will be allowed to carry over into the next calendar year 120 hours of vacation. Any unused vacation in excess of 120 hours will be forfeited. Leave may be taken only after it is earned; no advance leave will be approved. Use of vacation time is subject to management approval, and requests should be made at least 2 weeks in advance. Only persons who remain employed are eligible for vacation. Upon voluntary resignation, employees may be paid for accrued vacation hours to a maximum of 120 hours. Leave hours of any kind will not be accrued on any overtime hours.¶

3. Save the project.

NOTES

NOTES

Guided Activity 44: Apply Table Templates

1. Ensure that the **tables_index** project is still open.

2. Apply Table Templates.

   ❒ still working in the **Vacation Policy** topic, click within the table

   ❒ from above the topic, click the **table** tag to select the entire table

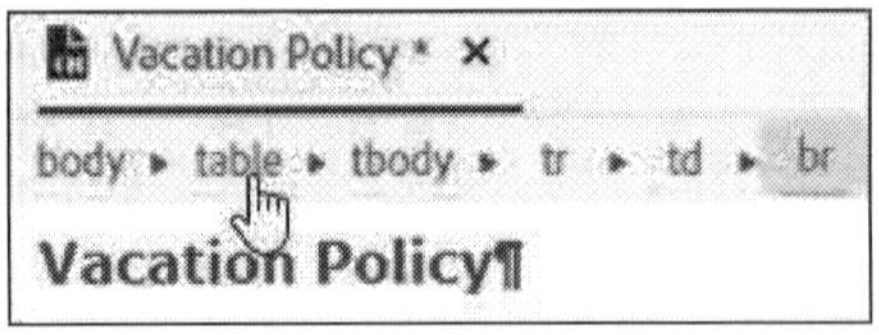

   ❒ from the **Table Properties** panel at the right, **Templates** area, click the **third** template in the first row

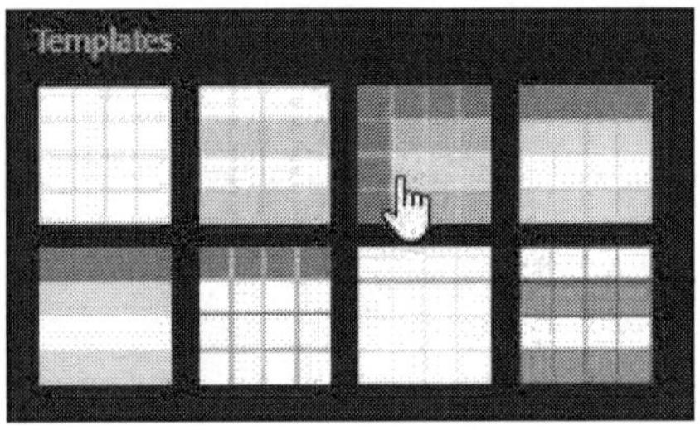

   ❒ click once in the table to deselect it

Notice that the appearance of the table changes to match the template.

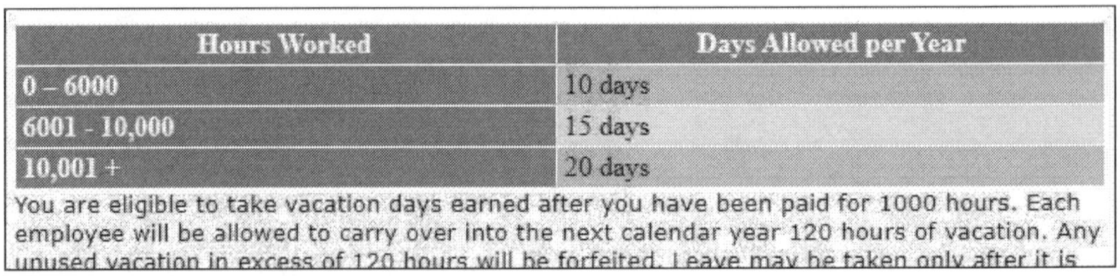

Hours Worked	Days Allowed per Year
0 – 6000	10 days
6001 - 10,000	15 days
10,001 +	20 days

You are eligible to take vacation days earned after you have been paid for 1000 hours. Each employee will be allowed to carry over into the next calendar year 120 hours of vacation. Any unused vacation in excess of 120 hours will be forfeited. Leave may be taken only after it is

   ❒ from above the topic, click the **table** tag to reselect the entire table

   ❒ from the **Content Properties** panel at the right, **Templates** area, click the **first** template (border only)

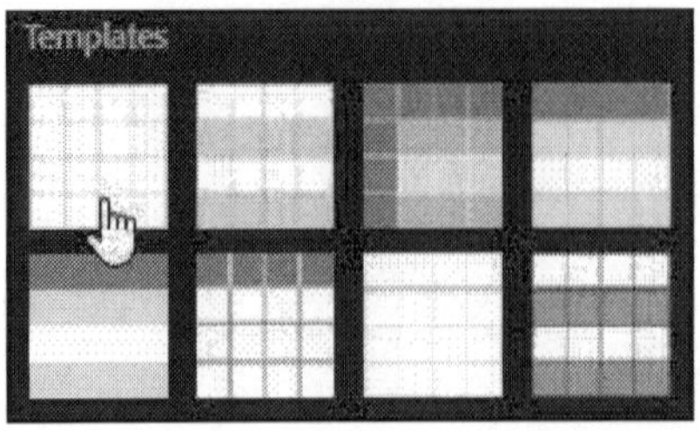

The table is reformatted again with simple cell borders.

Guided Activity 45: Edit Table Styles

1. Ensure that the **tables_index** project is still open and that you're editing the **Vacation Policy** topic.

2. Delete a CSS style.

❒ ensure that the table is still selected

❒ from the icons at the right, click **Styles**

❒ from the **Styles** drop-down menu choose **Table Styles**

When you applied the two templates to the table, RoboHelp added these two styles to the project.

❒ move your mouse over the **borderonly** style and click the **edit** icon

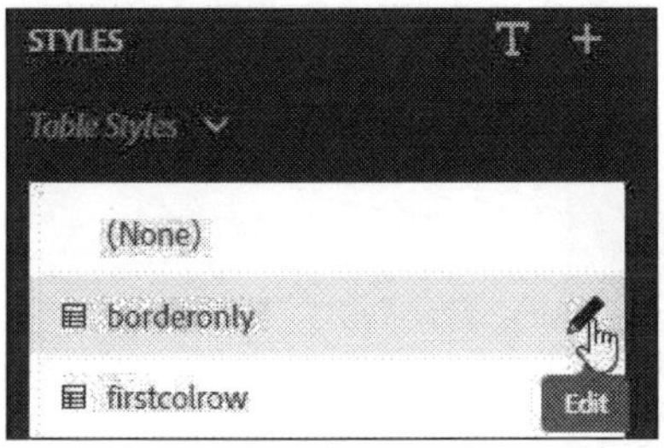

The policies style sheet opens for editing and the Table Style section is selected.

❒ right-click **table.firstrowcol** and choose **Delete Style**

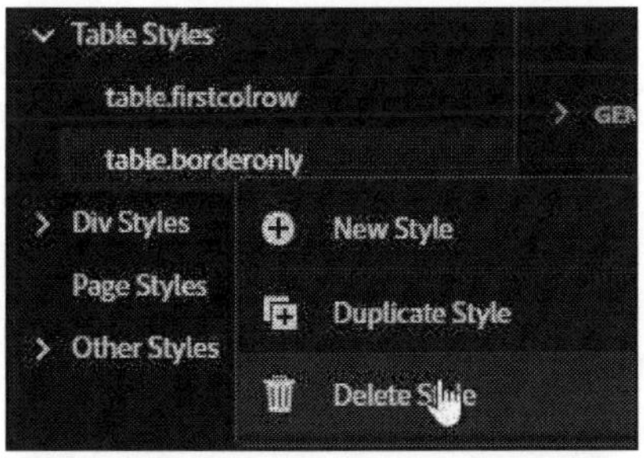

❒ click the **Yes** button to confirm the action

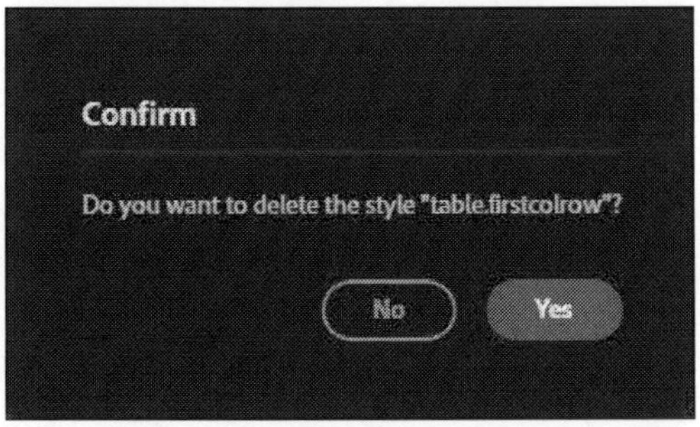

NOTES

The only remaining table style in the style sheet is **table.borderonly**.

3. Duplicate a style.

   ❒ right the **table.borderonly** style and choose **Duplicate Style**

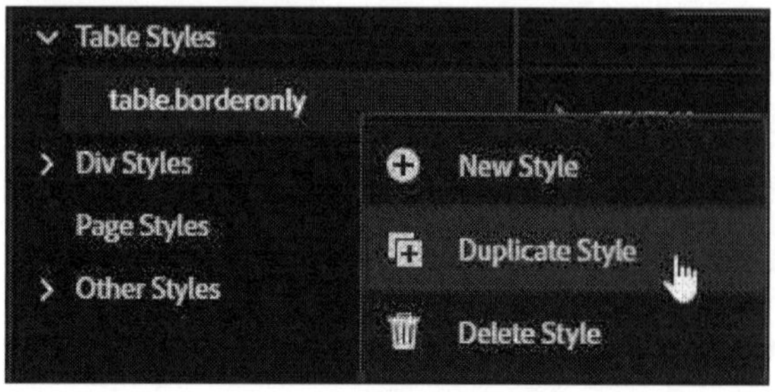

   The Add Style dialog box opens.

   ❒ change the class name to **custom**

   ❒ click the **Done** button

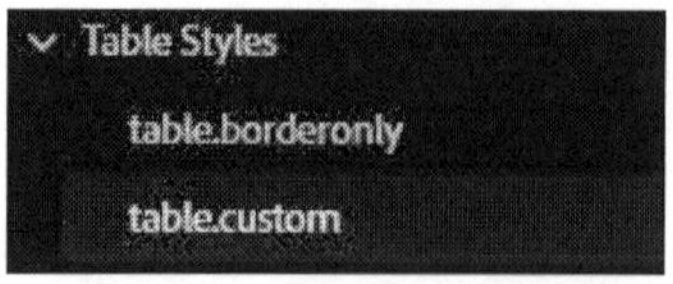

4. Edit the table border style.

   ❒ select the **table.custom** style

   ❒ expand the **Border** area

   ❒ from the **Border Side** area, click **All**

   ❒ from the **Style** drop-down menu, choose **Solid**

- ❒ click the **Border Color** box
- ❒ select any color that you like

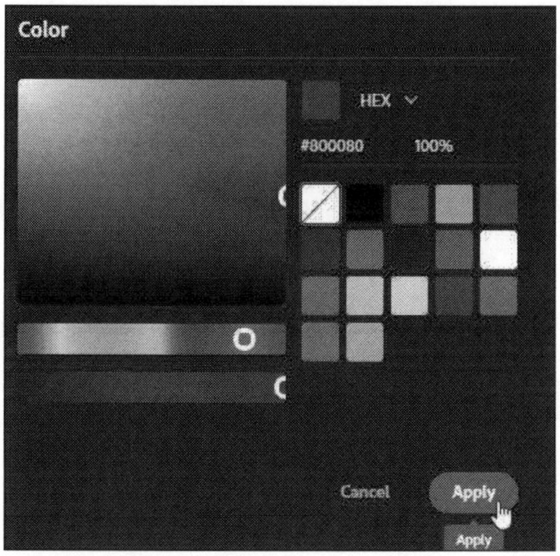

- ❒ click the **Apply** button
- ❒ change the **Border Width** to **3 px**

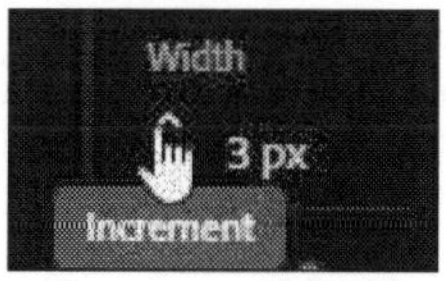

5. Save and close the policies style sheet.

6. Apply a table style.

   - ❒ if necessary, click within the table you added to the Vacation Policy topic
   - ❒ on the **Styles** panel, click the **custom** table style

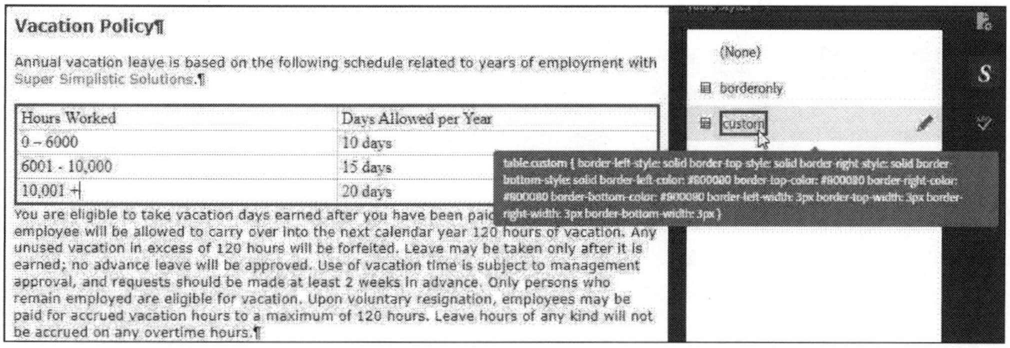

NOTES

Tables Confidence Check

1. Edit the **custom** table style.

2. From the **Apply Formatting to** drop-down menu, ensure that **Whole Table** is selected.

3. Expand the **Font** area.
4. Change the **Font Family** to **Verdana** and change the **Font Size** to **10 pt**.

5. Unlock the **Margin** options.
6. Change the **Bottom Margin** to **12px**.

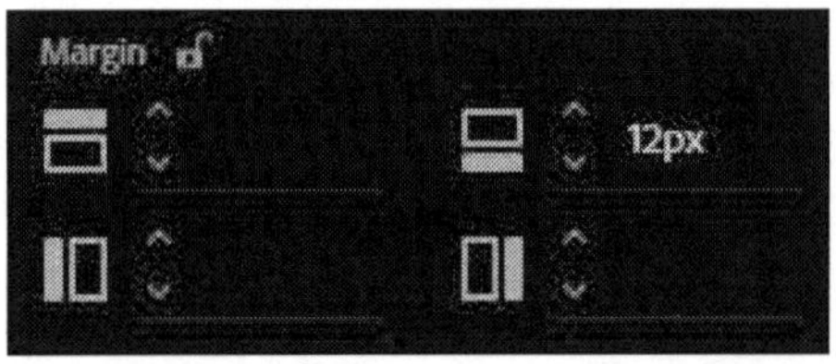

7. From the **Apply Formatting to** drop-down menu, select **First Row**.

8. From beneath the **Font Size** option, change the **Text Style** to **Bold**.

9. Save and close the style sheet.

   Thanks to the edit you just made to the table style, the appearance of the table updates.

Indexes

An index is a list of keywords that take users to project topics. Although often overlooked by novice Help authors, the index is the second most commonly used feature of a Help System (behind the Search feature).

Guided Activity 46: Add Index Keywords from Within a Topic

1. Ensure that the **tables_index** project is still open.

2. Copy and paste topic content into the Index.

   ❒ from the **Contents** area, **General Office Information** folder, open **About This Guide**

   ❒ highlight the heading, **About This Guide,** and **copy** it to the clipboard

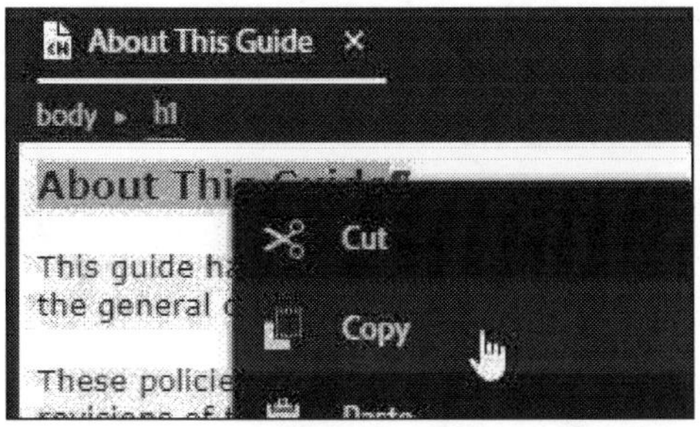

   ❒ at the right of the RoboHelp window, click **Topic Properties** 

   ❒ expand the **Index** section

   ❒ click in the **Index** text field and **paste** the text you copied to the clipboard

   ❒ press [**enter**] to add the pasted text as an Index keyword

3. Copy and paste more topic content into the Index.

   ❒ from within the **About This Guide** topic, highlight the phrase **Super Simplistic Solutions** and **copy** it to the clipboard

   ❒ click in the Index text field and **paste** the text you copied to the clipboard

   ❒ press [**enter**] to add the pasted text as an Index keyword

NOTES

Index Entries Confidence Check

1. From within the **About This Guide** topic, copy and paste the following keywords into the Index (or type the entries into the Index manually).

   Policies and Procedures

   Employment Contract

   At Will

   Note: When you copy/paste the text as an Index Keyword, consider manually capitalizing the initial letters (which is typical of index entries).

   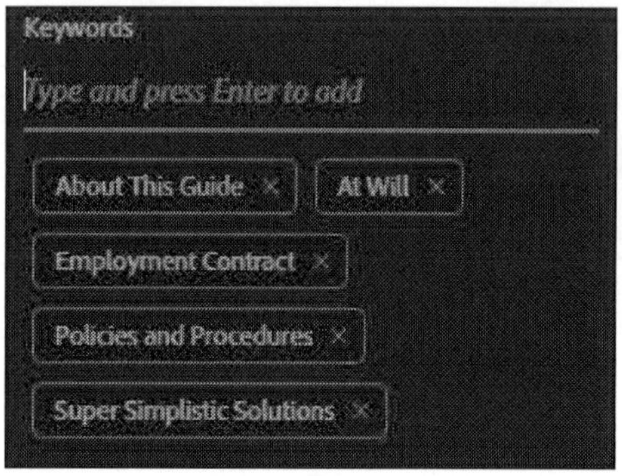

2. Save the project.

Guided Activity 47: Add Index Keywords on the Index Panel

1. Ensure that the **tables_index** project is still open.

2. Add an Index entry on the Index panel.

❒ from **Author** area at the left, click **Index**

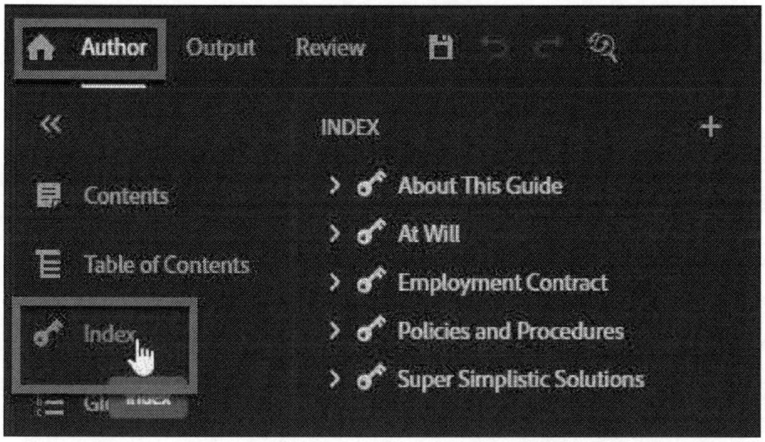

The keywords you added during the last activity appear in the Index.

❒ from the top of the Index, click the **New Keyword** icon

❒ type **Officers** and press [**enter**]

The new Index keyword has been added but is not yet associated with any topics. Note there is **no arrow** to the left of the keyword. Arrows appear when a keyword is associated with one or more topics.

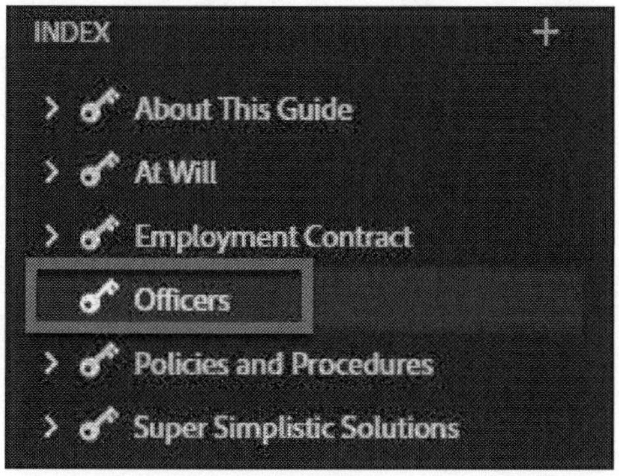

NOTES

3. Associate topics with an Index keyword.

❒ from within the Index, right-click the **Officers** keyword and choose **Add Topic**

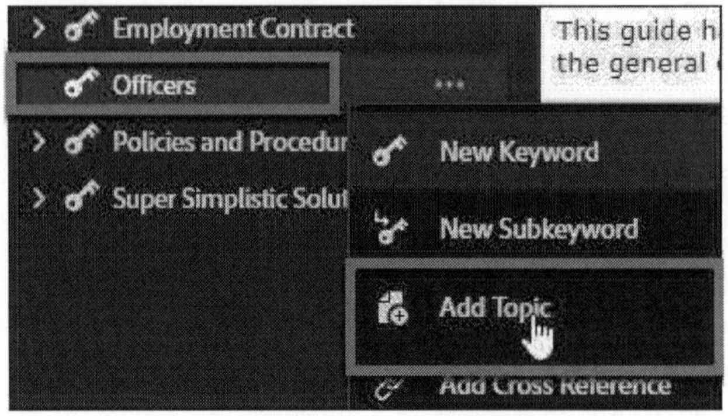

The Add Topic dialog box opens.

❒ from the **Company Officers** folder, select **Human Resources**

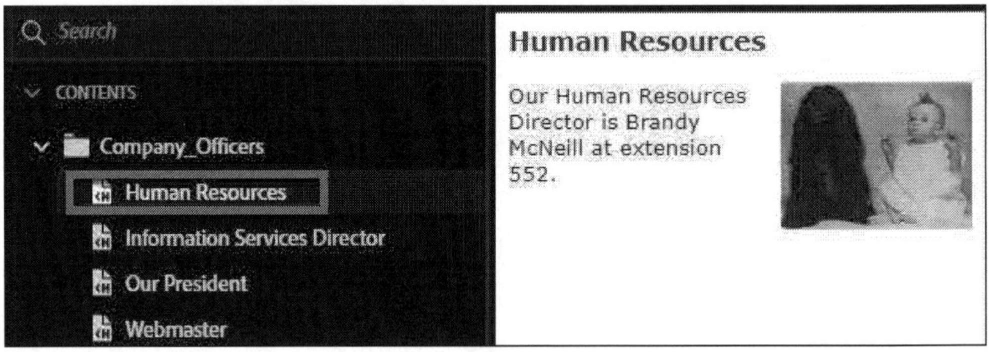

❒ click the **Link** button

The topic has been added beneath the **Officers** Index keyword.

Guided Activity 48: Add Index Entries to Multiple Topics at Once

1. Ensure that the **tables_index** project is still open.

2. Use the Topic List pod to add an Index keyword to multiple topics.

   ❒ choose **View > Topic List**

   A list of all project topics appears.

   ❒ from within the **Topic List**, select **IS**, **Our_President**, and **webmaster** (put checks in each topic box)

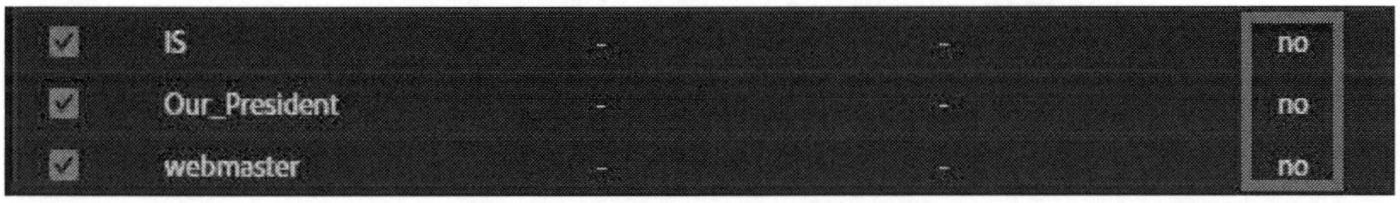

   At the right of the selected topics, notice the word "no" in the Index column. These topics are not currently represented in the Index.

   ❒ from within the **Topic List**, right-click any of the selected topics and choose **Properties**

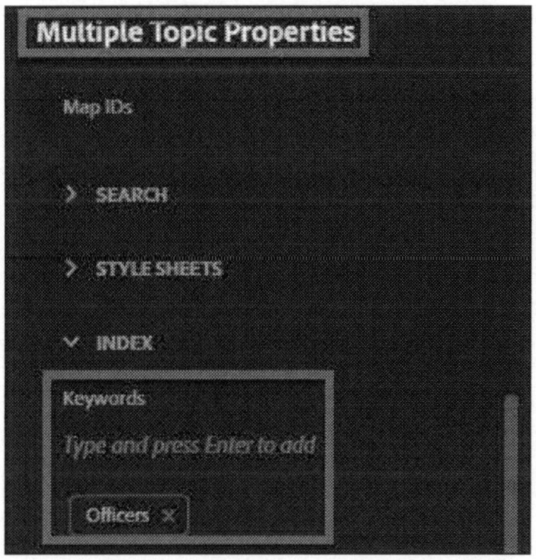

   The **Multiple Topic Properties** dialog box opens. Any change you make from here will affect all three selected topics.

   ❒ scroll down and, if necessary, expand the Index area of the dialog box

   ❒ click in the **Index** text field, type **Officers**, and press [**enter**] on your keyboard

   Check your spelling carefully. "Officers" is an existing Index keyword. If you typed the keyword differently from the existing keyword, you'll end up with a new keyword.

   ❒ click the **Apply** button

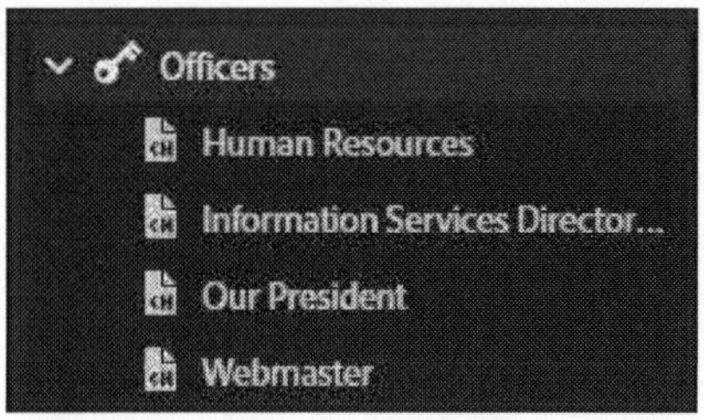

3. On the Index, notice that the selected topics have been added to the Officers keyword.

4. Save the project.

5. Refresh the Topic List.

   ❒ from above the Topic List, click the **Refresh** icon 

   In the **Index** column of the Topic List, notice that the word "yes" has been added, an indication that the three topics appear in the index at least one time.

NOTES

Index Confidence Check

1. From the **Output** area, open the **Responsive HTML5** Output.
2. Change the Output's **Title** to **Policies and Procedures**.
3. Change the Output path to **RoboHelp2022Data > output > Responsive HTML5**.
4. Save, Generate, and then View the Responsive HTML5 Output.
5. Click the **Index** icon A-Z to see the Index you created.

6. Close the browser and return to RoboHelp.

See Also Links

You have now learned about index entries and how to create them. Every index entry that you associate with a topic appears on the Index pane of the generated project. But there is a second type of keyword known as See Also. See Also keywords allow you to place related topics into one common group. See Also keywords do not appear on the Index when you generate the output. One popular way to get a See Also to appear is to use See Also Links.

In the next activity, you will create a See Also keyword and associate some topics with it. Then you will create a Link Control in a topic that tells the See Also links to appear in a topic.

Guided Activity 49: Create a See Also Keyword

1. Ensure that the **tables_index** project is still open.

2. Create a See Also keyword.

   ❒ from the **Author** area, click **See Also**

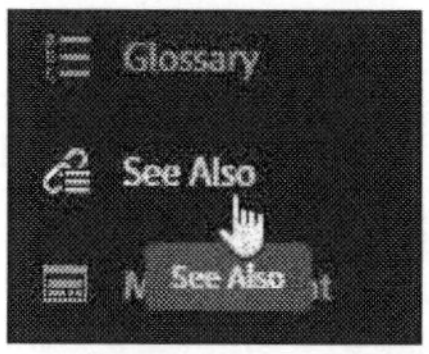

   ❒ from the top of the **See Also** panel, click the **New See Also Keyword** icon

   The **New See Also Keyword** dialog box opens.

   ❒ name the See Also Keyword **Managers**

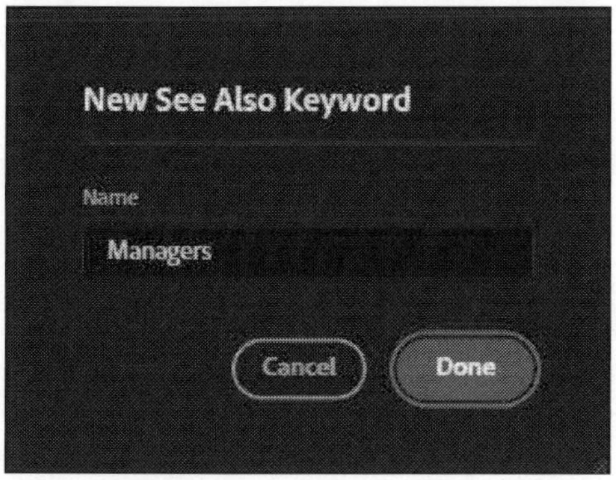

   ❒ click the **Done** button

NOTES

NOTES

3. Associate topics to a See Also Keyword.

   ❒ double-click the **Managers** See Also keyword you just added

   Two options appear beneath the Managers See Also keyword: **Associated Topics** and **Used In Topics**.

   ❒ click the **Add Associated Topic** icon

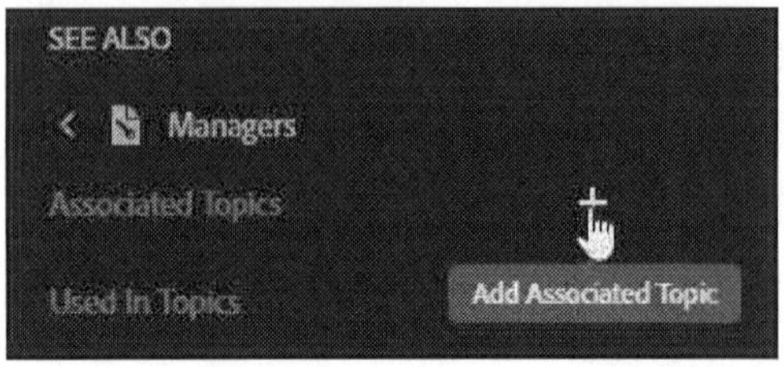

   The **Add Associated Topic** dialog box opens.

   ❒ expand the **Contents** folder

   ❒ from the **Company Officers** folder, select **Human Resources**

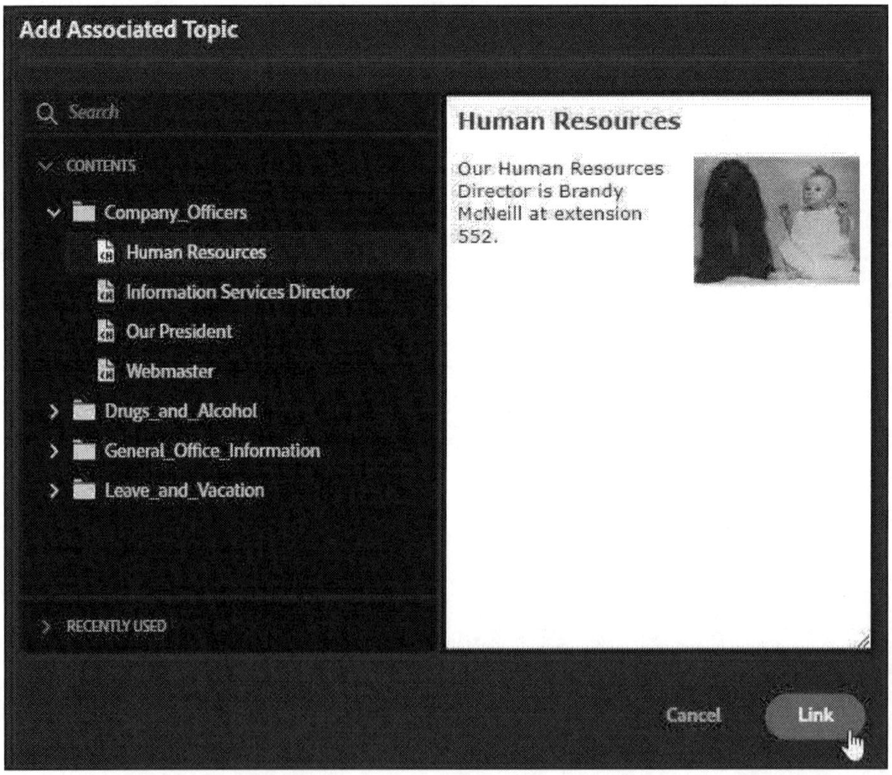

   ❒ click the **Link** button

   The Human Resources topic appears in the Associated Topics area.

Index Confidence Check

1. Add the following three topics to the **Managers** See Also Keyword:

   Information Services Director

   Our President

   Webmaster

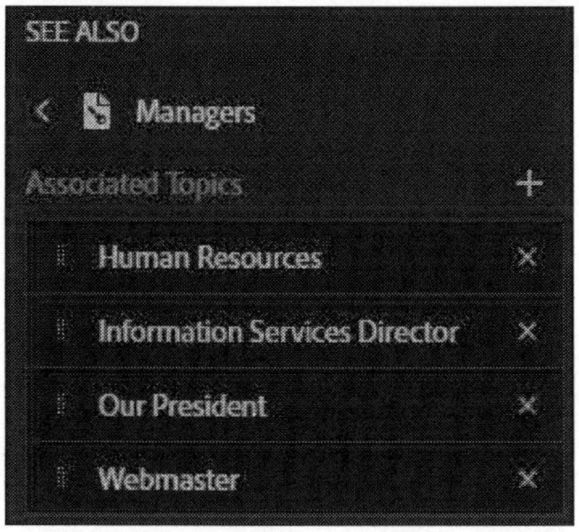

2. Add the four Company Officers to the **Used In Topics** area.

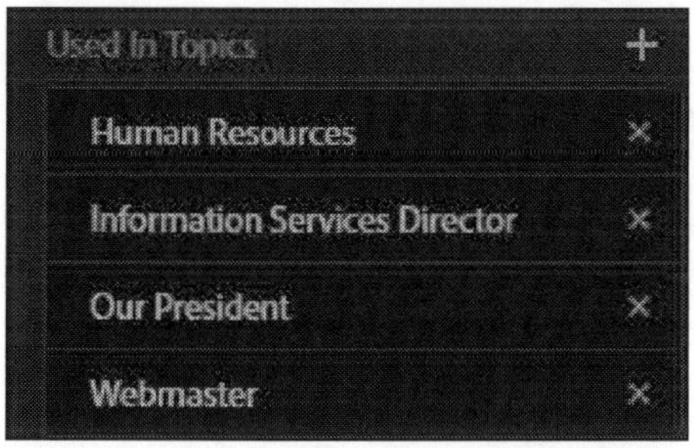

Now that you've created the Managers See Also keyword, associated the keyword with the four Company Officers, and used the keyword in some topics, all that's left to do is add a placeholder into a topic so that users will be able to see the related topics in the output.

NOTES

NOTES

Guided Activity 50: Insert a See Also Placeholder into a Topic

1. Ensure that the **tables_index** project is still open.

2. From the **Contents** area, **Company_Officers** folder, open the **Our President** topic.

3. Insert a See Also Placeholder.

   ❒ click at the end of the topic text and press [**enter**] to create a new paragraph

   ❒ from above the topic, click the **Insert Placeholder** icon

   ❒ choose **See Also**

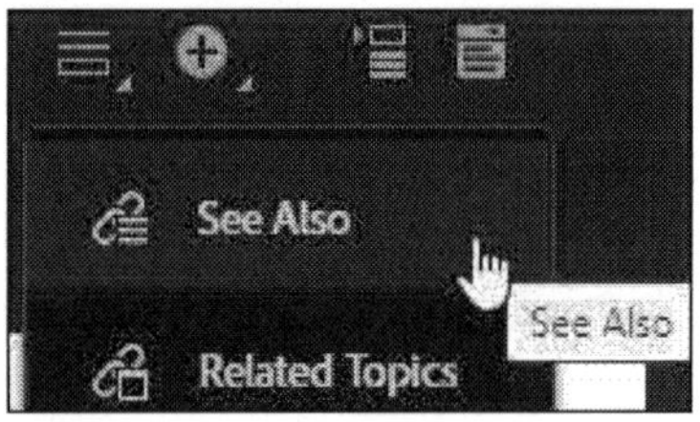

   The placeholder is added to the topic. Because you assigned the Managers See Also to this topic (and the other three managers), the placeholder loads the related topics when you generate output.

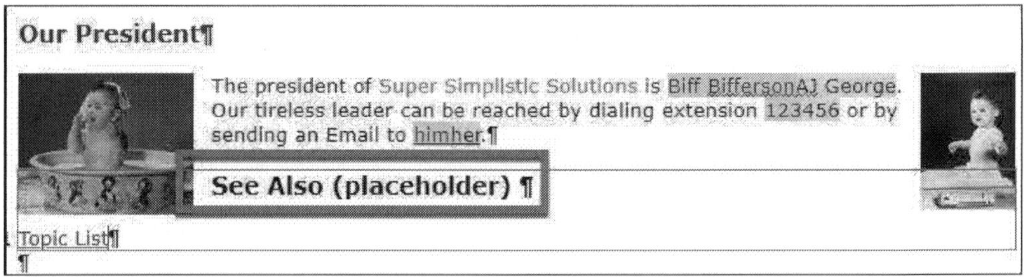

4. Save the project.

See Also Confidence Check

1. Add the **See Also** placeholder to the Human Resources topic.

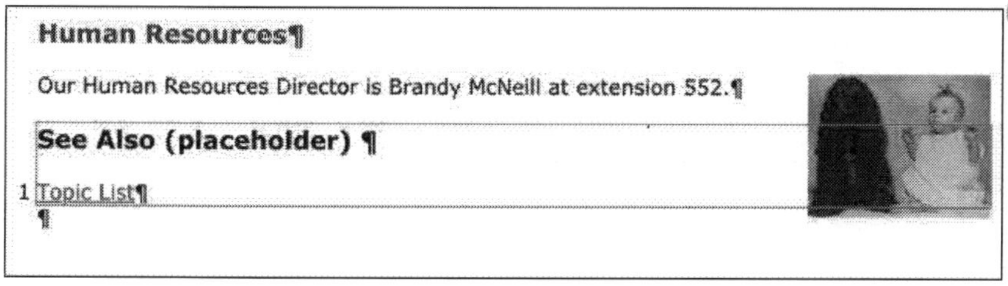

2. Add the **See Also** placeholder to the **Information Services Director** topic.
3. Add the **See Also** placeholder to the **Webmaster** topic.
4. From the **Output** area, open the **Responsive HTML5** output.
5. On the **Content** tab, **Dynamic Content Filter** drop-down menu, choose **Regions**.

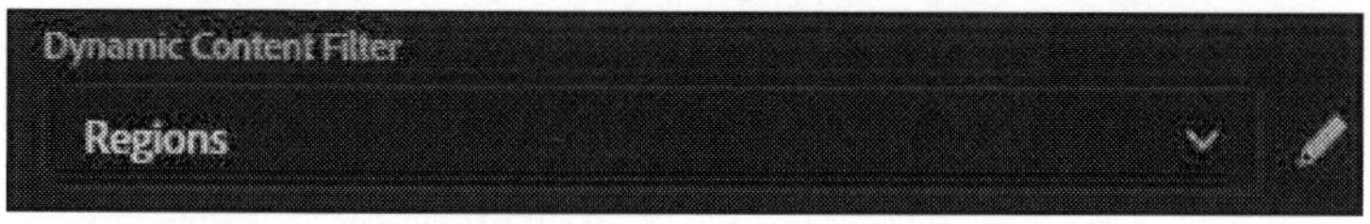

   You learned how to work with Dynamic Content Filters on page 108. By choosing the Regions filter, users will be able to choose between viewing one set of content or another.

6. Save the project.
7. **Generate** and **View** the Output.
8. Click in the **Search** field, type **president** and press [**enter**].

   The Help System is searched and topics containing the word "president" display in the results area (the results are ranked in order of relevance).

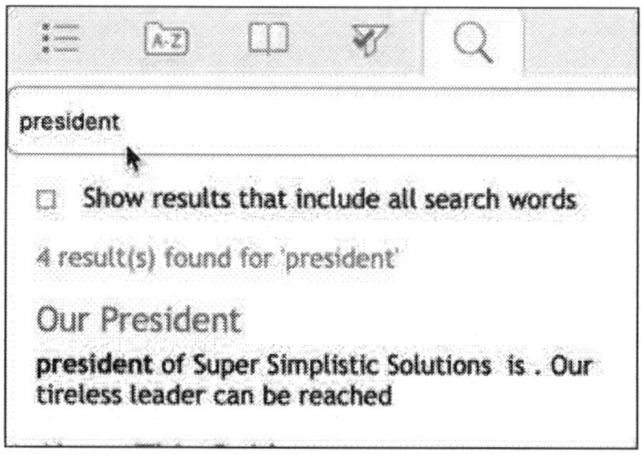

9. Click the first result (**Our President**) to open the Our President topic.

Thanks to the **Managers** See Also placeholder you added to the topic, there are links to the company's managers. However, notice that the currently open topic, Our President, does not appear in the list of managers even though the president is one of the Associated See Also Topics.

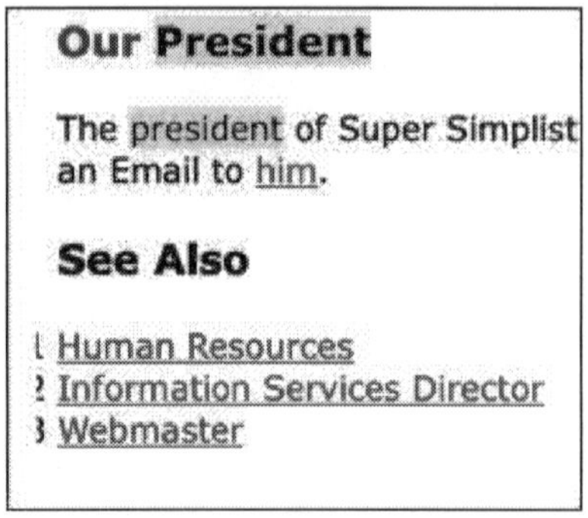

The omission of the Our President topic from the list of related topics makes sense because users are already viewing the topic. I love that the See Also feature automatically removes the current topic from the list.

10. Select any of the topics in the list to open the topic.
11. Notice that the link to the topic you're in is again automatically removed from the list of related topics.
12. Notice the appearance of the See Also content. The appearance is controlled by styles, which you will edit next.
13. Close the browser and return to the RoboHelp project.
14. Open the **Our President** topic.
15. From the right of the RoboHelp window, click the **Styles** icon.
16. From the **Styles** drop-down menu, choose **Paragraph Styles**.
17. Notice that there is a style named **seealso-caption**. This style controls the formatting of the words "See Also placeholder."

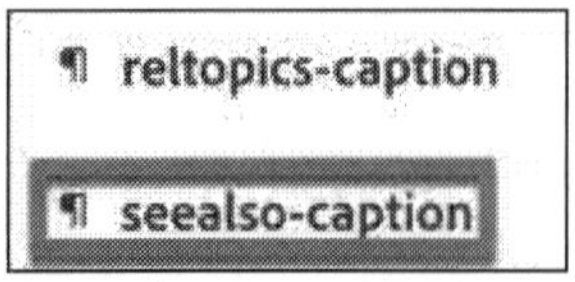

18. From the list of **Styles**, edit **seealso-caption**.

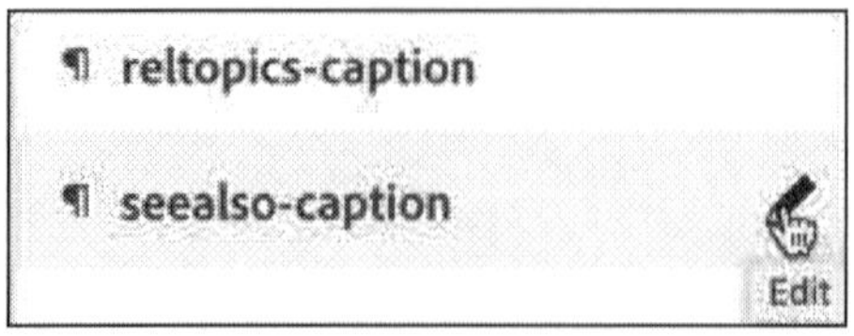

The policies.css file opens for editing and the seealso-caption is selected.

19. Expand the **Font** category.
20. Change the **Font Size** to **10 pt**.

21. Change the Font Color to **dark red**.
22. From the list of styles, expand **List Styles**.
23. From the list of **List Styles**, select **ol.seealso-list**.

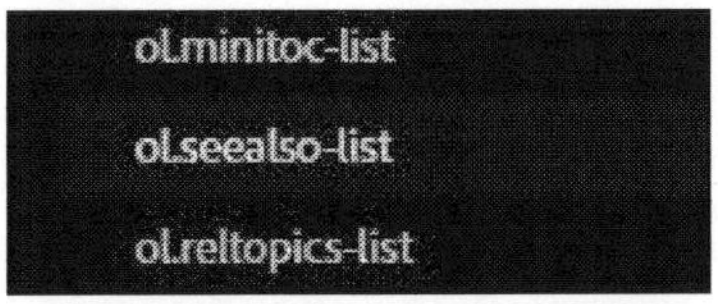

    This style controls the items listed beneath the See Also caption. Currently, the list items are numbered. You'll change the indentation of the text and remove the list numbers next.

24. From the **Level** area at the top of the style's Properties, click **Clear Level Formatting** (click the **Yes** button when prompted).

25. From the top of the Properties, select **Advanced Formatting**.
26. Ensure that **Numbering** is selected from the **Apply Styling to** drop-down menu.

27. Expand the **Layout** category.
28. From the **Display** drop-down menu, choose **none**.

29. In the **Preview** area, notice that the list numbers have been removed.
30. Save the project and then close policies.css.
31. Generate and View the **Responsive HTML5** output.
32. Search for and open the **president** topic to see the updated See Also formatting.
33. Close the browser and return to the RoboHelp project.

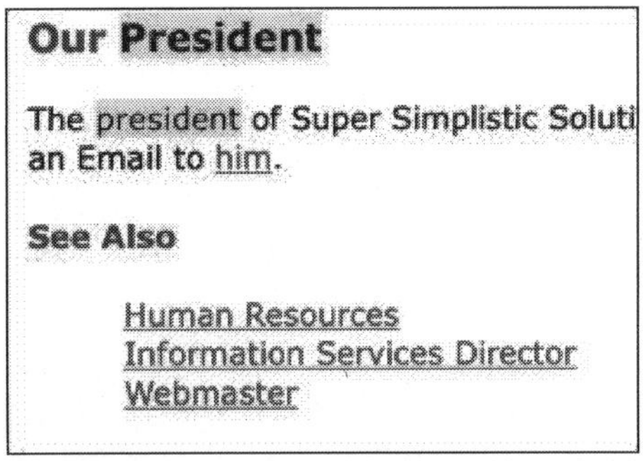

NOTES

NOTES

Search

During the last few activities, you used the Search feature in the output to find specific content. You may have noticed that the Search results were ranked based on relevance. If a word being searched appears in the title of a topic, its rank is higher than the word appearing in the body of a topic. In addition, a topic with the word appearing in a paragraph using a Heading 1 style ranks higher than the same word appearing in a paragraph using a Heading 2 style.

During the following activity, you will learn how to add search terms to a topic when those terms do not actually appear in the topic. Topics with custom search terms will appear higher in the search results than topics without these search terms set.

Guided Activity 51: Add Custom Search Terms

1. Ensure that the **tables_index** project is still open.

2. From **Contents > Company_Officers**, open the **Human Resources** topic.

   There isn't much content in the topic. Anyone searching for Brandy, McNeill, Human Resources, or Human would correctly find the Human Resources topic. However, if someone searches for a word that is not physically in the topic, such as **conflict**, they won't find anything. Let's test that.

3. Generate **Responsive HTML5** and **View** the output.

4. Use the Search field to search for **conflict**.

   Notice that no topics are found because the word "conflict" does not appear in any topic.

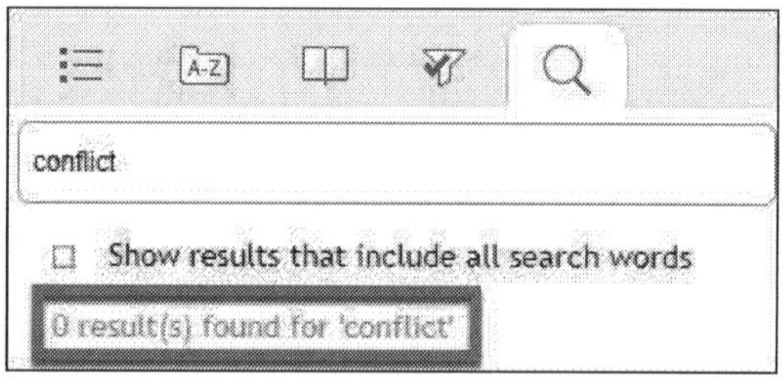

5. Close the web browser and return to the RoboHelp project.

6. Add a custom Search term to a topic's Properties.

   ❐ if necessary, open the **Human Resources** topic

   ❐ from the right of the RoboHelp window, click the **Topic Properties** icon 

   ❐ expand the **Search** options

   ❐ type **conflict** into the **Search Keyword** text field and then press **[enter]**

7. Save the project.

8. Generate **Responsive HTML5** and **View** the output.

9. Use Search to search for **conflict**.

   This time, the Human Resources topic is found even though the word "conflict" is not a word in the topic's content.

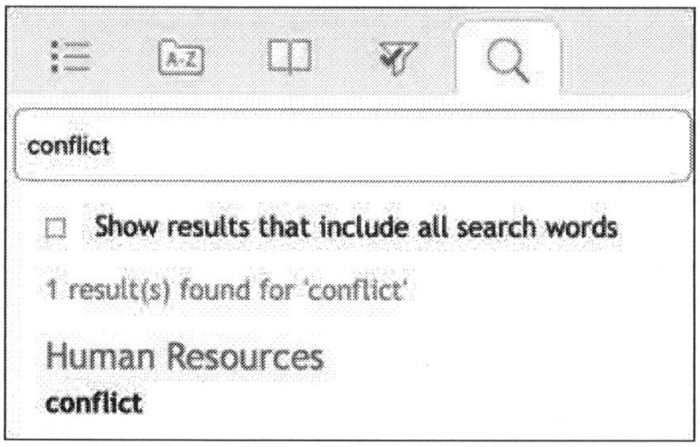

   Note: If you want to exclude a topic from appearing on the Search tab, you can go to the Search area for the topic's Properties and select **Exclude this topic from search**.

10. Close the browser and return to the RoboHelp project.

NOTES

NOTES

Guided Activity 52: Add a Search Synonym

1. Ensure that the **tables_index** project is still open.

2. From **Contents > Drugs_and_Alcohol**, open the **Alcohol Policy** topic.

   This topic contains the word "Alcohol" in the heading. When searching for the word "alcohol," a user will find this topic. However, one common misspelling of "alcohol" is "alchohol." If someone searches for "alchohol," they won't find any related topics. By adding a search synonym, you take misspelled search terms into account.

3. Create a search synonym.

   ❒ from the **Output** area, click **Synonyms**

   ❒ from the **Synonyms** area, double-click **English (US)**

   ❒ in the **Word** column, type **alcohol**

   ❒ in the **Synonym** column, type **alchohol** and press [**enter**]

4. Save the project.

5. Generate **Responsive HTML5** and **View** the output.

6. Use the Search tab to search for **alchohol**.

   All topics with the text "alcohol" will be found even though the word **alchohol** was the Search term.

7. Close the browser, return to the RoboHelp project and close all open topics.

Glossaries

A glossary gives your users a list of words and their definitions related to content presented in your Help System. Most users rely heavily on both the Index and Search features. Because access to the Glossary is conveniently located next to both of those tools, it's a good bet that it gets plenty of use.

Guided Activity 53: Add Glossary Terms

1. Ensure that the **tables_index** project is still open.

2. View the Glossary.

   ❒ from the **Author** area, click **Glossary** 

   ❒ double-click the existing Glossary (**policies**) to open it

   There are no glossary terms. You add glossary entries similarly to how you added index keywords earlier.

3. Add a New Term to a glossary.

   ❒ at the top of the policies Glossary, click the **New Term** icon

   ❒ type **SSS** as the Term

   ❒ click in the **Definition** area and type **Super Simplistic Solutions**

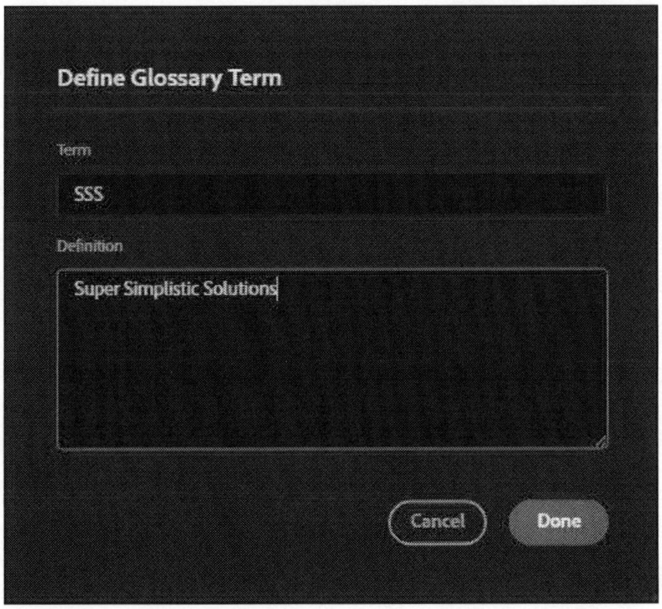

   ❒ click the **Done** button

NOTES

NOTES

Glossary Confidence Check

1. Add the following Glossary terms and definitions to the Glossary pod.

   EAP

   Employee Assistance Program

   ECT

   Earned Compensatory Time

   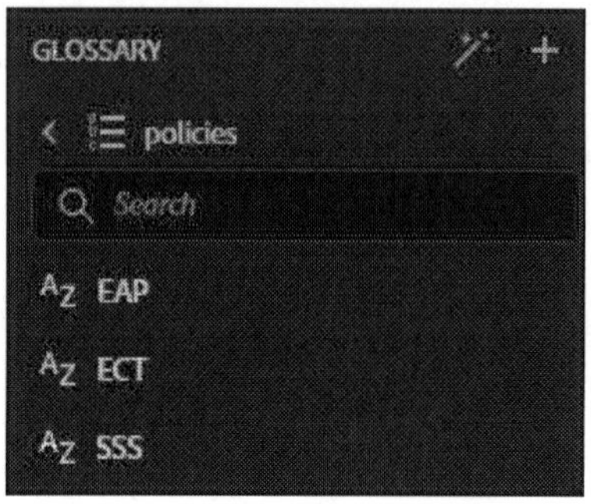

2. Save the project.

3. Generate **Responsive HTML5** and **View** the output.

   Notice that there is now a **Glossary** tab.

4. Click the **Glossary** tab and spend a moment clicking on the Glossary Terms and reviewing the definitions that expand.

   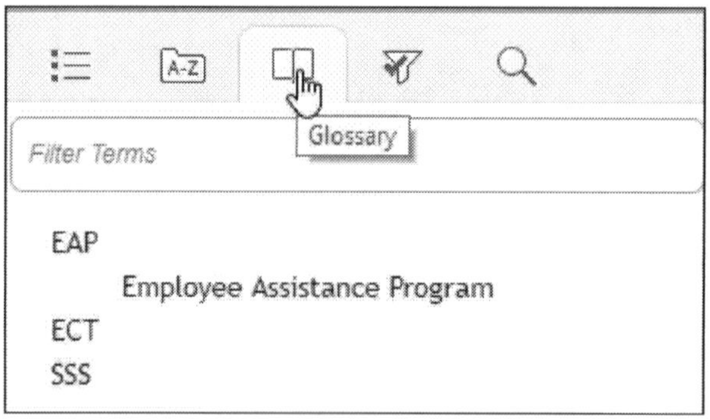

5. Close the browser and return to the RoboHelp project.
6. Save the project.

Scripts

You can create JavaScripts that automate any number of RoboHelp processes. However, I expect that most of you reading this book are not programmers and have little to no desire to create scripts on your own.

Fortunately, RoboHelp comes with a handful of scripts. You can edit the scripts to see how they work. And you can work with a programmer to create more scripts. (Scripts can easily be imported into RoboHelp.)

During the next activity, you'll use a script to convert plain topic text to interactive expanding text.

Guided Activity 54: Use the Glossary Term Converter Script

1. Ensure that the **tables_index** project is still open.

2. Add a glossary term to a few topics.

   ❐ open any topic and press [enter] to add a new paragraph

   ❐ type the letters **SSS**

   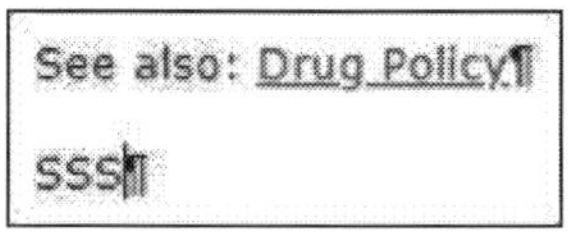

   You added these letters to the Glossary a few moments ago.

   ❐ open another topic and press [**enter**] to add a new paragraph

   ❐ type the letters **SSS**

   ❐ open another topic and press [**enter**] to add a new paragraph

   ❐ type the letters **SSS**

3. Review a script.

   ❐ from the **Author** area, click **Scripts** 

   ❐ right-click **GlossaryTermConverter**, and choose **Edit**

   The script opens. You won't be making any changes, but you could.

   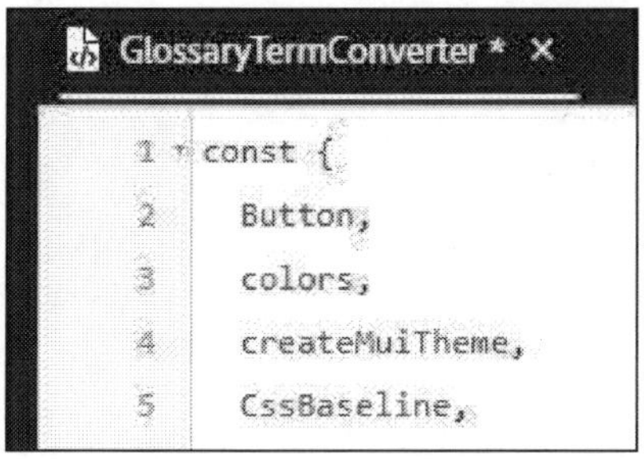

   ❐ close the script window (without saving any changes)

4. Run a script.

❒ right-click **GlossaryTermConverter** and choose **Execute**

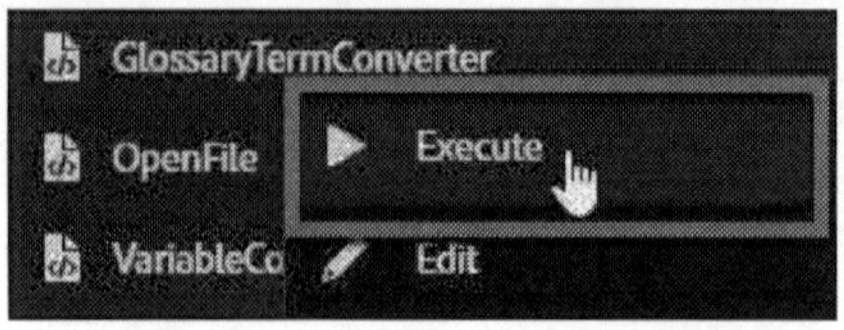

The Glossary Hotspot window opens.

❒ from the Glossary File drop-down menu, choose **policies.glo** (this is the RoboHelp support file containing the glossary terms you added earlier)

❒ from the Glossary Term drop-down menu, choose **SSS** (you added this term to the glossary earlier)

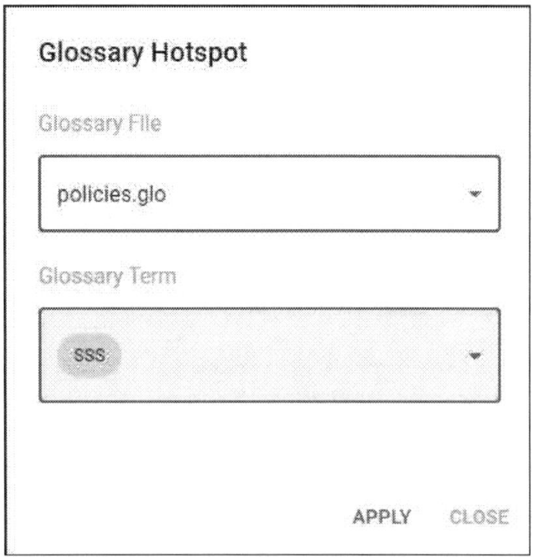

❒ click the **Apply** button

The **Replace Glossterm** screen opens. The "SSS" text you typed within the topics a moment ago has been converted to expanding text.

❒ click **Done**

❒ click **Close**

5. Preview the expanding glossary term.

   ❒ open one of the topics where you typed “SSS” earlier

   ❒ preview the topic

   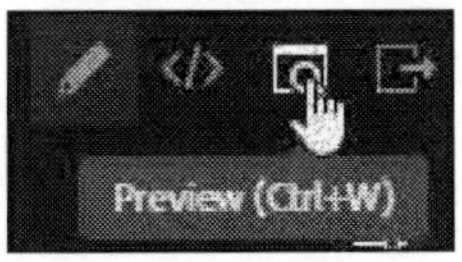

   ❒ click the letters “SSS”

   The text expands to display the definition you added to the Glossary earlier.

   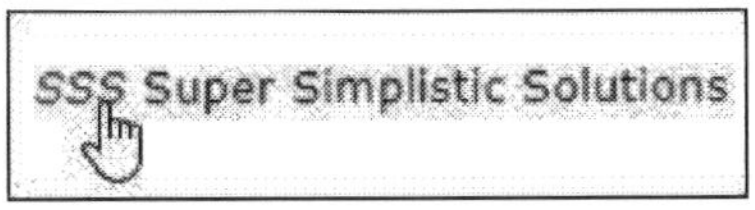

6. Save and close the project.

NOTES

Notes

iCONLOGiC
"Skills and Drills" Learning

Module 8: Templates, Layouts, and Word/PDF Output

In This Module You Will Learn About:

And You Will Learn To:

Templates

When generating output files, there are quite a few layouts available on the Output panel from which to choose. Most of the Output Presets allow for a significant amount of customization. In fact, the icons, the colors, the fonts... just about everything regarding the appearance of an output is controlled by its Template (formally known as a Skin in older versions of RoboHelp). Think of templates as the clothing for your Help System.

Favicons and Default Topics

Favicons became popular several years ago. They are tiny images that appear to the left of a web address on browser tabs. In the images below, notice the IconLogic favicon to the left of the web address at iconlogic.com and the Amazon favicon for amazon.com.

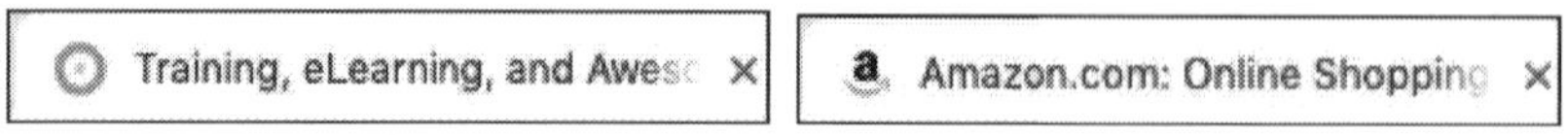

The Default Topic is the topic that appears when users first access the Help System.

During the activities that follow, you'll create a Frameless output and assign both a favicon and a default topic. Then you'll spend some time editing the template.

Guided Activity 55: Add a Favicon and Select a Default Topic

1. Using RoboHelp, open the **templates_layouts** project file.

   Note: Click the **Upgrade** button if prompted.

2. Create an Output.

   ❒ from the **Output** area, click **Output Presets**

   ❒ from **Output Presets**, click the **New Preset** icon

   The New Preset dialog box opens.

   ❒ from the **Type** drop-down menu, ensure **Frameless** is selected

   ❒ name the preset **Policies Output**

   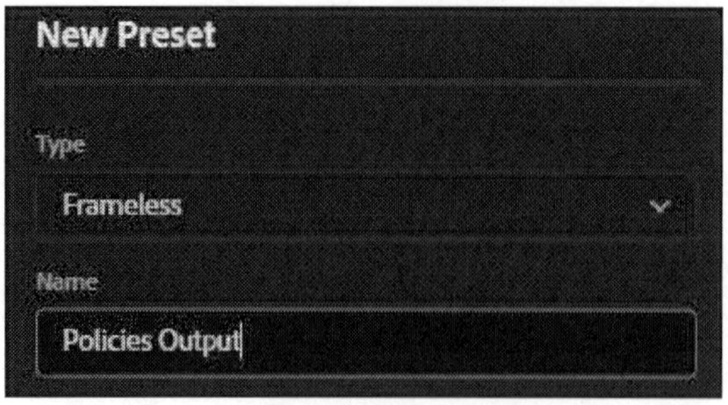

   ❒ click the **Done** button

   The new Policies Output opens for editing.

3. Change the output Title and add a Favicon.

   ❒ with the **General** category selected, change the **Title** to **Policies and Procedures**

   ❒ in the **Favicon** area, click the **Select Favicon** icon

   The **Select Favicon** dialog box opens.

   ❒ if necessary, select **Project Files**

   ❒ expand **assets** and then expand **images**

   ❒ select **Super_Favicon**

   ❒ click the **Select** button

4. Specify an Output location.

   ❒ from the **Output path** area, click the **Browse** icon 

   ❒ from **RoboHelp2022Data** > **output**, open **Frameless**

   ❒ click the **Select Folder/Open** button

5. Specify a default topic.

   ❒ still working within the **Policies Output**, select the **Content** category

   ❒ from the **Default Topic** area, click the **Select Default Topic** icon 

   ❒ from the **General Office Information** folder, select the **Mission Statement** topic

   ❒ click the **Select** button

6. Select a Dynamic Content Filter.

   ❒ from the **Dynamic Content Filter** drop-down menu, choose **Regions**

   Note: You learned about Dynamic Filters on page 108.

NOTES

7. Select a template.

❒ still working within the **Policies Output**, select the **Layout** category

❒ from the **Template** area, click the **Select from gallery** icon 

The New Frameless Template dialog box opens. Templates are made up of the components that surround your Help System (the appearance of the TOC and Index icons for instance). In the Preview area, you can see how content might look on a desktop, a mobile device, and a tablet.

❒ from the **Templates** list, select **Oceanic**

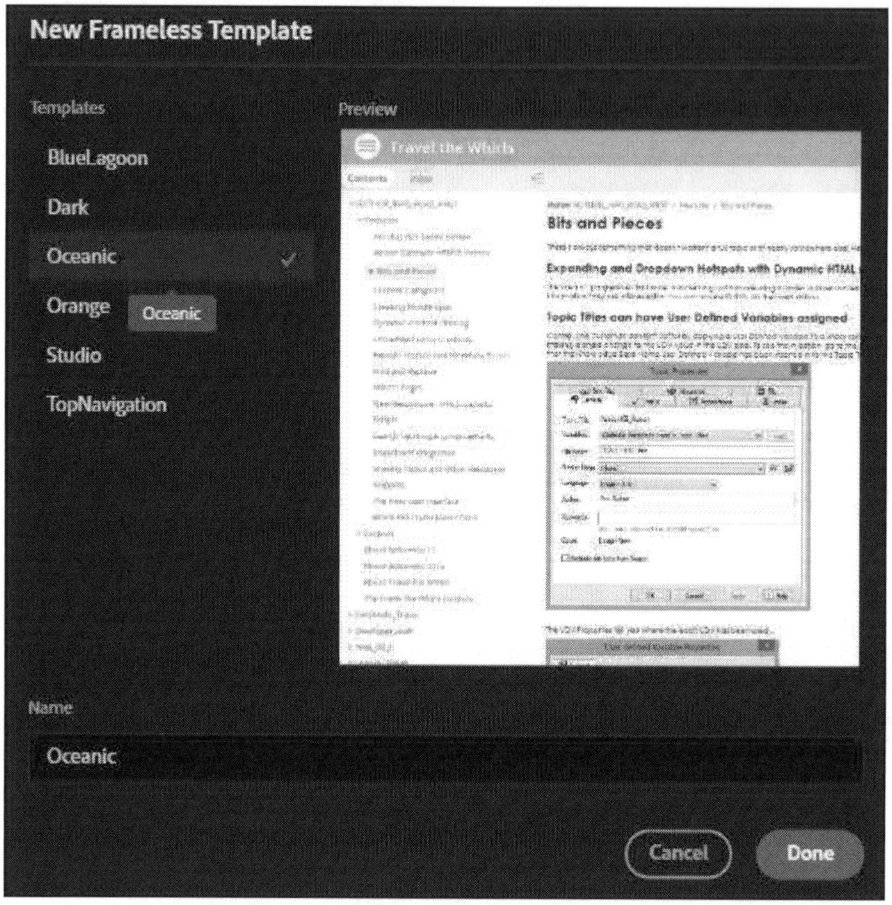

❒ click the **Done** button

The Oceanic Template is added to the output.

8. Save the project.

9. Generate and View the Policies Output.

   The first thing you'll see in the browser is the output's **Home Page**. The images you see in the tiles are controlled by the **Properties** of the items on the Table of Contents. You'll change the tile images in a moment.

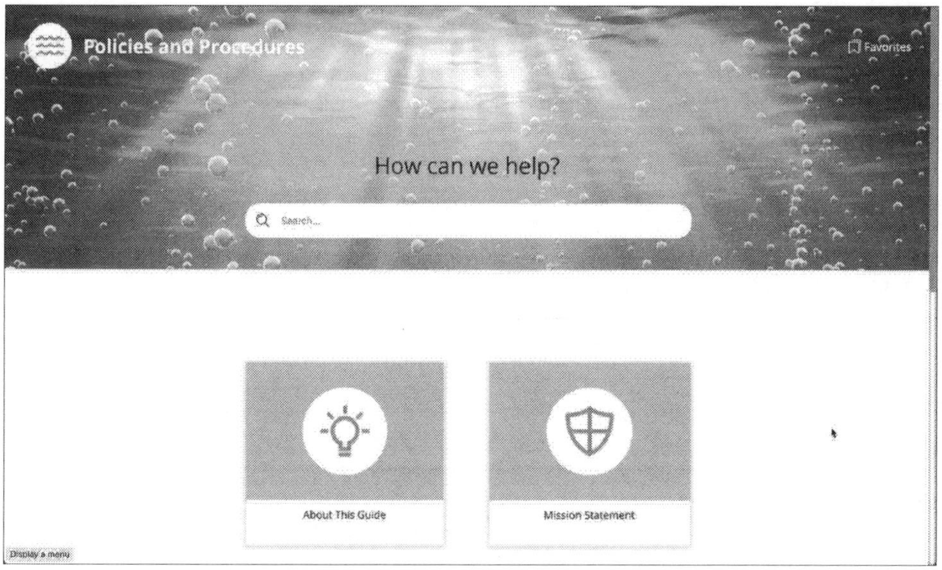

10. Click the **About This Guide** tile.

    The appearance of the interior pages of the output are controlled by the Topic Page area of the template.

11. Notice the Favicon image in the browser's page tab.

12. Close the browser and return to the RoboHelp project.

NOTES

Guided Activity 56: Modify a Home Page Tile Image

1. Ensure that the **Templates and Master Slides** project is still open.

2. Change a tile image used on the Home Page.

   ❑ from the **Author** area, select **Table of Contents**

   ❑ open the **policies** TOC

   ❑ on the **policies** TOC, right-click **About This Guide** and choose **Properties**

   The Properties dialog box opens.

   ❑ expand the **Tile Image** area

   ❑ click the **Update Link URL** icon

   ❑ if necessary, select **Project Files**

   ❑ expand **assets** and then expand **images**

   ❑ select **AboutThisGuide.png**

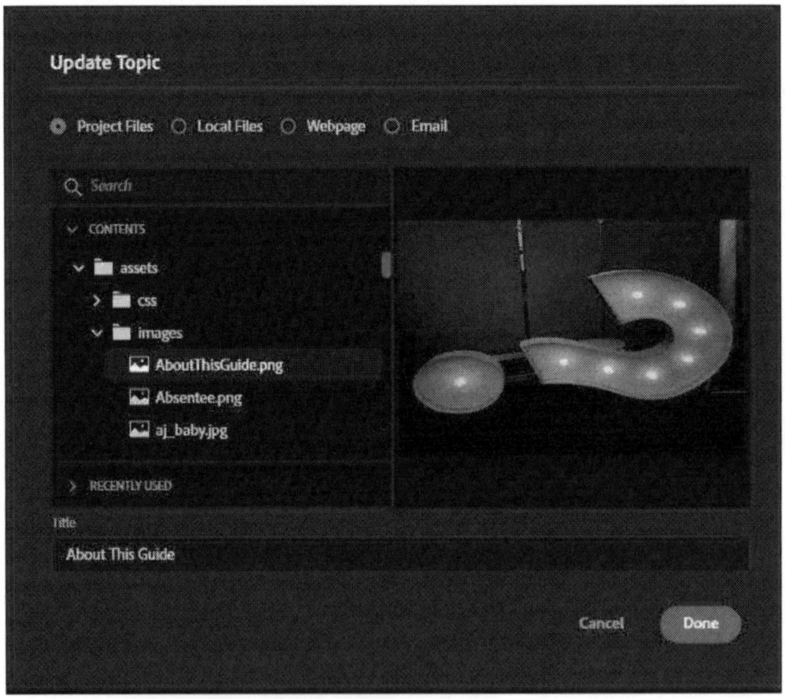

   ❑ click the **Done** button

   ❑ click the **Apply** button

3. Save the project.

4. Generate and View the Policies Output.

   The new image is being used on the **About This Guide** tile.

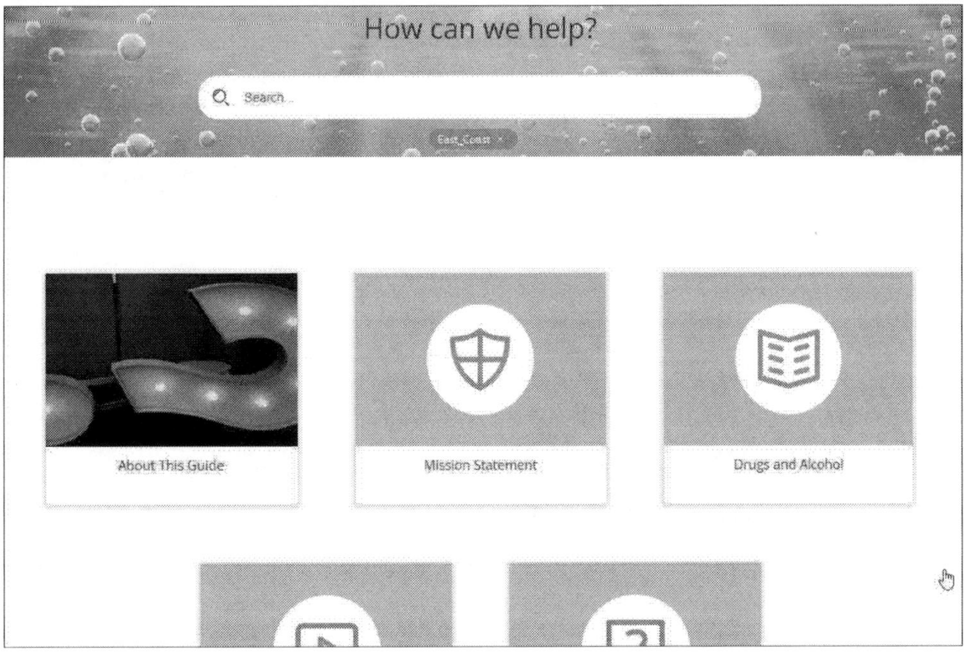

5. Close the browser and return to the RoboHelp project.

NOTES

Guided Activity 57: Change Output Home Page Logo

1. Ensure that the **Templates and Master Slides** project is still open.

2. On the **Output** tab, open the **Policies Output** preset for editing.

3. Edit the Oceanic template.

   ❒ select the **Layout** category

   ❒ from the **Template** area, click the **Edit selected template** icon 

   The template editor opens.

   ❒ select the **Home Page** tab

   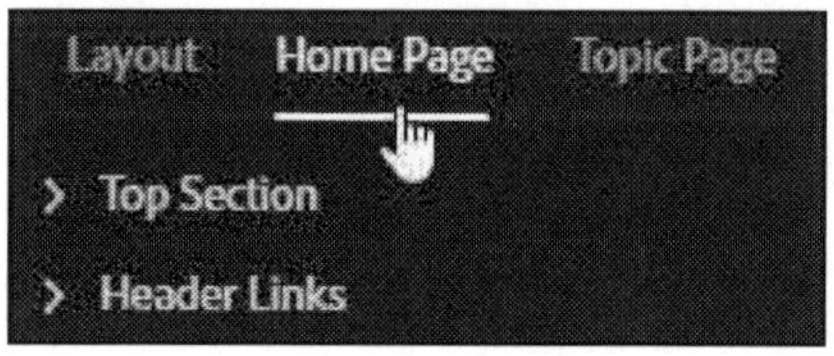

   ❒ expand the **Top Section** options

   ❒ select **logo**

   ❒ scroll down and expand the **Background** category

   ❒ from the **Image Path** area, click the **Browse** icon 

   The **Insert Image** dialog box opens.

   ❒ if necessary, select **Project Files**

   ❒ expand **assets**

   ❒ expand **images**

   ❒ select **Frameless_HTML5_Superlogo**

   ❒ click the **Insert** button

4. Save the project.

5. Generate and View the Policies Output.

   The new image is being used as the logo on the Home Page.

6. Close the browser and return to the RoboHelp project.

Templates Confidence Check

1. Edit the Oceanic template again.
2. Change the logo used on the **Topic Page**, **Header** area, to **Frameless_HTML5_Superlogo**.

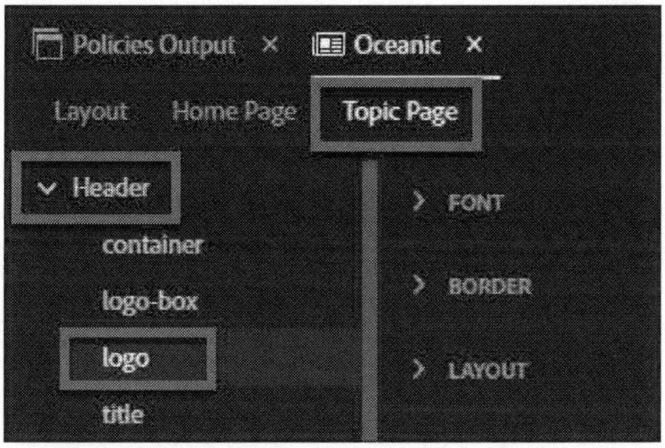

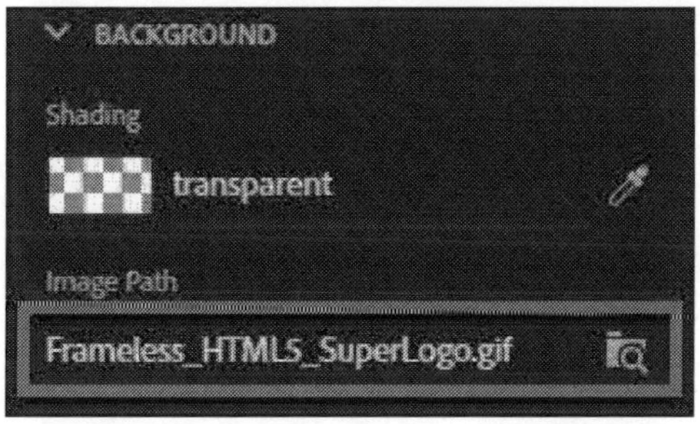

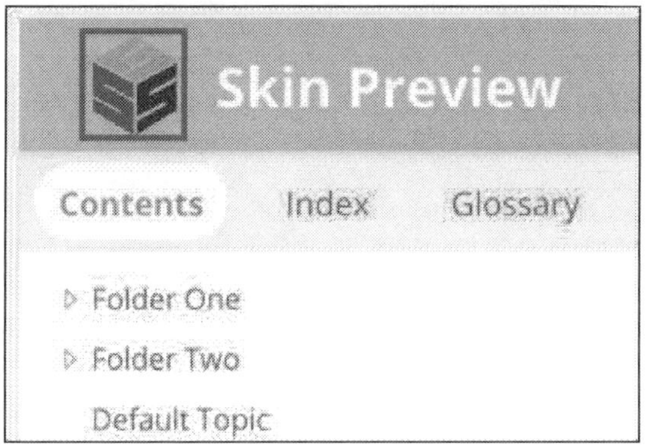

3. Save and close the Template.
4. Save and close the Output Preset.
5. Open the policies TOC.
6. Add **Tile Images** to all of the items on the policies Table of Contents.

   Note: The images are within **assets/images**. You can assign the available images to the TOC items as you see fit. For the Drugs and Alcohol section, I've

NOTES

NOTES

included two drug images: drugs.jpg and drugs2.jpg; one for use on the Drugs and Alcohol item, one for use on the Drug Abuse Policy item.

7. Generate and View the Policies Output to see the changes to the Image Tiles.

8. Close the browser and return to the RoboHelp project.

Topic Layouts

A Topic Layout is a background that can be used on a topic. Layouts can contain style sheets and page elements, such as headers and footers.

Once created, a Layout can quickly be attached to one or more project topics. Should you make changes to the Topic Layout, any topics using the Layout are updated. Using this concept, you can make a change on a Layout and update thousands of topics in seconds.

Guided Activity 58: Create a Topic Layout

1. Ensure that the **templates_layouts** project is still open.

2. Create a new Topic Layout

❒ from the **Author** area, click **Topic Layouts**

❒ from the top of the **Topic Layouts** area, click the **New Topic Layout** icon

The New Topic Layout dialog box opens.

❒ change the **Title** of the new Topic Layout to **Copyright Notice in Footer**

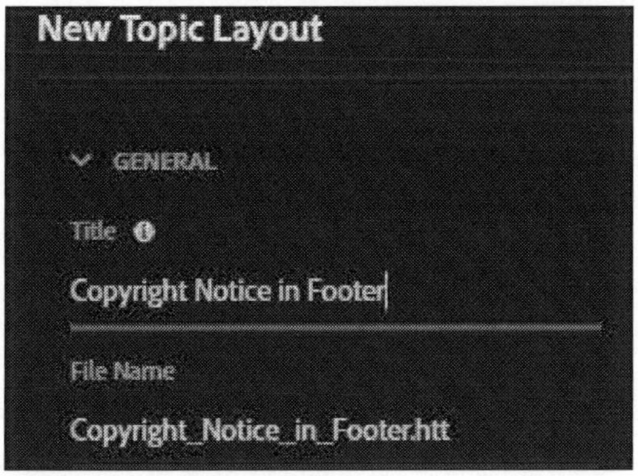

❒ click the **Create** button

NOTES

NOTES

The new Topic Layout appears in the Topic Layouts area and automatically opens for editing. Notice that the Topic Layout contains an empty Header and Footer.

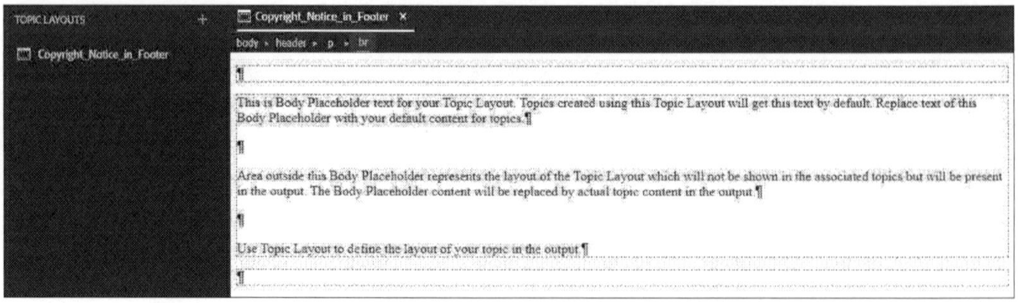

3. Assign a style sheet to a Topic Layout.

   ❑ from the right of the RoboHelp window, click the **Topic Properties** icon

   ❑ expand **Style Sheets**

   ❑ from the **Style Sheets** drop-down menu, choose **policies.css**

4. Insert a copyright symbol and some text into the Footer.

   ❑ at the bottom of the **Topic Layout**, click within the **Footer** area

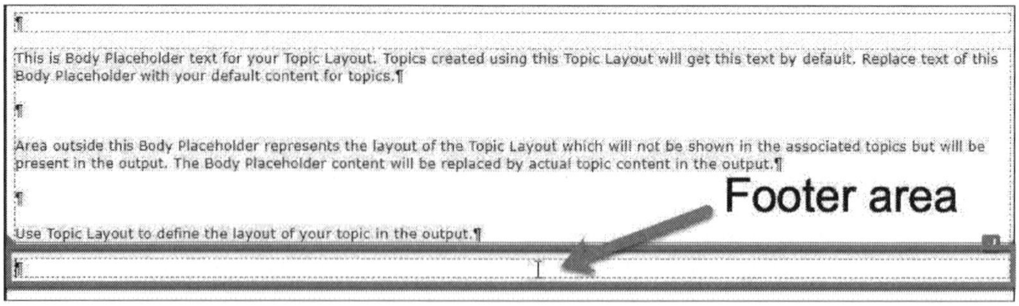

   ❑ from the toolbar above the layout, click the **Insert Special Character** icon

❒ from the **Select Category** drop-down menu, choose **Special Characters**

❒ double-click the **Copyright** symbol

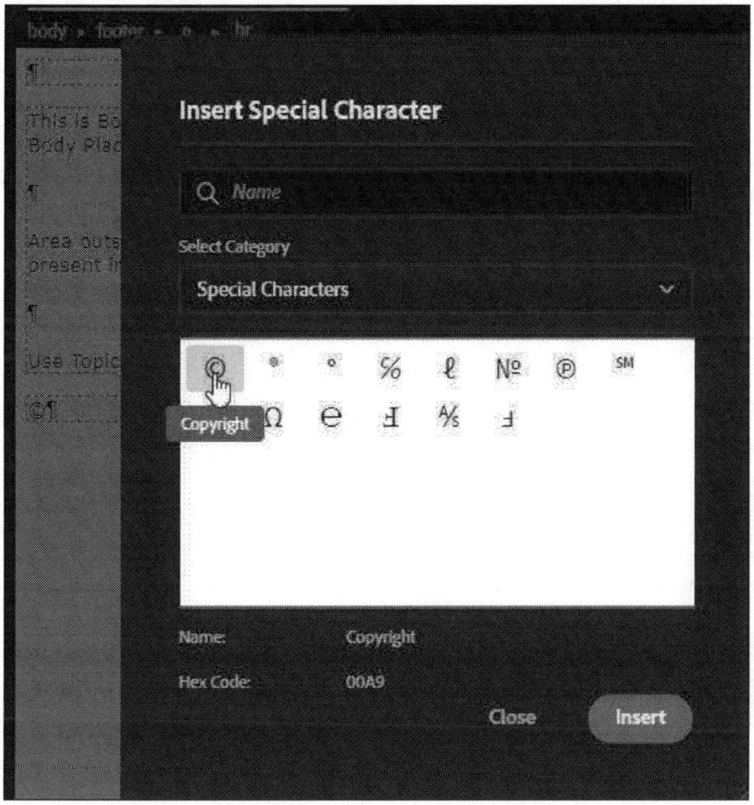

❒ click the **Close** button

A copyright symbol is added to the footer.

❒ press [**spacebar**] after the copyright symbol and then type **Super Simplistic Solutions, All Rights Reserved**

5. Center the Footer text.

❒ from the right of the RoboHelp window, click the **Content Properties** icon

❒ expand the **Font** area

❒ from the **Text Alignment** area, click the **Align Center** icon

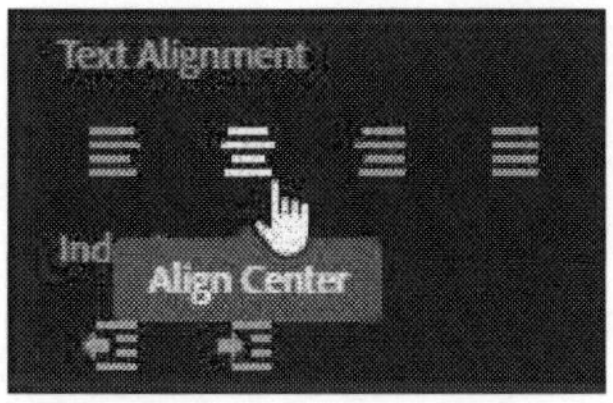

NOTES

The Topic Layout Footer should look like this:

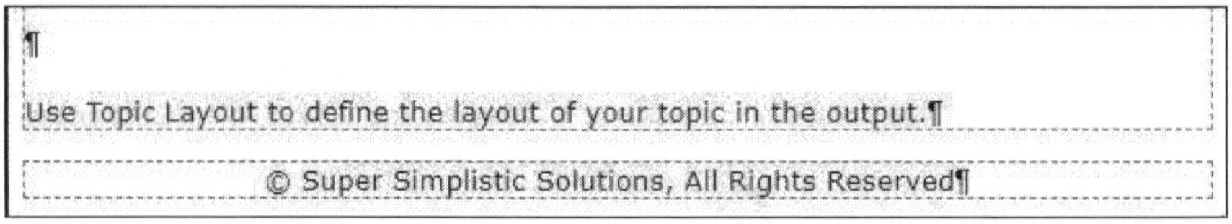
¶

Use Topic Layout to define the layout of your topic in the output.¶

© Super Simplistic Solutions, All Rights Reserved¶

6. Save the project.

7. Close the Topic Layout.

8. Apply a Topic Layout to a topic.

   ❒ from the **General Office Information** folder, open the **Special Benefits** topic

   ❒ from the right of the RoboHelp window, click the **Topic Properties** icon

   ❒ expand the **General** area

   ❒ from the **Topic Layout** drop-down menu, choose **Copyright Notice in Footer**

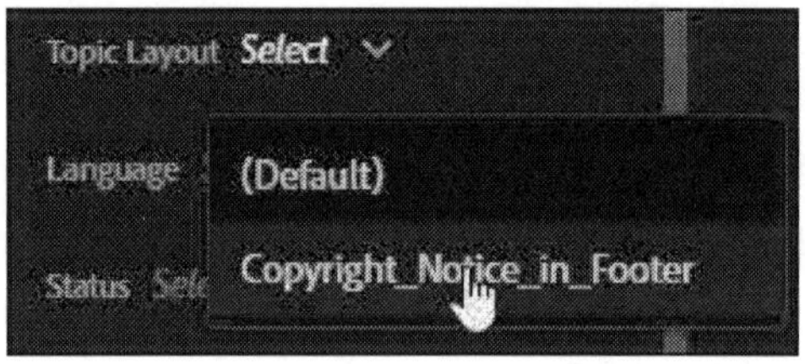

9. **Preview** the topic.

   Notice that the footer you set up in the Topic Layout appears at the bottom of the topic.

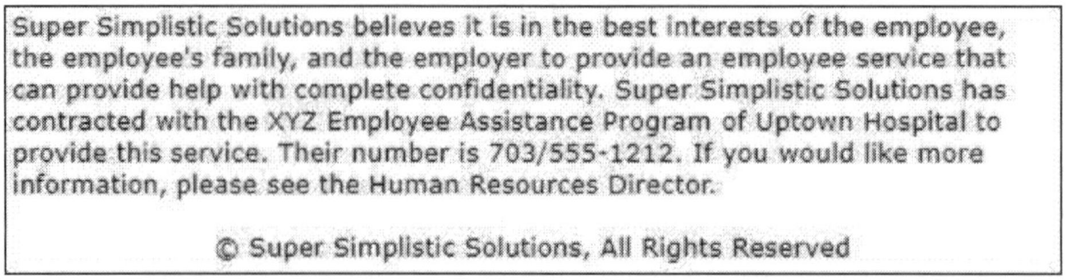
Super Simplistic Solutions believes it is in the best interests of the employee, the employee's family, and the employer to provide an employee service that can provide help with complete confidentiality. Super Simplistic Solutions has contracted with the XYZ Employee Assistance Program of Uptown Hospital to provide this service. Their number is 703/555-1212. If you would like more information, please see the Human Resources Director.

© Super Simplistic Solutions, All Rights Reserved

10. Return to **Author** mode.

11. Save and close all topics.

12. Filter the Topic List.

    - ❒ choose **View > Topic List**
    - ❒ from the right of the Topic List, **Folder** drop-down menu, choose **Drugs and Alcohol**

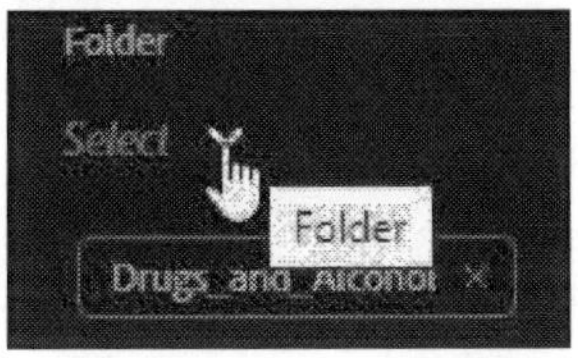

Only the two topics in the Drugs and Alcohol folder are shown in the Topic List.

13. Apply the Topic Layout to more topics.

    - ❒ in the **Topic List** window, select both the **Alcohol** and **Drug** Policy topics
    - ❒ right-click the selected topics and choose **Properties**

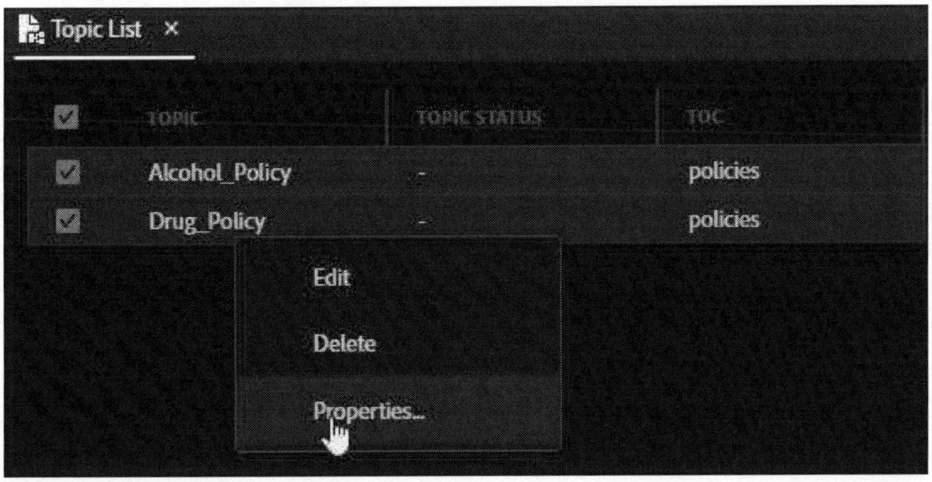

The **Multiple Topics Properties** dialog box opens.

- ❒ from the **Topic Layout** drop-down menu, choose **Copyright Notice in Footer**

NOTES

❒ click the **Apply** button

Both topics are now using the Copyright Notice in Footer Topic Layout.

14. Open the **Alcohol Policy** topic.

15. Preview the topic to see the copyright notice.

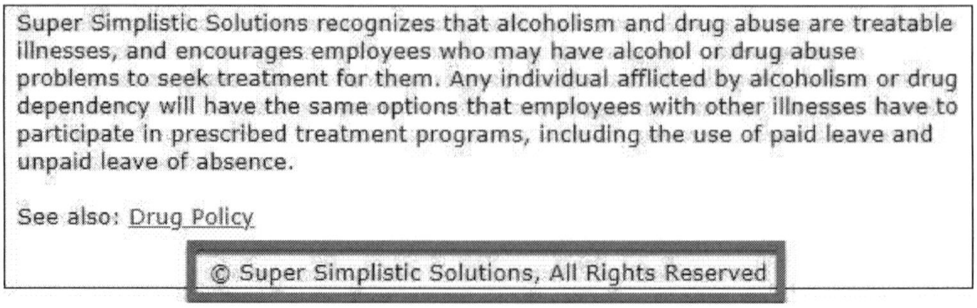

16. Return to **Author** mode.

17. Save the project.

Guided Activity 59: Edit a Topic Layout

1. Ensure that the **templates_layouts** project is still open.

2. Edit the footer on the Topic Layout.

   - ❒ from the **Author** area, click **Topic Layouts**
   - ❒ double-click the **Copyright Notice in Footer** Topic Layout (to open the Topic Layout for editing)
   - ❒ click in the Footer
   - ❒ click after the word **Solutions,** press [**spacebar**] and type **Inc.**
   - ❒ add a period after the phrase **All Rights Reserved**

   © Super Simplistic Solutions, Inc. All Rights Reserved.¶

3. Save and close the Topic Layout.

4. If necessary, open the **Alcohol Policy** topic.

5. Preview the topic.

   The topic displays the updated footer. In fact, any topics in your project using the Copyright Notice in Footer Topic Layout now have the updated footer.

6. Return to **Author** mode.

7. Save the project.

NOTES

Topic Layout Confidence Check

1. Apply the **Copyright Notice in Footer** Topic Layout to the topics in the following two folders: **General Office Information** and **Leave and Vacation**.
2. Remove the Copyright Notice in Footer Topic Layout from the **Mission Statement** topic. (Show the topic's Properties and set the Topic Layout to **Default**.)
3. Save the project.
4. Generate the Policies Output and then View the Output.

   All of the Help System topics, except Mission Statement, should now contain footers, and those footers should contain the copyright notice.
5. Close the browser and return to the RoboHelp project.
6. Open the **Copyright Notice in Footer** Topic Layout for editing.
7. Click in the **Header**.
8. From the toolbar above the page, click **Insert Variables/Snippet/Fields** icon and choose **Fields**.

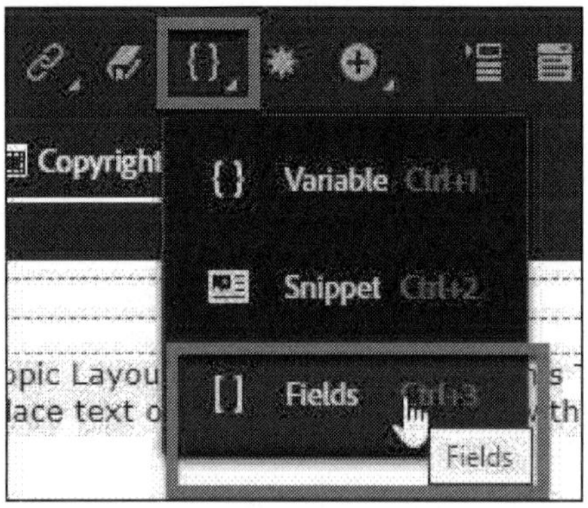

9. From the **Fields** list at the left, choose **Project Title**.

10. From the **Format** area, choose the first format (**Templates and Layouts**) and then click the **Insert** button.

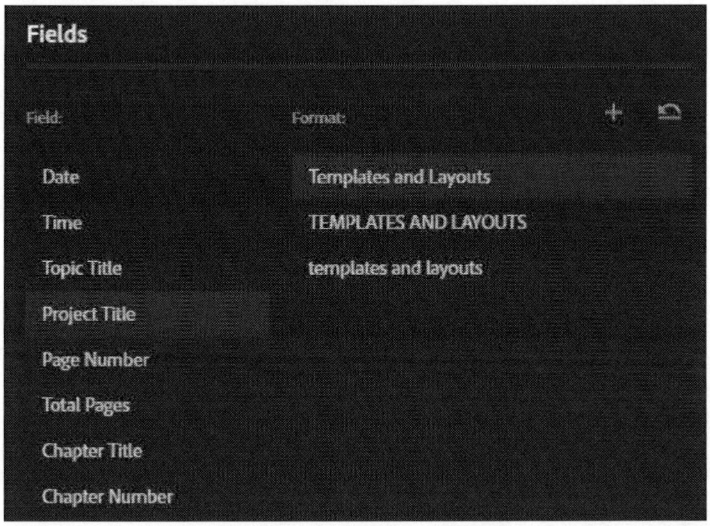

11. The project's title is inserted into the Header.
12. Change the **Text Alignment** for the Header text to **Right**.
13. Save and close the Topic Layout.
14. Open the **Alcohol Policy** topic.
15. Preview the topic to see the Project Title in the Header.
16. Return to Author mode.
17. Choose **File > Project Settings**.
18. Change the project's Title to **Policies and Procedures**

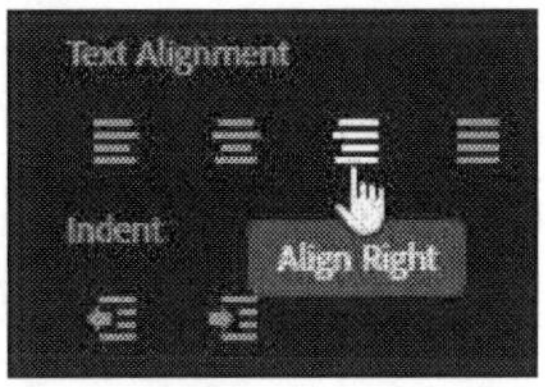

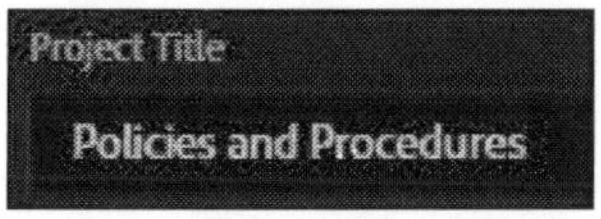

19. Click the **Done** button.

    The updated Project Title field is updated on the **Copyright Notice in Footer** Topic Layout. All of the topics that are using the **Copyright Notice in Footer** Topic Layout instantly get the updated title.

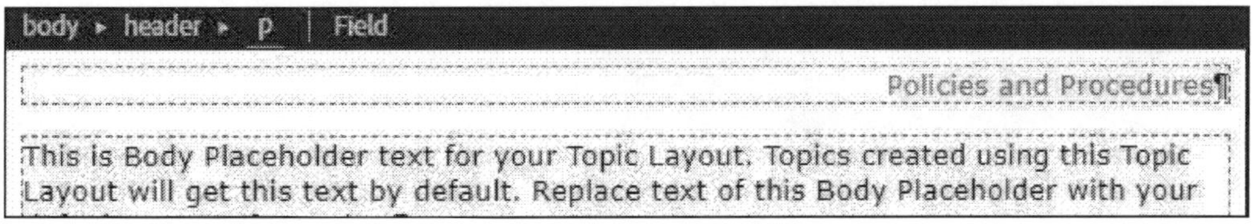

20. Save the project.

NOTES

Word/PDF Output

You may need to output your help system as a Word or PDF so it can be printed or emailed. In the following activities, you will create a TOC specifically for the print and PDF outputs, and you'll learn how to assign and edit templates. Then you'll output the project as both Word and PDF.

Guided Activity 60: Create a Book TOC

1. Ensure that the **templates_layouts** project is still open.

2. Create a Book TOC.

   ❒ on the **Author** tab, click **Table of Contents**

   ❒ click **New Table of Contents**

The New Table of Contents dialog box opens. There are two types of TOCs: **Online** and **Book**. You learned how to edit an Online TOC back on page 39. Online TOCs are perfect if you generate Responsive HTML or Frameless output. However, a Book TOC includes specific options, such as Front Matter and Back Matter, that are not used by an Online TOC. Print TOCs are appropriate if you are creating a Word document, PDF, or an eBook.

   ❒ **name** the TOC **Print and PDF TOC**

   ❒ from the **Type** area, select **Print TOC**

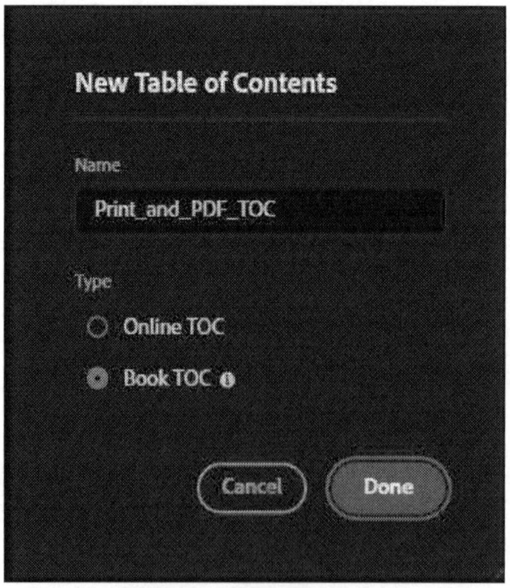

   ❒ click the **Done** button

3. Auto-create a TOC.

   ❒ with the **Print_and_PDF_TO**C open, click the **Auto-create TOC** icon

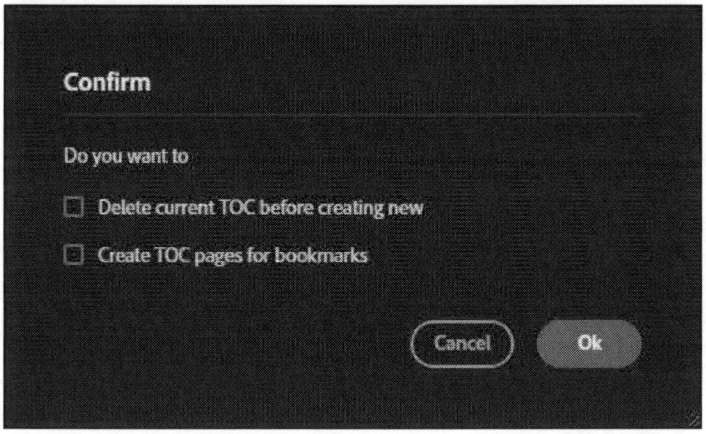

   ❒ click the **OK** button

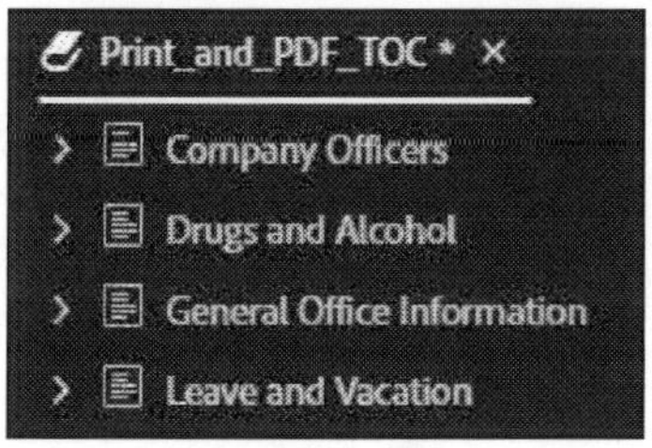

4. Save the project.

NOTES

NOTES

Print TOC Confidence Check

1. Edit the Print TOC as necessary so that the TOC matches the TOC shown in the image below.

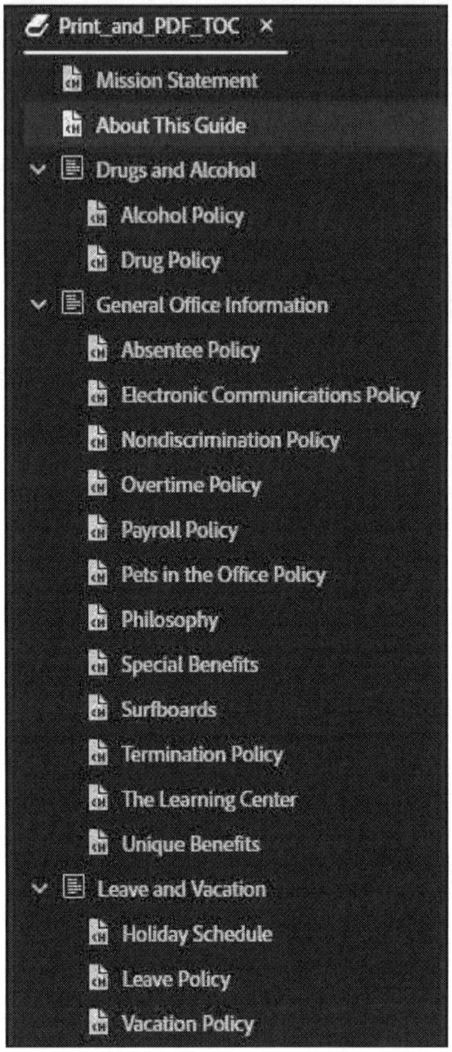

2. Save the project.

Guided Activity 61: Add TOC Front and Back Matter

1. Ensure that the **templates_layouts** project is still open.

2. Add a TOC Page as Front Matter.

   ❒ with the **Print_and_PDF_TO**C open, click the **Front Matter** icon

   ❒ click **TOC Page**

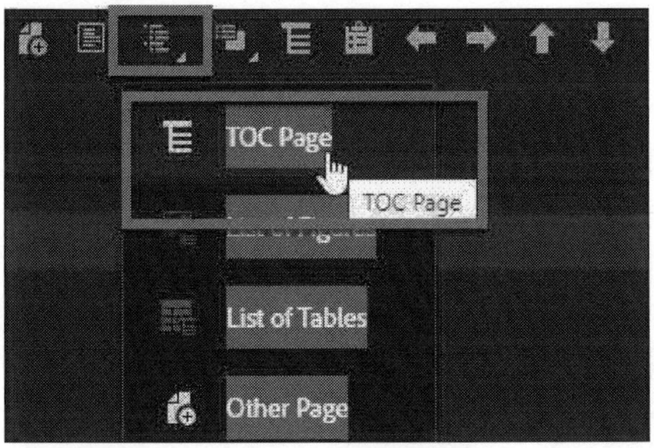

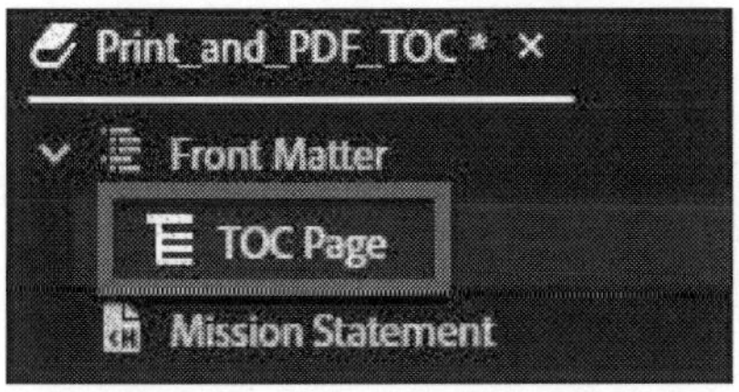

3. Add an Index as Back Matter.

   ❒ with the **Print_and_PDF_TO**C open, click the **Back Matter** icon

   ❒ click **Index Page**

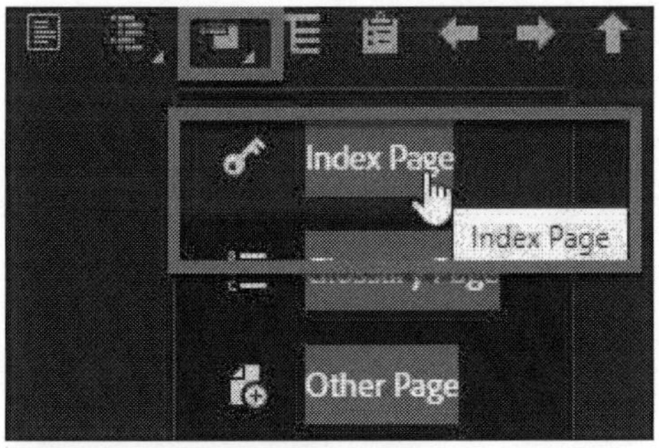

4. Save the project.

NOTES

NOTES

Guided Activity 62: Create a Word Template

1. Ensure that the **templates_layouts** project is still open.

2. Create a Word Template.

❒ click the **Output** tab

❒ from the list at the left, click **Templates**

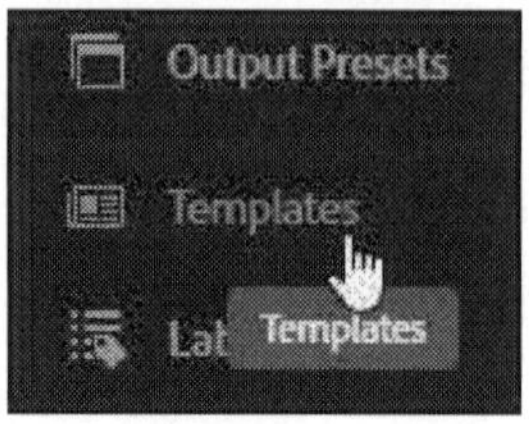

❒ from the **Templates** area, click **New Template**

❒ select **Word Template**

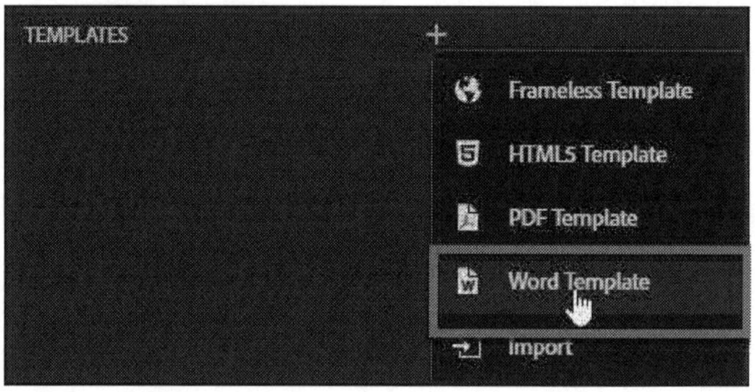

❒ from the list of **Templates**, select **Simple**

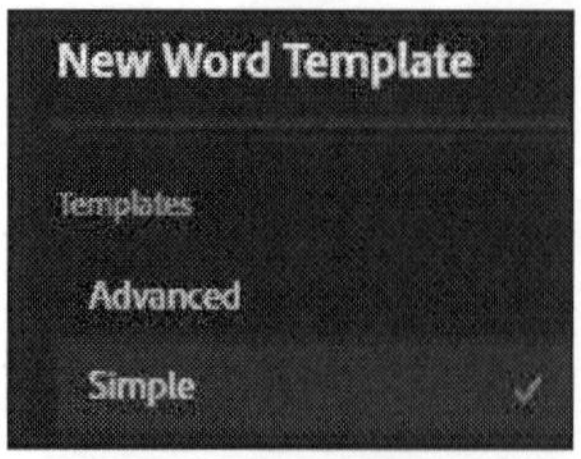

❒ click the **Done** button

Word/PDF Confidence Check

1. Using the Output tab, create a new **Word** Output Preset (title the preset **Word**).

2. On the **General** tab, change the **Output path** to **RoboHelp2022Data > Output > Word**.

3. On the **Content** tab, select **Print_and_PDF_TOC** as the Table of Contents.

4. On the **Content** tab, select **East Coast** as the Conditional Expression.

5. On the **Layout** tab, select the **Simple Template** you created a moment ago.

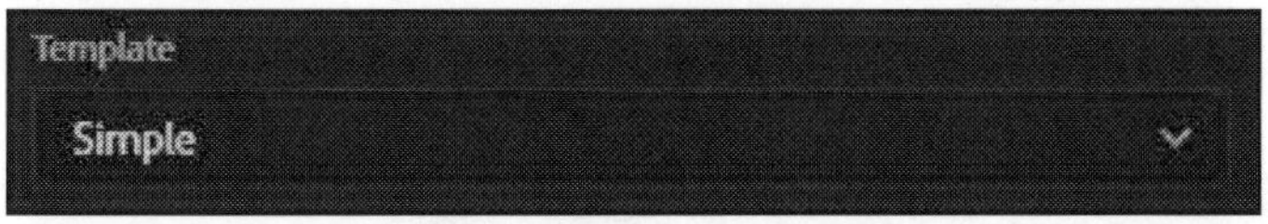

6. Save the project.

NOTES

7. **Generate** and **View** the **Word** output (click **Yes** when you are alerted about fields needing to be updated).

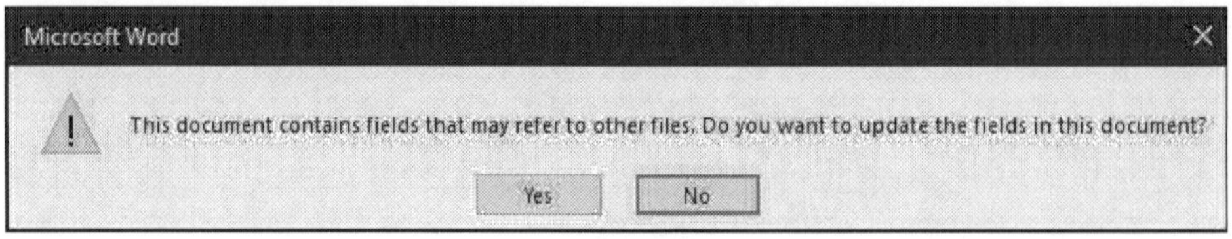

Your project opens in Microsoft Word and is complete with a Table of Contents and Index.

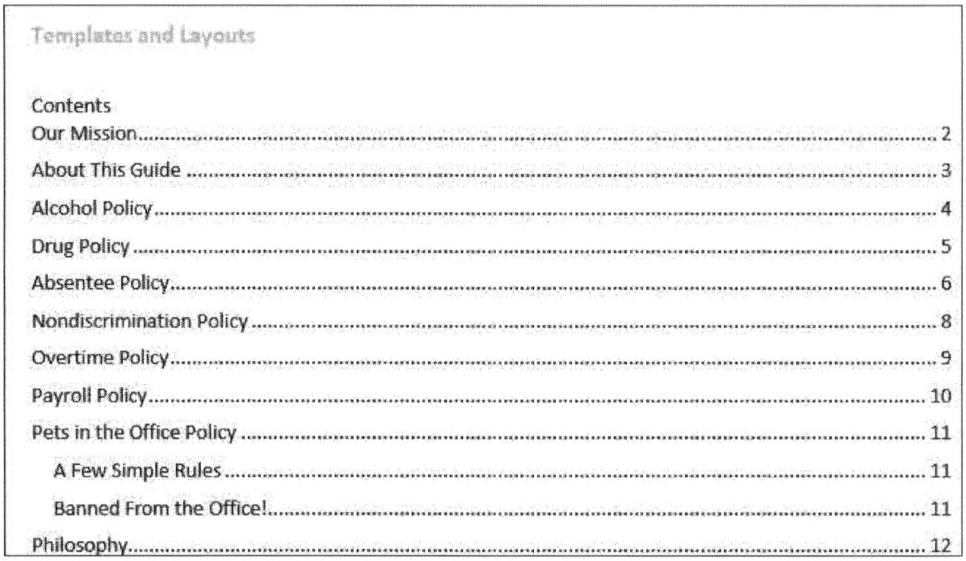
Templates and Layouts

Contents

8. Exit Word and return to RoboHelp.
9. Create a **new PDF** Template that uses the **Basic** layout.

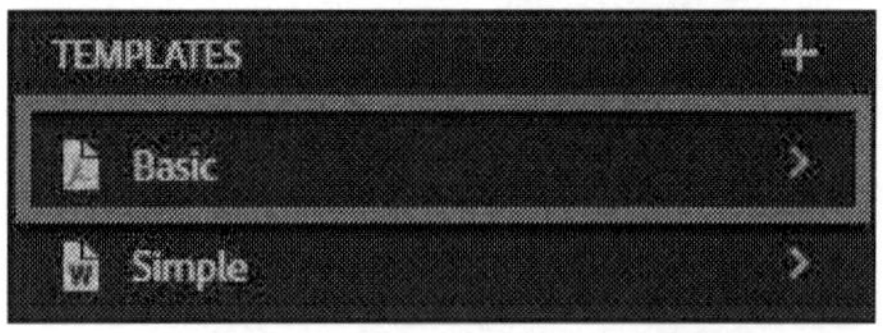

10. Create a new **PDF** Output Preset (name it PDF).

11. On the **General** tab, change the **Output path** to **RoboHelp2022Data > Output > PDF**.

12. On the **Content** tab, select **Print_and_PDF_TOC** as the Table of Contents.

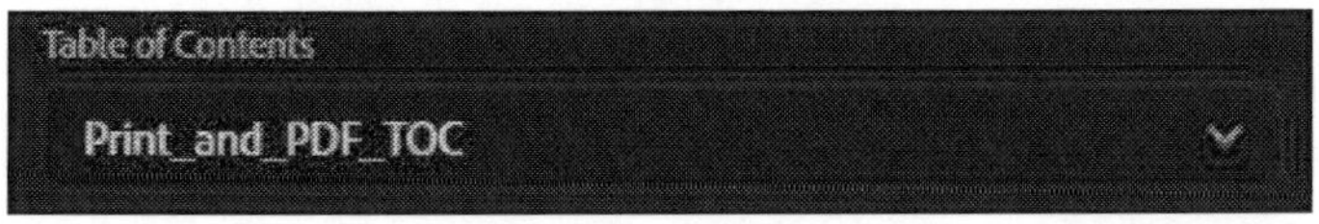

13. On the **Content** tab, select **East Coast** as the Conditional Expression.

14. On the **Layout** tab, select the **Basic Template** you created a moment ago.

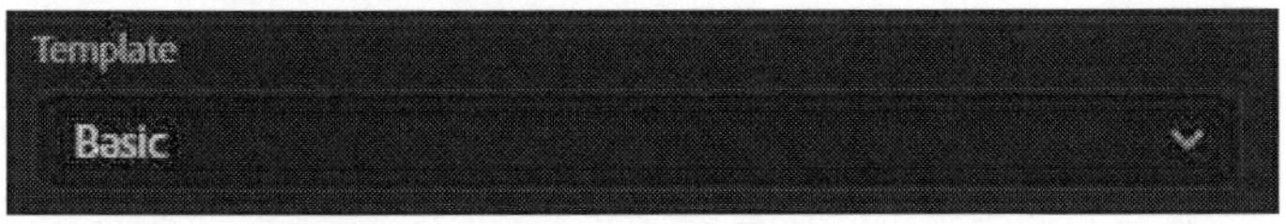

15. Save the project.
16. **Generate** and **View** the **PDF** output. As with the Word output, the PDF is complete with a Table of Contents and Index.

    Note: The Word and PDF outputs are customizable. You can edit either of the Template's Page Layouts and CSS files... skills you have learned during previous activities.

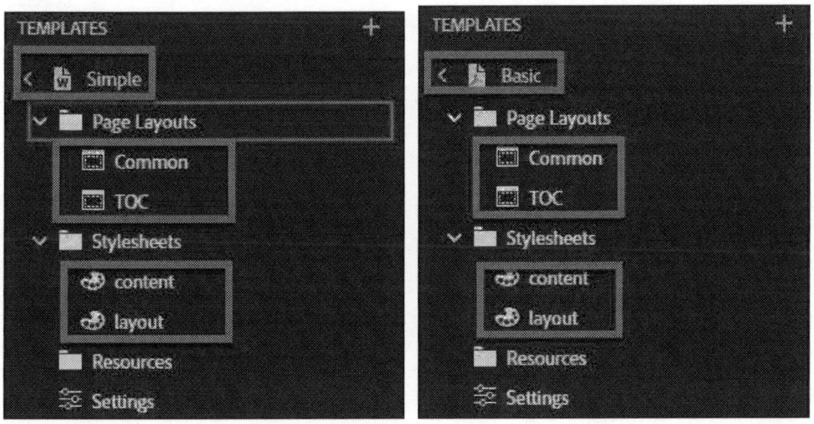

17. Exit the PDF and return to RoboHelp.
18. Close the project.

NOTES

Notes

iCONLOGiC

"Skills and Drills" Learning

Module 9: HTML Help, Application Help, and CSH

In This Module You Will Learn About:

And You Will Learn To:

NOTES

HTML Help Windows

Microsoft HTML Help isn't dependent upon a web browser to be opened by users like Frameless or Responsive HTML5 outputs. HTML Help, using a program called the Microsoft Help Viewer, opens your RoboHelp output on the user's display that is set to a specific size and width. You can control several HTML Help window features by creating a custom window and then attaching the window to the output prior to generating the output.For instance, in addition to controlling the placement and size of the window, you can add a search tab, browse sequence, and custom buttons to the Help window.

Note: HTML Help only works on Windows and cannot be output by RoboHelp for the Mac. Mac users, open the **Application_Help** RoboHelp project and skip to the "Browse Sequences" activity on page 183.

Guided Activity 63: Create an HTML Help Custom Window

1. From the **apphelp_csh** folder, open the **Application_Help** RoboHelp project file.

   Note: Click the **Upgrade** button if prompted.

2. Create a new window.

   ❐ from the **Output** area, click **Window Settings**

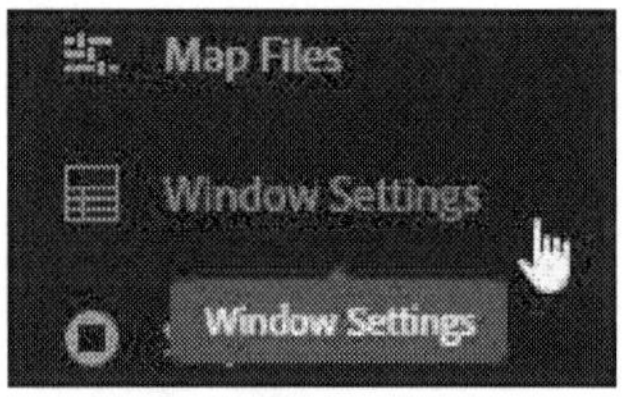

   ❐ from the top of the **Window Settings** area, click **New Window Setting**

   The Microsoft HTML Help dialog box opens.

   ❐ in the **Window Name** field, type **Super Simplistic Solutions Window**

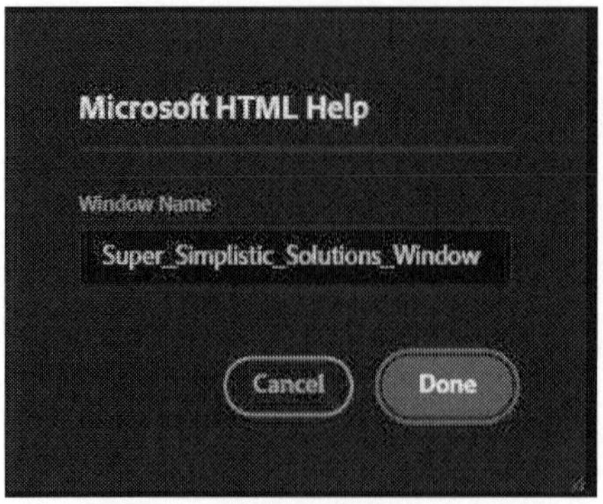

   ❐ click the **Done** button

The new window's settings open at the right of the RoboHelp window.

3. Set the Tri-pane Tabs and Windows options.

   ❐ if necessary, expand the **Window Properties**

   ❐ from the **Tri-pane Tabs and Windows** area, ensure that **TOC & Index** is selected

   ❐ ensure that **Glossary** is selected

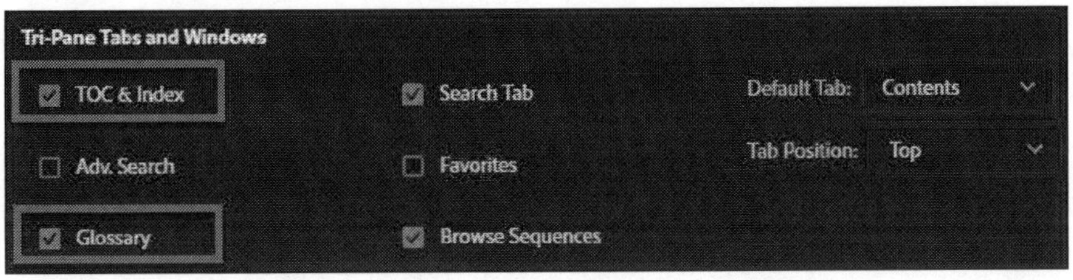

You learned how to create a TOC on page 39, an Index on page 127, and a Glossary on page 143. All of the options automatically appear in Responsive HTML5 and Frameless outputs. By ensuring that each of the options is selected here, they'll appear when you output HTML Help.

   ❐ ensure that **Search Tab** is selected

   ❐ ensure that **Browse Sequences** is selected

You will learn how to create a Browse Sequence on page 178. By selecting Browse Sequences now, the Browse Sequence you will create will appear in the Help window.

   ❐ ensure that the **Default Tab** is **Contents**

   ❐ ensure that the **Tab Position** is **Top**

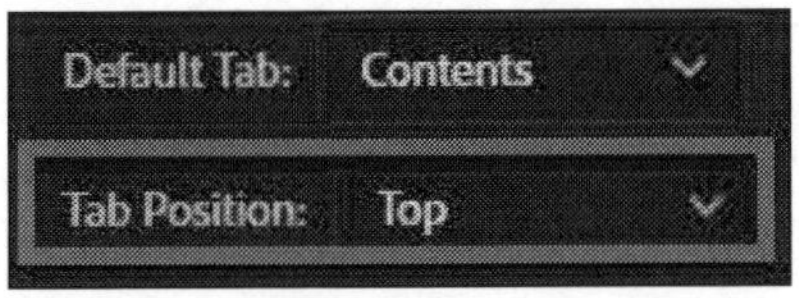

4. Change the screen location and size of the new window.

   ❐ from the **Window Placement** area, change the **Top** to **25 px**

   ❐ change the **Left** to **25 px**

When you generate the Microsoft HTML Help output, the Help window appears 25 pixels from the top and left of the users' display.

   ❐ change the **Height** to **720 px**

   ❐ change the **Width** to **1280 px**

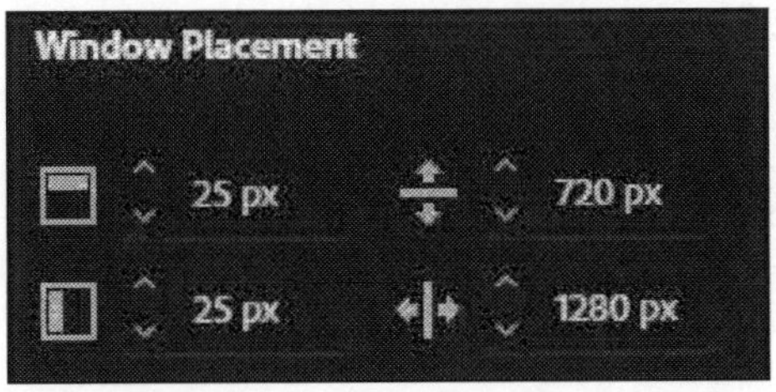

NOTES

5. Set the Tri-pane options.

   ❒ from the **Tri-pane Options** area at the bottom left of the window, ensure **Auto-synchronize TOC** is selected

   The Auto-synchronize TOC option synchronizes the left and right panes of your generated Help System so that selected books or pages on the TOC and topics match as the Help System is used.

   ❒ select **Remember Window Size and Position**

   You are controlling the exact size and display position of the Help window. If users move or resize the window after it opens on their display, **Remember Window Size and Position** ensures that the Help window remembers the users' settings and puts the Help window in the same place the next time they open the Help System.

6. Save and close the Super Simplistic Solutions Window settings.

   Next, you will instruct RoboHelp to use the **Super Simplistic Solutions** window when you output Microsoft HTML Help.

7. Set the Title, Output Path, and CHM name for the Microsoft HTML Help output.

   ❒ from the **Output** area, click **Output Presets**

   ❒ double-click **Microsoft HTML Help** to open the output for editing

   ❒ click the **General** category

   ❒ in the **Title** area, change the Title to **Policies and Procedures**

   ❒ in the **Output Path** area, browse to and select **RoboHelp2022Data > output > HTML_Help**

   ❒ change the name of the CHM File to **policies.chm**

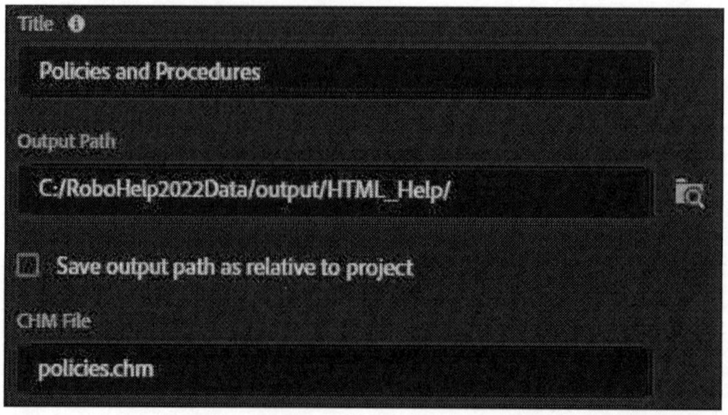

8. Ensure that the **Output** uses the Super Simplistic Solutions Window.

   ❒ select the **Layout** category

   ❒ from the **Default Window** drop-down menu, choose **Super Simplistic Solutions Window**

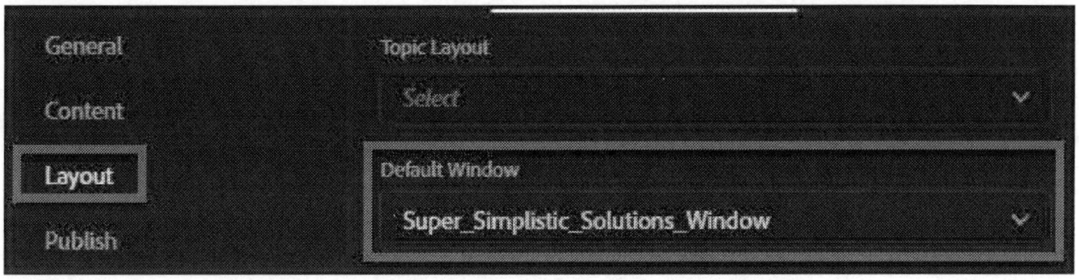

9. Save the project.

NOTES

NOTES

Help Window Confidence Check

1. Generate Microsoft HTML Help and View the Output.

   Notice the position and size of the Help window.

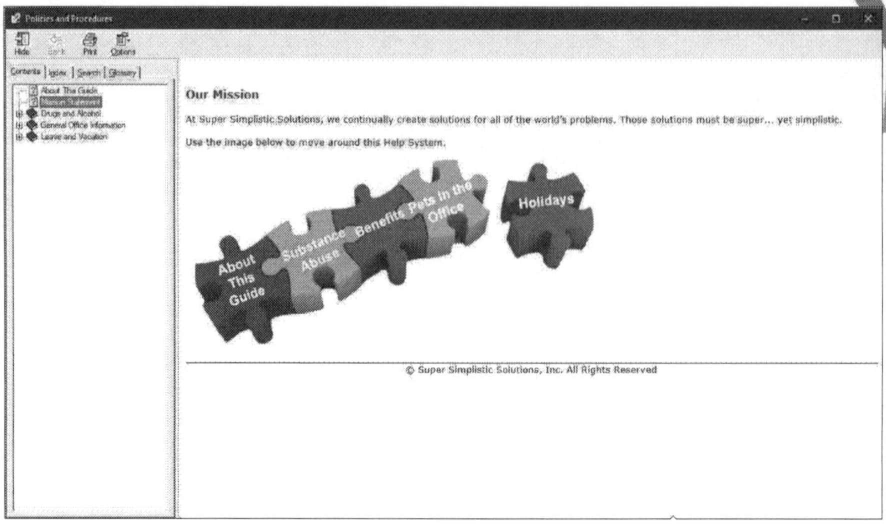

2. Close the Help window and return to RoboHelp.
3. From the Window Settings area, edit the **Super Simplistic Solutions** Window Placement Properties.
   - ❐ change the **Top** and **Left** Placement to **36 px**.
   - ❐ change the Window **Height** to **600 px**.
   - ❐ change the Window **Width** to **900 px**.

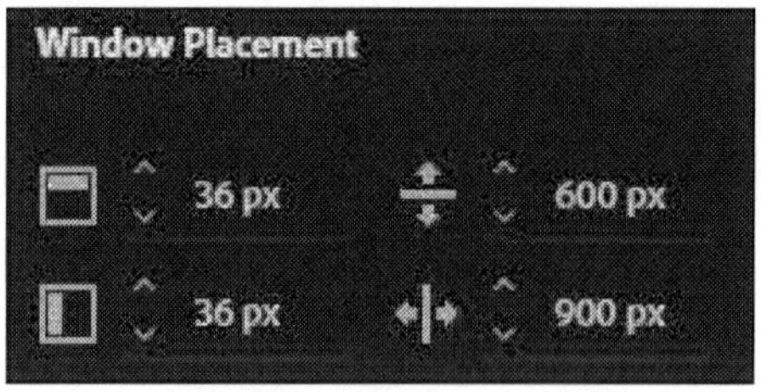

4. Deselect **Remember Window Size and Position**.
5. Save and close the Window Properties dialog box.
6. **Generate** Microsoft HTML Help again and **View** the Output.

   The resulting Help window should be resized smaller.

   Note: If you hadn't deselected **Remember Window Size and Position**, the size of your Help window would not have changed because you already viewed the window at the larger size.

7. Close the Help window and return to the RoboHelp project.

Browse Sequences

A browse sequence allows users to move forward and backward through your topics in a specific order. The grouping of topics added to a browse sequence can be based on anything you think might improve the usability of your output. Once created, a browse sequence can be added to Responsive HTML5, HTML Help, and Frameless outputs.

Guided Activity 64: Create a Browse Sequence

1. Ensure that the **Application_Help** project is still open.

2. Create a Browse Sequence.

❒ from the **Author** area, click **Browse Sequences**

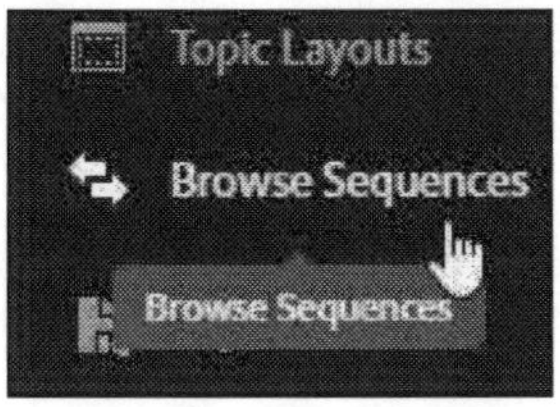

❒ from the top of the **Browse Sequence** area, click the **New Browse Sequence** icon

The New Browse Sequence dialog box opens.

❒ name the New Browse Sequence **Managers**

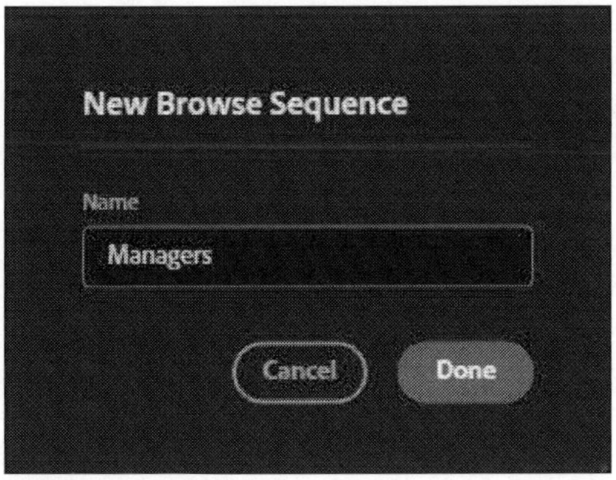

❒ click the **Done** button

The Browse Sequence appears in the Browse Sequence area and opens at the right of the RoboHelp window.

NOTES

NOTES

3. Add a topic to the browse sequence.

   ❒ from the **Contents** area, expand the **Company Officers** folder

   ❒ drag the **Our President** into the Managers **Browse Sequence** area

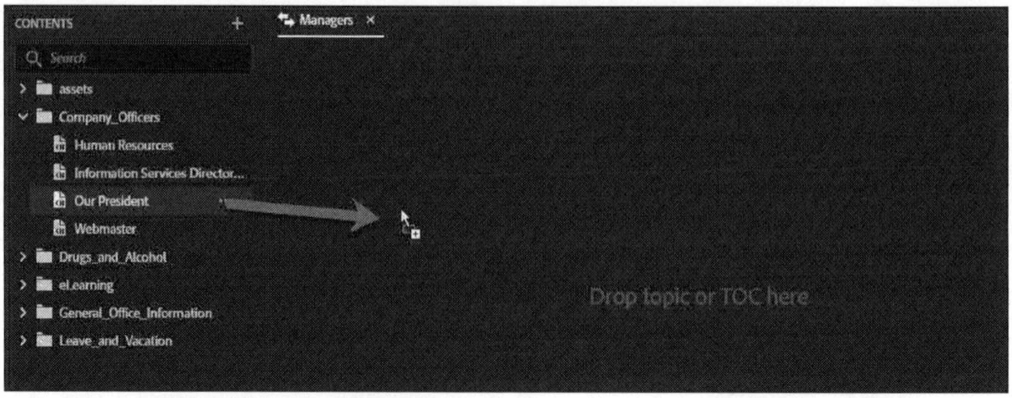

Browse Sequences Confidence Check

1. Add the remaining officers to the **Managers** browse sequence. (As you add topics, keep the following in mind: (1) If you want to change the order of the browse sequence, use the **Move** icons to move the topics up or down; (2) if you want to remove a topic from the sequence, right-click within the browse sequence and choose **Delete**.)

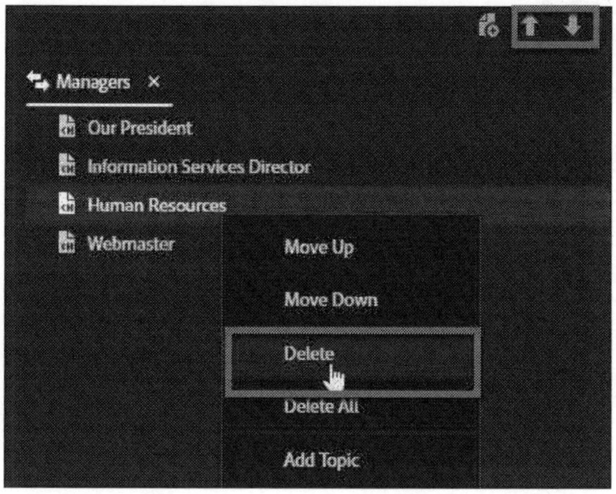

2. Save the project.
3. From the **Output** area, edit the **Policies Output**.
4. On the **General** tab, edit the **Output Path** so the output goes to **RoboHelp2022Data > output > Frameless**.
5. On the **Content** tab, **Browse Sequence** drop-down menu, choose **Managers**.

6. On the **Layout** tab, edit the **Oceanic** Template: on the template's **Layout** tab, select **Topic Page** and enable **Browse Sequence in Right Panel.**

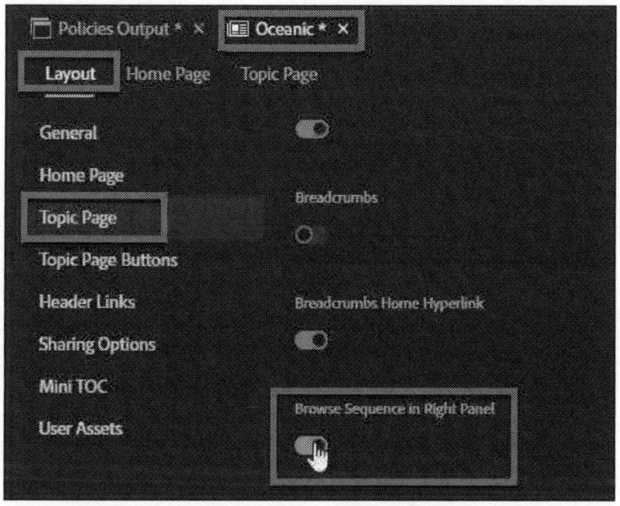

7. Save the project.
8. Close the template and the output.
9. Generate and View the Policies Output.
10. Use the **Search** feature to find and open the **Our President** topic.
11. Use the **Next** button in the lower right of the page to move through the Browse Sequence.

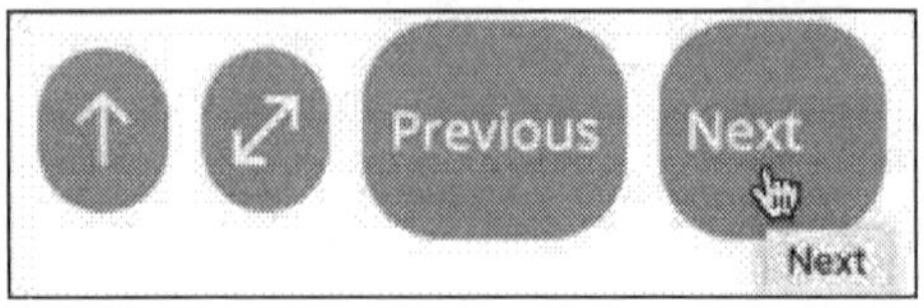

12. Close the web browser and return to the RoboHelp project.

Application Help

Up until now, your generated outputs have been Standalone Help Systems, meaning that anyone can double-click the generated CHM file (if you generated HTML Help) or the Start Page (if you generated Frameless or Responsive HTML5), and the Help System opens.

Application Help means that your generated output is intended to work from within a program. There isn't much you have to do to go from Standalone Help to Application Help, except hand the generated output to your application developer. From there, the application developer programs the application to open your generated and published Help System when the user clicks a Help link or icon.

To demonstrate Application Help, a web application is included within the **webapp** folder called **SimpleWebApplication**.

The **SimpleWebApplication** is looking for the Policies and Procedures Help System that you created during the previous modules in this book.

When one application attempts to communicate with another, the interaction is called an Application Programming Interface—API.

Guided Activity 65: Test an API Call for Help

1. Minimize/Hide RoboHelp.

2. Review the folder containing the published Help System files.

   ❐ using Windows Explorer or the Mac's Finder, open the **RoboHelp2022Data** folder

   ❐ open the **webapp** folder

   There are just a few things in the folder. There's an HTML file named SimpleWebApplication.htm that was created using basic HTML. The web page is communicating with the other assets within the webapp folder. The most important thing from your perspective as the Help author is the **helpsystem** folder.

3. Open a web application and test the link to the Help System.

   ❒ double-click **SimpleWebApplication.htm** to open the application in your default web browser

   There is a link on the web page that is looking for the Help System you've been building as you've moved through the lessons in this book. Because the output files have not yet been added to the **helpsystem** folder, the link to the Help System will fail if the link is clicked.

4. Attempt to get help from within the web application.

   ❒ in the **second paragraph**, click the link (the word **here**)

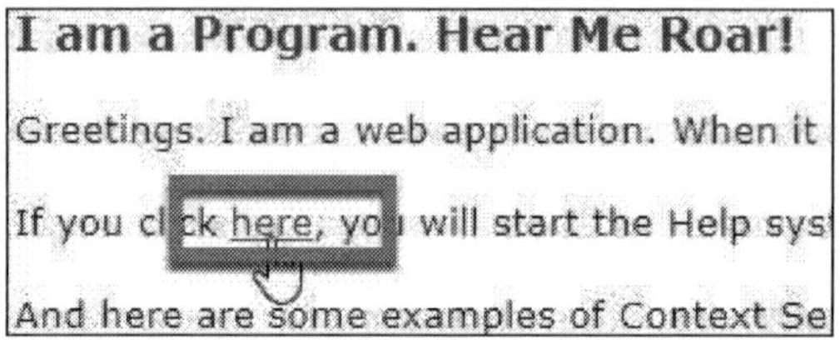

   The Help System does not open because you haven't yet published the RoboHelp output into the **helpsystem** folder. Depending upon your operating system and browser, you might see the **File not found** message, an alert similar to what is shown above might appear, or you might not see anything at all.

5. View an application's source code.

   ❒ close the tab containing the error message

   ❒ still working on the **SimpleWebApplication** file, use your mouse pointer to point to, but not click, the **link** in the **second paragraph** (the word **here**)

   In the status bar at the bottom of the browser window, the HTML tag that links the web application to the Help System appears.

   You do not have to be an HTML developer to get a feel for what the HTML tag is trying to do. The link is looking within the web application's **helpsystem** folder for a specific file named **index.htm**. Index.htm is the start page for the entire Help System's output, not a topic that you created. The start page is automatically created each time you generate Frameless or Responsive HTML5 output.

   If you Publish the output files to the **helpsystem** folder, the link to the Help system will work as designed. You will learn to Publish during the next activity.

6. Return to RoboHelp.

Publishing

You've generated your Help System output files multiple times during the activities in this book. When you generate output files, the generated files go into an output folder on your computer. To make the generated output available to your users, you need to copy the output files to a shared location (typically a corporate web server). Assuming users know and have access to the URL for the Help System's Start Page (the Start page is typically named index.htm and is created every time you generate), your job is done.

The most efficient way to get your generated output to the server is by **Publishing**. When your output files are published, RoboHelp copies and pastes the output files to the server for you. Depending upon the size and number of your project files, the first time you publish the project could take some time. However, after you edit the project, Generate, and then re-Publish, only the edited content (and required support files) is copied and pasted to the server, making the publishing process faster than manually copying and pasting all of the output to the server.

Guided Activity 66: Publish an Output

1. Ensure that the **Application_Help** project is still open.

2. Create a Publish Profile.

   ❒ from the **Output** area, double-click the **Policies Output** Preset to open it for editing

   ❒ on the **General** tab, ensure that the **Output Path** is **RoboHelp2022Data > output > Frameless**

   ❒ select the **Publish** tab

   ❒ click the **Publish Profiles** icon

   The Publish Profiles dialog box opens.

   ❒ click the **Create a new Profile** icon

   There are several Server Types available, and Adobe adds to the list from time-to-time. You will need to work with your IT department to determine the best type of server to use. For this example, you'll be using **File System**, a great option if you want to publish your files locally or to a network drive.

NOTES

NOTES

❒ from the **Server Type** drop-down menu, choose **File System**

❒ in the **Name** area, type **Publish to WebApp**

❒ from the **Destination Path** area, click the **Change** icon

The **Select a Folder** dialog box opens.

❒ navigate to and Select/Open **RoboHelp2022Data > webapp > helpsystem**

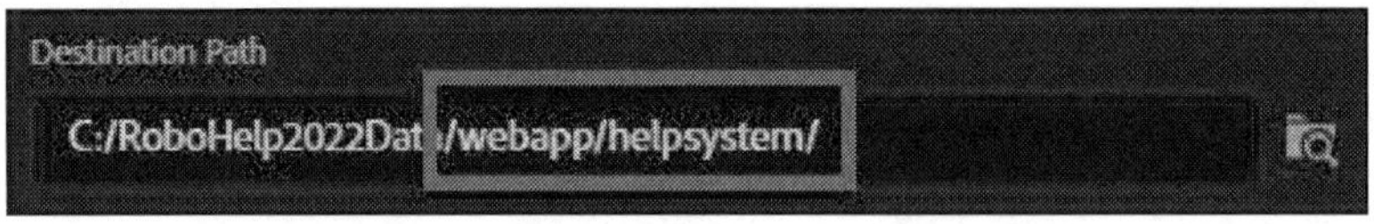

❒ click the **Save** button

Your new "server" now appears in the list of Servers.

❒ if necessary, select **Publish to WebApp** (ensure that there is a check mark in the box)

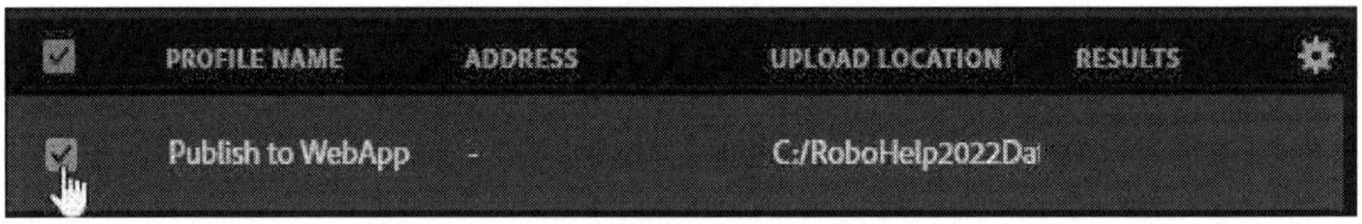

3. Save and Generate the Policies Output.

4. Publish the Policies Output.

❒ right-click the **Policies Output** output and choose **Publish** 

The destination you set up for the Published output is different from the Output Path for generated content. When you Generate, all of the output files are created within a folder on your computer. However, your users do not have access to that output. When you Publish, all of the output is copied to the server for user access. In this example, you've published to a folder on your own computer. In reality, you would set a publish destination appropriate for your users.

Publishing Confidence Check

1. Minimize/Hide RoboHelp.
2. Navigate to the **RoboHelp2022Data** folder
3. Open the **webapp** folder.
4. Open the **helpsystem** folder to see the published output files.

5. Go back to the **webapp** folder and, if necessary, reopen **SimpleWebApplication** in your web browser.
6. Click the link to the word “here.”

   This time, the Help System that you just published to the “server” opens. Congratulations! You are now a published Help author!

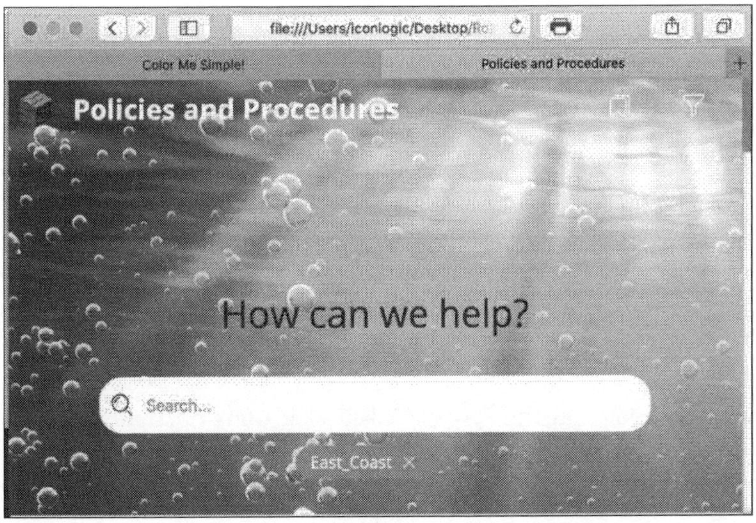

   Note: If the published Help System did not open when you clicked the word “here,” the issue is likely your web browser (some browsers misbehave when you test items such as local links). If you have an alternative web browser installed on your computer, open **SimpleWebApplication** there and retest the link.

7. Close the Help System tab (or window) but keep **SimpleWebApplication.htm** open.

NOTES

NOTES

Context Sensitive Help

Context Sensitive Help (CSH) allows users to get help about specific areas of a program. Users can quickly get help without having to use the Help System's TOC, Index, or Search.

Here is how context sensitive help works: To make a topic context sensitive, the topic needs a unique topic ID and a map number. This information is stored in a **map file**. The application's programmer can (and most probably will) create the map file (also known as an **H** or **HH** file).

Here's an example of a map file entry: **#define ID_AboutSSS 5001**. The text **ID_AboutSSS** is the topic ID; **5001** is the map number.

After the programmer is finished with the map file, you would import the map file into your RoboHelp project. Then you would match the topics in your project with the IDs from the map file. After that, Generate and Publish the output files.

You can also create the map file yourself from within RoboHelp. In the next few activities, you will review the areas of the Simple Web Application that are meant to be context sensitive, create a map file, assign map numbers to a few topics in your project, Generate, Publish, and test the results.

Guided Activity 67: Review CSH Source Code

1. Attempt to get Context Sensitive Help.

   ❒ still working within the **SimpleWebApplication.htm** web application, click the link **Open just the Leave Policy** topic

   The link you just clicked is supposed to start the Help System and then open just the **Leave Policy** topic in its own window. Instead, the entire Help System is started, and the Welcome topic opens. If you were the user looking for information on the Leave Policy, you would now have to manually search for the content.

2. Close the Help window but leave SimpleWebApplication.htm open.

3. Try to get additional Context Sensitive Help.

   ❒ click the link **Open just the Payroll Policy topic**

   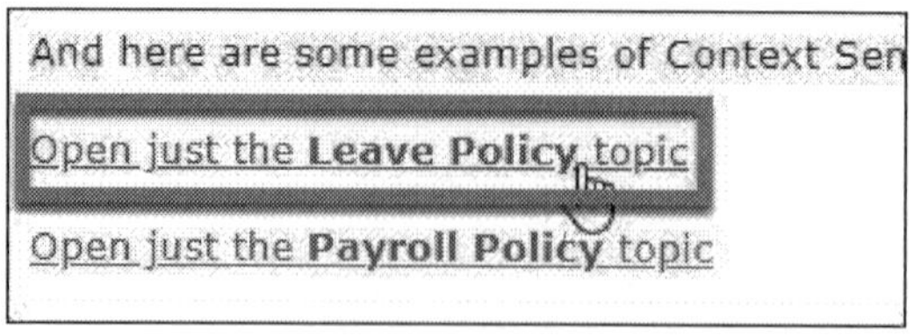

   The Help System starts again, but the Payroll Policy topic does not appear.

4. Close the Help window (or tab) but leave the SimpleWebApplication.htm page open in your browser so you can review some HTML code in the next step.

5. View the source code.

   ❒ point to (but don't click) the **Open just the Leave Policy topic** link

   HTML code displays in the browser's status bar (in most browsers, the status bar is at the bottom of the browser window).

In the HTML code, the text “javascript” causes the JavaScript file named RH_ShowHelp to activate. The next bit of text ('helpsystem/index.htm') is what opens the Help System.

Finally, the last bit of text (**45**) is what tells the Help System to display the topic with map ID number **45**. Soon, you will assign Map ID **45** to the **Leave Policy** topic in your project.

6. View another source code.

   ❒ using your browser, point to (but don’t click) **Open just the Payroll Policy topic**

   The end of the text (, **46**) is what tells the Help System to display the topic with map ID number **46**. Soon, you will assign Map ID **46** to the **Payroll Policy** topic.

7. Leave SimpleWebApplication.htm open and return to the RoboHelp project.

NOTES

NOTES

Guided Activity 68: Create and Edit a Map File

1. Ensure that the **Application_Help.rhpj** project is still open.

2. Create a Map file.

   ❒ from the **Output** area, click **Map Files**

   ❒ click the **New Map File** icon and choose **New Map File**

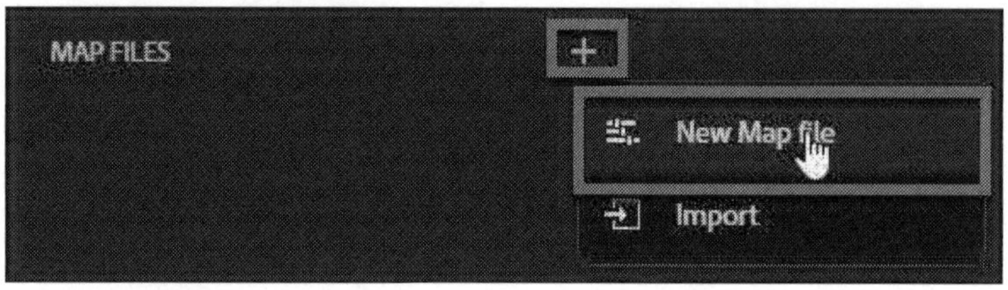

   The **New Map File** dialog box opens.

   ❒ type **CSHMap**

   ❒ click the **Done** button

   The new map file has been created within the Map Files area.

3. Assign a Map ID to a topic.

   ❒ if necessary, open the **CSHMap** for editing

   ❒ from the **CSHMap** area, open the **Leave and Vacation** folder

   ❒ drag the **Leave Policy** topic into the Drag and Drop area

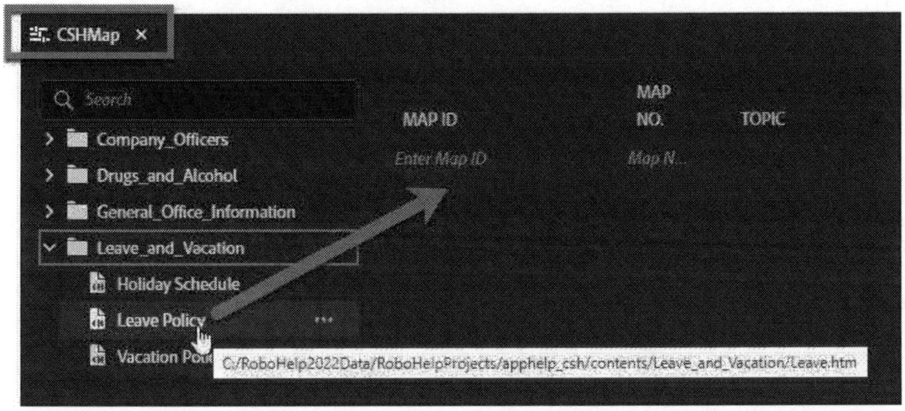

The **Leave Policy** topic is automatically assigned Map Number **1**. You need to change the number to **45** so it matches the reference in the web application's source code.

4. Edit a Map Number.

   ❒ in the **Map ID** area, double-click the existing Map Number (the number **1**) and change it to **45**

Map IDs Confidence Check

1. Add the **Payroll Policy** topic to the Map file.
2. Change the Map Number for the Payroll Policy to **46**.

NOTES

3. Save the project.

   Note: You've been prompted to save your work several times throughout this book. Reminding you to save doesn't mean that I am simply encouraging good saving habits and helping you prevent lost work... not that there's anything wrong with that. If you don't save RoboHelp project assets frequently, changes to things such as Map Files don't always appear within other areas of RoboHelp.

4. Open the **Policies Output** Preset for editing. On the **Content** tab, **Map Files** area, choose **CSHMap** from the **Map Files** drop-down menu.

   CSHMap is the map file you just created. If you had not saved the project as instructed above, it's possible that the Map File would not have been listed in the Map Files drop-down menu.

5. Save the project.
6. **Generate** and **Publish** the **Policies Output.**
7. Return to the **SimpleWebApplication.htm** window.
8. Reload/Refresh the **SimpleWebApplication** web page.
9. Test the links to the **Leave** and **Payroll Policy** topics.

   Clicking either link should result in the specific topic opening in the Help System.

   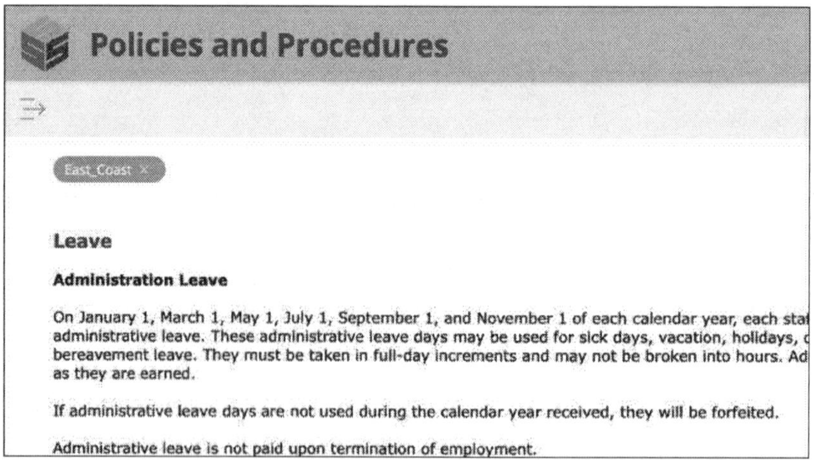

10. When finished, close the browser.
11. Return to RoboHelp and close the project.

Take a Bow!

Hey, look at that, you have completed this book. Congratulations, you're well on your way to becoming a help authoring rock star with Adobe RoboHelp! Here are some of the awesome skills you've gained as you worked through the activities in this book:

- ❒ Creating New Projects
- ❒ Adding, Deleting, Editing, Importing and Linking to Topic Content
- ❒ Creating Project Structure (Folders, TOCs)
- ❒ Working with CSS Files
- ❒ Generating Output
- ❒ Adding Images and Multimedia
- ❒ Creating Image Maps
- ❒ Adding Indexes
- ❒ Adding Conditional Build Tags and Expressions
- ❒ Adding Snippets and Variables
- ❒ Working with Templates
- ❒ Working with Topic Layouts
- ❒ Generating Word Documents
- ❒ Generating PDFs
- ❒ Publishing Output

and...

- ❒ Creating Context Sensitive Help

I hope you have enjoyed this learning journey. If you need additional help learning or working with RoboHelp, I offer instructor-led RoboHelp training, live online RoboHelp mentoring and support, and complete technical communication development services. You'll find me online at www.iconlogic.com. You can reach me via email at ksiegel@iconlogic.com.

NOTES

Notes

Index

NOTES

NOTES

NOTES

Notes

Made in the USA
Monee, IL
05 November 2026

67911919R00127